nd edition

CRIMINAL JUSTICE
policy and planning

WAYNE N. WELSH / PHILIP W. HARRIS
Temple University   Temple University

 LexisNexis®

 anderson publishing
A member of the LexisNexis Group

Criminal Justice Policy and Planning, Second Edition

Welsh, Wayne N., 1957-
    Criminal justice policy and planning / Wayne N. Welsh, Philip W. Harris. -- 2nd ed.
        p. cm.
    Includes bibliographical references and index.
    ISBN 1-58360-560-6 (softbound)
    1. Criminal justice, Administration of. 2. Criminal justice, Administration of--United States.
    3. Criminal justice, Administration of--Planning. I. Harris, Philip W. II. Title.
HV7419.W45 2004
364.973--dc22   2004021269

Cover design by Tin Box Studio, Inc.

Editor   Ellen S. Boyne
Acquisitions Editor   Michael C. Braswell

Acknowledgments

The authors are grateful to their families for all their love and patience, especially during those times when we sequestered ourselves to do the writing and research for this book. Thank you, Dea and Ilana, and Ellen and Elisabeth.

We appreciate the thoughtful guidance provided by Michael Braswell, Acquisitions Editor, and the helpful comments of Victor Kappeler at Eastern Kentucky University during the developmental stages of the first edition. Comments by Professor Frank Cullen at University of Cincinnati on an earlier version were most valuable in shaping this work and bringing it to fruition. We also thank Ellen Boyne for her careful and thoughtful editing on both the first and second edition. Of course, any errors or omissions are the responsibility of the authors alone.

We express great appreciation to the many students who have served as "clients" for this book in our university classes, and who gave us extremely helpful comments and feedback each step along the way.

Last but not least, we thank the many fine men and women in criminal justice agencies, community programs, the private sector, and local, state, and federal government whom we have had the good fortune to work with and learn from in our criminal justice research.

Contents

Acknowledgments   *iii*
Preface   *vii*

Chapter 1
Introduction   1

Chapter 2
Analyzing the Problem   33

Chapter 3
Setting Goals and Objectives   91

Chapter 4
Designing the Program or Policy   125

Chapter 5
Developing an Action Plan   151

Chapter 6
**Developing a Plan for Monitoring Program/
Policy Implementation**   177

Chapter 7
Developing a Plan for Evaluating Outcomes   215

Chapter 8
Initiating the Program or Policy Plan   249

**Appendix 1 A Seven-Stage Checklist for Program
          and Policy Planning**   267

About the Authors   273

Index   277

Preface

The purpose of this book, broadly speaking, is to acquaint students, practitioners, and policymakers with scientific techniques for analyzing criminal justice problems and developing solutions. We offer guidelines for developing new programs and policies, but we also analyze existing criminal justice interventions, asking to what degree such efforts were guided by logic and planning, rather than partisan politics and untested hunches.

Change, some of which is planned, touches every aspect of our lives. In criminal justice, new interventions aimed at reducing crime constantly seem to spring up. Some notable interventions of recent years have included mandatory sentencing, "three strikes and you're out" laws (aimed at incapacitating repeat felony offenders), the Brady Act (requiring waiting periods and background checks for prospective firearm purchasers), drug courts, boot camps, "weed and seed," prisoner reentry initiatives, and others. But to what degree are such interventions guided by a rational planning approach? What problems do they attempt to address, and what causal theory about crime do they assume? What difficulties could have been anticipated (e.g., a shortage of prison space; criticisms that programs or policies are inconsistent, unfair, or even unconstitutional)?

Our point is this: what we call "planned change" encompasses a multitude of criminal justice policies, programs, and projects that are developed, implemented, revised, torn down, and recreated every year. We are interested in how such policies, programs, and projects are currently developed, and in how they *should be* developed. Poor planning and faulty problem analysis, we argue, are the primary reasons that so many criminal justice interventions fail to live up to their promises.

Consider the example of three-strikes laws. Evidence suggests that the laws are unfair, expensive, and ineffective. As Walter Dickey[1] argued, "When the law's hidden costs and unintended consequences are assessed, its simple goal is obscured by effects that are alarming in their scope" (p. 62). We illustrate some of the pitfalls of poor planning below, using the seven-stage framework that guides our work.

The Pitfalls of Poor Planning: Three-Strikes Legislation

1. Problem Analysis

The proper starting point for program or policy planning is to ask what problem needs to be addressed. How does a specific issue become targeted for change, and why? How big is the problem, where is it, who is affected by it, and so on? What evidence has been used to demonstrate a need for change?

There is a widespread misconception that crime rates have been steadily rising in recent years, and that a larger and larger portion of serious crimes is committed by recidivating felons. Nowhere in state or federal three-strikes legislation can any evidence for such conclusions be found. In fact, crime rates remained stable or decreased since the early 1990s, while recidivism rates remained remarkably stable. It is doubtful that any coherent problem analysis guided policy development in this arena.

Assumptions speak faster and louder than facts, and politicians may too eagerly cater to the perceived public will rather than documented problems. Three-strikes laws were a rapid and visible response to public outcries following heinous or well-publicized crimes.[2] "We have a serious crime problem in this country," according to Walter Dickey, a University of Wisconsin law professor. "We are sold this as a solution. It gets all kinds of energy and attention, and yet it is relatively ineffectual."[3]

2. Goals and Values

Before designing programs or policies, we must be clear about the specific outcomes they are expected to achieve, and what specific values guide choices to select one course of action over another.

The intent of three-strikes laws is to incapacitate violent offenders for long prison terms—25 years to life. If the law successfully increases the imprisonment rate, according to this logic, fewer offenders will be free to victimize the population. The laws have no *specific* deterrent effect if those confined will never be released, but their *general* deterrent effect could, at least in theory, be substantial. Legislators convey the message that certain crimes are deemed especially grave and that people who commit them deserve harsh sanctions.

Such laws may compromise values such as *equity* (fairness). A California study[4] found that blacks were sent to prison under the "three-strikes" law 13 times more often than whites. Forty-three percent of the third-strike inmates in California were African-American, although they made up only 7 percent of the state's population and 20 percent of its felony arrests. Controversy still ensues over exactly what outcomes three-strikes laws were expected to achieve, and whether numerous unintended consequences, including racial disparity, could have been avoided.

3. Program or Policy Design

For any program or policy to have a chance at being effective, it is absolutely essential that the target population and all provisions, procedures, and services be clearly spelled out ahead of time. In other words, there should be absolutely no doubt about who does what to whom, in what order, how much or how often. This has clearly not been the case with three-strikes laws.

One might expect some consistency between three-strikes laws in different states and between state and federal three-strikes laws. In reality, laws vary widely across states in terms of the definition of a "strike," the conditions under which the law is triggered, and the severity of the sanctions. Some state laws call for third-time offenders to receive life without parole. In others, prisoners are eligible for parole after 30 or 40 years.[5]

Target populations for three-strikes laws seem particularly poorly defined. During the first few years of the law's implementation in California, about 1,300 offenders were imprisoned on third-strike felonies and more than 14,000 criminals for "second-strike" felonies. California's law calls for a doubling of the prison sentence for a second felony and for a sentence of 25 years to life for a third conviction. The California law was written to cover 500 felonies, including many nonviolent offenses. Some of the felonies include petty theft, attempted assault, and burglary. Thus, about 85 percent of all those sentenced under the three-strikes laws were involved in nonviolent crimes. For instance, 192 marijuana possessors were sentenced for second and third strikes, compared with 40 murderers, 25 rapists, and 24 kidnappers[6].

4. Action Planning

Prior to implementing a new policy such as three-strikes laws, a systematic plan is needed that assigns responsibilities for communication, coordination, and completion of specific tasks required to enact the new law. Everyone involved must clearly understand his or her roles and responsibilities. Possible obstacles and sources of resistance should be anticipated and sought out. By the time the new three-strikes laws were implemented, everyone should have understood and accepted their roles. Evidence suggests the opposite.

State prosecutors avoided the three-strikes laws because they saw little need for them with existing sentencing laws.[7] Another reason is that the laws were narrowly written, making them difficult to apply. Plea-bargaining and charge bargaining became increasingly common methods for circumventing three-strikes laws.

The criminal courts typically rely on a high rate of guilty pleas to speed case processing and avoid logjams. Three-strikes laws disrupt established plea-bargaining patterns by preventing a prosecutor from offering a short prison term (less than the minimum) in exchange for a guilty plea. However, prosecutors can shift strategies and bargain on charges rather than on sentences. The findings of research on the impact of mandatory sentencing laws are instructive.[8] Officials make earlier and more selective arrest, charging, and diversion decisions; they also tend to bargain less and to bring more cases to trial[9].

5. Monitoring

Following implementation of a policy such as three-strikes, it is essential to *monitor*, that is, collect data to determine to what degree the actual provisions, procedures, or services are actually being implemented as designed. Adjustments may be needed, but absolutely no valid evaluation can be conducted if the laws are not being properly implemented. That would be tantamount to arguing that "x caused y" when we have no idea what "x" (the policy) was. Three-strikes laws fare badly on this criterion also.

At the federal level, where a three-strikes law was included in the 1994 crime bill, the law had been used on only nine occasions two years later. Twenty-four other federal cases were pending.[10] At the federal level, the long-term impact was minimal because less than 2 percent of violent felonies are resolved in federal courts.

Three-strikes statutes simply weren't being used in many of the 25 states that passed similar laws.[11] Some states have not used them at all; others have applied their laws infrequently and inconsistently. Even within a single state such as California, there was considerable variability in how state laws were interpreted and used across different counties.

6. Evaluation

We need measurable evidence that any policy, particularly an expensive one such as three-strikes laws, effectively and efficiently achieves what it was intended to do (i.e., reduce crime, protect public safety). Three-strikes laws were intended to reduce serious crime by incapacitating repeat offenders and by deterring others from becoming repeat offenders.

A 1994 report by RAND predicted a 28 percent decrease in crime over the 25 years following passage of the law. RAND also predicted tremendous increases in criminal justice costs, mainly through the construction and operation of additional prison cells necessitated by three-strikes laws. Three-strikes laws, researchers expected, would also result in defendants mounting more rigorous defenses to avoid severe sanctions, leading to fewer guilty pleas and more trials, greater court workloads and backlogs, and increased jail overcrowding. The existing evidence, so far, is mixed.[12]

- States with three-strikes laws did not experience greater declines in crime than states without such laws.

- Three-strikes states did not experience greater increases in statewide incarceration rates (e.g., number of adults incarcerated per 10,000 population), although the likelihood of incarceration *per conviction* (e.g., number of adults incarcerated per 10,000 convictions) has increased substantially.

- The California prison population certainly increased in terms of *total numbers*, but at a *rate* no faster than before the implementation of three-strikes laws. California already had one of the highest incarceration rates in the country, and three-strikes laws did not significantly change this rate of incarceration.

- No consistent effects in terms of dramatic workload increases or court backlogs were found in California. Counties varied dramatically in how the law was implemented. For example, some District Attorneys followed the letter of the law more strictly than others. Strikes were dismissed in one-quarter to one-half of all strike-eligible cases in some counties.

While effects of three-strikes laws on crime rates so far have been negligible, RAND researchers cautioned that the full effects of the laws will remain unknown until offenders imprisoned under three-strikes laws have been incarcerated longer than they would have been under previous laws. It is also difficult (in any research study) to control for the many other social, political, and economic factors (aside from three-strikes laws) that may affect crime rates. In sum, the data required to adequately evaluate the effects of three-strikes laws are simply not available at this time.[13]

7. Reassessment and Review

Better planning in each of the areas discussed above could have reduced widespread inconsistency and failures in implementation, and could have helped reduce the number of unknown or unintended consequences of the laws (e.g., impacts on court workloads and backlogs, impacts on jail and prison crowding). Auerhan (2001) carefully illustrates how sentencing reforms such as three-strikes laws and California's Proposition 36 (intended to provide treatment to California's incarcerated drug offender population) result in impacts that are often far less (or far different) than what political pundits claim.[14]

The Focus of This Book

Where the costs of unsuccessful intervention are high in terms of human suffering as well as finances, we can and must do better in devising solutions to criminal justice problems. One should be skeptical, even critical, but not cynical. In spite of the pitfalls of poor planning, it is possible to address and reduce even the most pressing problems in criminal justice. We invite students, practitioners, politicians, academics, and planners to subject their own assumptions, decisions, and plans to scrutiny.

In this revised second edition, we discuss several successful (and unsuccessful) programs and policies. We have added new case studies and examples that examine more recently identified problems (e.g., club drugs, terrorism) and innovations (e.g., restorative justice, performance-based standards for juvenile justice, prisoner reentry, the USA Patriot Act, homeland security, drug courts, Operation Weed and Seed, prison-based drug treatment, policing illegal gun markets). We have also updated research findings relevant to numerous other programs and policies (e.g., the Brady Act, three-strikes legislation).

As authors, the challenge we face is to present and communicate the *methods* of analyzing problems and interventions in a clear, concise manner. We have found no existing book adequate to the task. Some are simply far too jargonistic or technical; others are idiosyncratic, abstract, or unfocused. Moreover, to make life even more difficult for us, no existing book presents these methods using criminal justice problems and interventions. This book attempts to meet these challenges. No doubt, even in its second edition, it is less than perfect, and we welcome all comments and suggestions for improvements. Could advocates of planned change do any less?

Endnotes

[1]   Dickey, Walter J. (1997). "The Impact of "Three Strikes and You're Out Laws: What Have We Learned?" *Corrections Management Quarterly*, 1(4):55-64.

[2]   Parent, Dale, Terence Dunworth, Douglas McDonald, and William Rhodes (1997). *Key Legislative Issues in Criminal Justice: Mandatory Sentencing* (NCJ 161839). Washington, DC: U.S. Department of Justice, Office of Justice Programs, National Institute of Justice.

[3]   Cannon, Angie (1996). "Survey: 'Three-Strikes' Laws Aren't Affecting Crime. The Federal Government and States Aren't Hastening to Use Them. California is the Notable Exception." *The Philadelphia Inquirer*, Tuesday, September 10, 1996.

[4]   Greenwood, Peter W., C. Peter Rydell, Allan F. Abrahamse, Jonathan P. Caulkins, James Chiesa, Karyn E. Model, and Stephen P. Klein (1994). *Three Strikes and You're Out: Estimated Benefits and Costs of California's New Mandatory-Sentencing Law*. Santa Monica, CA: RAND. Available at: *http://www.rand.org/ publications/MR/MR509/* (retrieved March 6, 2004).

[5]   Greenwood, Peter W., Susan S. Everingham, Elsa Chen, Allan F. Abrahamse, Nancy Merritt, and James Chiesa (1998). *Three Strikes Revisited: An Early Assessment of Implementation and Effects* (NCJ 194106). Washington, DC: U.S. Department of Justice, Office of Justice Programs, National Institute of Justice.

[6]   Ibid, note 4.

[7]   Ibid, note 4.

[8]   Tonry, Michael (1987). *Sentencing Reform Impacts*. Washington, DC: U.S. Department of Justice, National Institute of Justice.

[9]   Ibid, note 2.

[10]   Ibid, note 3.

[11]   Ibid, note 6.

[12]   Ibid, note 6.

[13]   See also: Stolzenberg, Lisa and D'Alessio, Stewart J. (1997). "'Three Strikes and You're Out': The Impact of California's New Mandatory Sentencing Law on Serious Crime Rates." *Crime and Delinquency*, 43:457-469; Zimring, Franklin E., Sam Kamin, and Gordon Hawkins (1999). *Crime & Punishment in California: The Effect of Three Strikes and You're Out*. Berkeley, CA: Institute of Governmental Studies Press.

[14]   Auerhahn, Kathleen (2001). *Incapacitation, Dangerous Offenders, and Sentencing Reform*. Albany, NY: State University of New York Press.

CHAPTER 1

Introduction

CHAPTER OUTLINE

▶ *Examples of criminal justice interventions* include gun control and regulation (e.g., the Brady Act), "three strikes and you're out" legislation, juvenile waiver laws, and comprehensive drug courts and prisoner reentry courts.

▶ *Planned change versus unplanned change*: Any project, program, or policy, new or revised, intended to produce a change in some specific problem. It is limited in scope, it is aimed at improving quality of life for its clients, it includes a role for consumers, and a "change agent" guides it.

▶ *There are three approaches to planned change: policy, program, and project.*

▶ *The need for planned change has been sharpened by three trends: declining resources, accountability, and expansion of knowledge and technology.*

▶ *The perils of planned change:* Any change to existing procedures and conditions is likely to be resisted. Two broad approaches to change should be carefully considered: *collaborative strategies* versus *conflict strategies.*

▶ *A seven-stage model for planned change* specifies the sequence of steps required for analyzing a problem, determining its causes, and planning and carrying out some intervention. The seven stages consist of (1) analyzing the problem, (2) setting goals and objectives, (3) designing the program or policy, (4) developing an action plan, (5) developing a plan for monitoring program/policy implementation, (6) developing a plan for evaluating outcomes, and (7) initiating the program or policy design.

There are many different types of "programs," "policies," and "projects" in criminal justice: different interventions within government (federal, state, and local), community, and private agencies. In fact, one could argue that these many interventions comprise a majority of what "criminal justice" really is all about: a series of constant innovations and experiments attempting to discover "what works" to meet the goals of criminal justice (e.g., to reduce criminal behavior, to protect public safety). These numerous innovations attempt to change *individuals, groups, organizations, communities,* and even *societal and cultural norms* in some cases, in order to improve the achievement of criminal justice goals. Criminal justice, then, is much more than just the daily business of police, courts, and corrections, which forms the grist for many university courses and professional training in criminal justice. Figure 1.1 offers just a few examples of recent criminal justice interventions.

Figure 1.1

Examples of Criminal Justice Interventions

- Prisoner reentry initiatives and programs, including prison-based drug treatment and community aftercare, vocational and basic education, post-release employment assistance, and reintegration assistance.

- Drug Awareness Resistance Education (DARE) for elementary, middle school, and high school students.

- Federal "weed and seed" program (dual policy of first stamping out drug sales in specific communities, then "seeding" the communities with protective, economic, and social resources)

- Shelters, counseling, and victim assistance for abused women.

- Mandatory arrest policies for suspected spouse abusers.

- "Three strikes and you're out" legislation that aims to put away repeat offenders for long periods of time.

- Juvenile waiver laws (serious juvenile offenses may be transferred to adult courts, or automatically tried as adult offenses)

- Comprehensive prisoner reentry and drug courts that provide assessment and treatment services in conjunction with traditional criminal sanctions.

The problem is that many criminal justice interventions often fall short of their goals because of poor planning, poor implementation, and poor evaluation. It is fair to say that we have not yet discovered "what works" to reduce crime. What we truly need, though, is not more programs, or new programs, per se: we need *better* programs. We need a better understanding of planned change to improve the effectiveness of such interventions. Such change is ubiquitous in governmental, community, private, and nonprofit agencies. This book provides a systematic framework for analyzing and improving existing interventions, but also for planning new ones so as to maximize chances of success.

Planned Change versus Unplanned Change

Planned change involves *planning*. Planning means that some person or group of persons has explicitly thought about a problem and developed a specific solution. However, solutions (interventions) vary considerably in the degree to which thorough, explicit, or deliberate planning has been undertaken.

Planned Change

Any project, program or policy, new or revised, intended to produce a change in some specific problem. The intended change may occur within individuals, groups, organizations, systems of organizations, communities, cities, regions, states, or, much more rarely, within entire cultures or societies.

Figure 1.2

The Birth of a Program or Policy: Examples

1. A nonprofit organization working with juveniles in poor neighborhoods applies for state funding after reading a solicitation for proposals to develop after-school delinquency prevention programs.

2. Following several tragic school shootings during the 1990s, hundreds of school districts across the United States announce that they are revising their disciplinary policies and installing tougher security measures.

3. A parolee shoots and kills a police officer after a routine traffic stop. Intensive scrutiny and revision of state parole policies immediately follows.

4. A local police agency adopts a crime-mapping approach to detect crime "hot spots" and reallocates police resources to address specific problems in specific neighborhoods.

5. Following the "9/11" terrorist attacks, the U.S. federal government passes the USA Patriot Act (P.L. 107-56) on October 26, 2001, granting federal officials widespread investigative powers into suspected terrorist activities. Provisions included expanded electronic surveillance capabilities, nationwide search warrants issued in one jurisdiction but valid in any jurisdiction where evidence may be found, seizure of suspected terrorist assets, and detention of noncitizens for at least seven days without filing any charges.

How much planning do you think guided the development of these interventions?

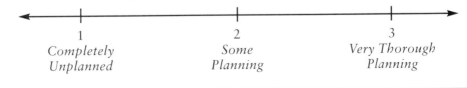

1	2	3
Completely Unplanned	*Some Planning*	*Very Thorough Planning*

As the examples and case studies in this book will illustrate, interventions are often poorly planned or even unplanned. *Unplanned change* means that little explicit or proactive planning has been undertaken at all. Instead, unplanned change often comes about as a reaction to a crisis, a dramatic incident publicized by the media, a political opportunity, a lawsuit against criminal justice officials, or an untested set of assumptions about a specific problem. Unplanned change, even if it is motivated by sincere intentions, is likely to be ineffective *and* expensive.

Planned change improves the likelihood of successful intervention, but it cannot guarantee it. Even when planned change is successful, it may not be permanent. Planned change is *dynamic*, like the problems it seeks to address. People who play critical leadership roles come and go over time, initial shock about a problem and enthusiasm about an intervention abates, the political environment changes, other problems demand greater attention, and the impact of the intervention may be unknown. Good planning, however, increases the odds of success by explicitly considering such factors.

In general, planned change differs from unplanned change in at least three ways:[1]

1. *Planned change is limited in scope, and specific.* It is confined to specific goals and achievable objectives; it seeks to develop clear, precise definitions of problems before developing solutions.

2. *It includes a role for consumers.* Programs and policies must consider the unique perspectives and needs of the people affected by the intervention. In addition to the "targets" of the intervention (ex-offenders in a halfway house for example), "consumers" include those within a specific area likely to be affected by an intervention. Neighbors, local schools, and crime victims are examples of consumers who may be affected by a halfway house program. Cooperative planning of the intervention is an important part of program planning, monitoring, and evaluation.

3. *A "change agent" guides planned change.* Some individual must be responsible for coordinating the planning and development of a new program or the revision of an old one. Such an individual will guide the analysis of the problem to be solved, search for causes of the problem and review similar interventions in use elsewhere, and facilitate the collaboration of clients, staff, and consumers involved in the planning process. This individual may come from various backgrounds: he or she may be a program director appointed by a specific agency such as county probation, a university professor with a research grant, a director of a nonprofit agency such as an ex-offender program, a consultant hired by a criminal justice agency to formulate a plan, or perhaps even a state representative who introduces new legislation authorizing the use of boot camps for certain offenders as an alternative to incarceration.

Three Approaches to Planned Change: Policy, Program, and Project

There are three general approaches to planned change, which differ in terms of their specificity and complexity. The most specific type of intervention is a *project*, the next most specific is a *program*, and the most complex and comprehensive is a *policy*.

Policies vary on the complexity of the rule or guidelines *(simple-complex)* and the amount of *discretion* afforded to those who apply policies *(constrained-flexible)*. How an instructor calculates grades in a course is a matter of policy, and students are typically informed of this policy at the start of a course. The existence of a grading policy helps to ensure that all students are treated fairly. Similarly, police officers are required to read *Miranda* warnings to people they have arrested, before beginning to ask questions that might be used in court against the defendant. Both of these examples pertain to relatively simple rules designed to protect the interests of individuals. Discretion is relatively constrained, although the Supreme Court has formulated specific exceptions. Sometimes policies are much more complex: the federal government may construct a "social" policy, such as President Lyndon Johnson's "War on Poverty" in the 1960s, designed to address large-scale social and economic problems. Organizations, too, create policies specifying how they are going to expend their resources: the U.S. Health Department's emphasis on juvenile violence prevention was tied to its budget in such a way that specific resources were set aside to deal with this problem. The policy was relatively complex (different rules and guidelines applied to different situations, and guidelines were quite broad), and flexible (the policy allowed decision makers to use discretion to develop or fund specific programs). Complexity and flexibility do not always correspond: for example, state sentencing guidelines are generally complex (different rules apply to different offenders and offenses), but vary considerably in the amount of discretion afforded to the sentencing judge. We address these issues in more depth in Chapter 4.

Policy

A rule or set of rules or guidelines for how to make a decision.

An example of a program would be a local Boys and Girls Club that decides to address the problem of minority overrepresentation in juvenile justice by creating an after-school program for minority juveniles residing in a high-risk community. Another example is a boot camp correctional program that is created to reduce the amount of time that offenders spend in custody. Offenders are sentenced to an intensive, short program of rigorous physical and academic services that is followed by probation rather than years

Program

A set of services aimed at achieving specific goals and objectives within specified individuals, groups, organizations, or communities.

in prison. Theoretically, such programs reduce the cost of corrections, increase the rehabilitative impact of corrections and satisfy the aim of retributive punishment. Programs, then, consist of services that are linked together by a single set of goals and an organization.

Project

A time-limited set of services provided to particular individuals, groups, organizations, or communities, usually focused on a single need, problem, or issue.

Projects are usually intensive efforts by groups within an organization, system of organizations, or a community to achieve a short-term objective. Evaluating a community corrections program, instituting a crackdown on drunk driving, or conducting an assessment of needs for a computerized information system are examples of projects.

While the distinction between programs and projects is sometimes ambiguous, depending on whether the intervention is permanent or short-term, the distinction between programs and policies deserves more careful attention. Two examples illustrate the differences between a program and a policy, the two most common types of change. In each of the two cases below, a program is but one small component of a much larger policy formulated at the local, state, or federal level. In each case, a *policy* (legislation in these two examples) authorized or mandated the use of specific *programs* for certain populations.

Figure 1.3

Problem	Program	Policy
• Jail overcrowding	Boot camps	Federal Crime Bill
• Drug abuse	Operation Weed and Seed	The federal "War on Drugs"

Boot camps, rigid military-style drill camps intended as an alternative to incarceration for certain offenders, were mandated and funded by the Violent Crime Control and Law Enforcement Act of 1994. The federal government allocated $24.5 million in competitive funds available for boot camps in 1995, and authorized $7.9 billion in the time period 1996-2000.

Operation Weed and Seed, a U.S. Department of Justice initiative launched in 1992 as part of President Bush's continuing "War on Drugs" campaign, is a two-pronged community intervention. First, law enforcement agencies and prosecutors cooperate in "weeding out" criminals who participate in violent crime and drug abuse and attempt to prevent their return to the targeted area. Second, "seeding" involves the development of community services including prevention, intervention, treatment, and neighborhood revitalization. In each case, federal policy led to the formulation and funding of specific programs.

Policies, therefore, often contain the authorization or impetus for many specific programs, but policies often provide only very general prescriptions for what kind of approach should be used to solve specific problems. We can begin to see that the development of many programs and policies arises out of a political process that determines not only which problems will receive attention and priority in the first place, but also what kind of intervention approach (e.g., changing individuals versus changing specified conditions in a community) will be used to address those problems.

The Need for Planned Change

The quest to find "what works" to achieve the goals of criminal justice has not yet been fulfilled and will not likely be anytime soon. In fact, many people (policymakers, academics, politicians, and citizens) disagree profoundly about the desirability of certain intervention approaches (e.g., drug treatment for convicted offenders versus tougher criminal sanctions to reduce drug abuse). Even if there were not such strong disagreement in *values*, it would still be difficult to find widespread agreement about how effective specific interventions have been (e.g., school-based drug prevention campaigns such as DARE).

Several factors fuel the debates over program effectiveness. For one thing, it is usually difficult to evaluate the long-term effects of social interventions. There are many different social variables to measure and control for, and this complexity often defies measurement. In addition to difficulties involved in measuring the objectives of specific interventions, the objectives themselves may be poorly defined. Or, the problem may be poorly defined. Or, both the problem and the goals are well defined, but the intervention was not implemented correctly, and thus we cannot have faith in any outcome results obtained by evaluation, whether they point to program success or failure. Indeed, evaluation results that do not address implementation problems should be treated suspiciously.

We will address all of these issues in more detail in subsequent chapters, but our point is that there is currently very little consensus about "what works" in criminal justice. A major reason for this lack of consensus, we argue, is a lack of sufficient attention to principles of planned change. At least three trends have sharpened our needs for planned change over the past 20 years:[2] (1) declining resources, (2) accountability, and (3) the expansion of knowledge and technology.

Declining Resources

Beginning about 1980, and continuing into the twenty-first century, there have been huge cuts in social services, especially programs affecting the poor and minorities (e.g., subsidized health care, welfare reform, daycare for working parents). Part of the explanation for these changes lies in the increased public concern over high taxes. However, as taxes are the basis for the provision of public services, cuts in taxes mean cuts in services (somewhere). Cuts in social services, according to some, may have magnified social problems that already existed. For example, the problem of homelessness was likely exacerbated by huge cuts in funds available for mental health care, inadequate funding for substance abuse treatment programs, and rising healthcare costs.[3]

Partly as a consequence of declining resources, many groups have organized to promote change, both legally (through lawsuits) and politically (by advocating for changes in laws and government programs). Advocacy efforts have often succeeded in raising awareness about a particular problem and stimulating change. A good example is provided by the problem of domestic violence. Women's groups have organized and protested for numerous changes throughout history, including the rights to vote and to work. Advocacy by women's groups in the 1970s and 1980s led to changes in police and court policies for dealing with sexual harassment, rape, and domestic violence. Such advocacy contributed greatly to the perception that existing programs and policies were not working, and that some kind of change was needed.[4] One can find numerous examples of other groups that have campaigned for change and contributed to changes in existing policies and programs (e.g., groups protesting welfare reforms that restrict eligibility and benefits; groups advocating for programs and policies to address problems of homelessness, AIDS, and so on).

Accountability

As public resources have dwindled, agencies have increasingly been called upon to demonstrate their effectiveness and efficiency in meeting their goals. There has been suspicion by many that public money is not always being spent wisely. There has been a renewed dialogue over the past decade about how to make public institutions more effective and accountable, although the means for achieving this goal are subject to debate.[5] This is especially the case within the public sectors of education, human services, and welfare, where one finds considerable public expenditure, conflicting values and goals, and high stakes.[6] Annual budget hearings at the state and federal levels are tense events for directors of publicly funded agencies, who must justify their funding needs with specific and detailed evidence.

According to a recent report to the U.S. Congress, the effectiveness of most crime prevention strategies will remain unknown until the nation invests more in evaluating them.[7] Using rigorous, scientifically recognized standards and methodologies, a review of more than 500 impact evaluations revealed only a handful of definitive conclusions. Congress can solve this problem, the authors suggested, by limiting the scope of required evaluations but requiring that evaluations that are funded receive sufficient funding to answer questions about effectiveness. In order for this approach to be effective, Congress should match the funding earmarked for program spending with corresponding funding to pay for the evaluations.

Current thinking about improving government services suggests that at a minimum public institutions must do four things: (1) work smarter, particularly with better information; (2) constantly monitor the shifting demands of constituents and clients; (3) link themselves with other agencies and support functions; and (4) evaluate their work processes and the results of their programmatic efforts.[8]

Expansion of Knowledge and Technology

We have greater technological abilities than ever before, and these changes have created both new opportunities and new problems. Improvements in computing technology over the past 20 years have dramatically increased our information collection, storage, and retrieval capabilities. We now have ready access to many types of criminal justice data, including information about reported crimes, police arrests, convictions, sentencing, prison time served, parole, and recidivism. Improved data collection and access mean that our ability to analyze specific needs and problems has improved.

For example, improved justice information systems have contributed to our understanding of problems such as racial disparities in sentencing.[9] High-powered computers and statistical packages make it possible to collect and compare data on the processing of thousands of defendants in different regions over time, and statistically control for various legal (e.g., previous criminal record) and nonlegal factors (e.g., race, socioeconomic status) that influence sentencing. There are no longer disputes about whether sentencing disparities exist or not, but about where, why, and how much. Computers have also increased the ability of researchers to discover what works. The effects of juvenile and adult correctional programs are increasingly the subjects of sophisticated outcome-based evaluations and meta-analyses (see Chapter 7).

Other technological changes have improved our ability to detect crime and monitor offenders. Computerized fingerprint identification systems have greatly reduced the amount of time required to scan and match individual prints, and both regional and national databanks of criminal information and fingerprints are now available to criminal justice agencies for investigation. DNA testing and analysis technologies have become increasingly sophisticated, and forensic DNA evidence has been used with increasing frequency to both convict the guilty and exonerate the innocent.[10] Many previously unsolvable cases became solvable because viable suspects could be identified and arrested or removed from suspect lists.

Electronic monitoring equipment made it possible for probation and parole agencies to supervise certain offenders more cost-effectively in a community rather than a prison setting, at least as part of their sentence. However, increasingly sophisticated drug-testing equipment has also made it possible to detect minute amounts of drugs in an individual's body, leading to huge increases in the number of parolees who fail to successfully complete their parole terms and return to jail.[11]

As computerized information systems have grown, a whole new field of crime dubbed "computer crime" has evolved, where perpetrators attempt to break into secure computer systems of individuals and corporations, usually for the purpose of illegally obtaining classified information or money. Methods of detecting, investigating, and prosecuting this whole new category of crime are evolving rapidly, but seemingly slower than the rate of growth in the crime itself.[12]

The Perils of Planned Change

Any change to existing procedures and existing conditions carries a certain amount of risk. The proposed change is likely to be resisted by someone, perhaps even its intended beneficiaries (e.g., a city successfully lobbies for state funds to build a new prison, but then faces vigorous protests from different communities being considered for the location of the new prison). Regardless of the specific change proposed, universal consensus is rare; resistance is the norm.

In many cases, people fear and resist change because it may threaten their job security or bring about unwanted scrutiny (e.g., citizen review boards of complaints against police). There is often a fear that the change might only make things worse. For example, the USA Patriot Act passed in October of 2001 has been criticized by many civil rights advocates who fear that tough new government powers have led to the unwarranted detention of large numbers of legal immigrants. Regardless of the many varied reasons for which resistance emerges in any specific case, those who propose change must be prepared for disagreement and resistance. Again, *planned* change, rather than unplanned or poorly planned change, can go a long way toward minimizing resistance, especially if the "change agent" (the person or agency that has introduced the proposed intervention) has involved different constituents in the planning process from the beginning.

Even prior to beginning work on planning a specific intervention, the change agent should have identified potential sources of resistance and considered the potential costs and benefits of two very different approaches to handling resistance: (1) *collaborative* strategies; or (2) *conflict* strategies.[13] While the actual outcomes of either strategy are impossible to predict without knowing detailed circumstances of the case in question, there are several serious costs associated with conflict strategies that generally make them unattractive options:

- They create greater resistance;

- They require greater resources;

- They create more unexpected effects; and

- Change tends to be temporary (capitulation) rather than long-term.

Collaborative strategies seek involvement from all parties concerned. For example, a police commissioner might ask police officers about their views on community policing before it is adopted as a department policy and imposed on them. State sentencing commissions might ask judges about perceived difficulties in sentencing before drafting, adopting, or imposing sentencing guidelines on them.

Collaborative Strategies

Collaborative strategies emphasize participation from those affected by change. Individuals, groups, or organizations known to oppose the intervention in part or *in toto* are included in the design and planning of the intervention.

Conflict strategies are more likely to come into play where opposing parties have a strong history of disagreement; leaders favor a dictatorial, authoritarian style of management; resources are scarce and there is much disagreement over allocation; the stakes of the proposed change are high (i.e., large benefits to certain parties and perhaps large costs to others); time pressures are great; and the likelihood of successfully suppressing the opposition is perceived (correctly or incorrectly) as high. A good example is provided by brutality lawsuits launched against local police

Conflict Strategies

Conflict strategies approach resistance in an adversarial manner. Those who resist the proposed change are seen as opponents who must either be persuaded or coerced to change their views.

departments. Because citizens perceived the existing system of reviewing complaints as ineffective and heavily biased in favor of police,
legal reform in complaint review procedures has evolved. Another
example is provided by lawsuits against local, state, and federal prisons for overcrowding and other conditions of confinement. Such lawsuits, some lasting as long as 13 years, usually followed a period of
unsuccessful and rancorous discussion and negotiation.[14] Changes
eventually resulted, but at considerable cost to human and fiscal
resources.

A Seven-Stage Model For Planned Change

A "model" specifies the sequence of steps required for (1) analyzing a problem, (2) determining its causes, and (3) planning and carrying
out some intervention. For our purposes, a model may be used to plan
new interventions, analyze existing interventions, or both (e.g., revising a current program). In the first case, certain critical activities can
be enacted (or avoided) so as to increase the likelihood that a proposed
intervention will effectively produce a desired change in a specific
problem. In the second case, critical activities and decisions that
informed the planning process can be identified and analyzed so as to
help us to understand why a particular intervention did or did not produce effective results.

Our model of planned change is based on a "problem-solving
model" (i.e., developing solutions to specific problems through a
rational process of planning). The 1968 President's Commission
report,[15] *The Challenge of Crime in Free Society*, was extremely influ-
ential in shaping current conceptions of criminal justice as a "system,"[16]
and it stimulated attempts to improve criminal justice programs and
policies through *comprehensive, coordinated* planning. As Mark
Moore[17] suggests, ". . . The Crime Commission had two big things in
mind: (1) how to produce an effective, decent criminal justice system
and (2) how to deal with crime . . . They also had a *managerial or implementation vision* [emphasis added], which was a theory about how the
processes and institutions of the criminal justice system needed to be
developed . . . (167-168)." This vision was to be guided by data and
knowledge rather than ideology and passion.

The Commission's report was the major impetus for passage of the
Omnibus Crime Control and Safe Streets Act of 1968 and the creation
of the federal Law Enforcement Assistance Administration (LEAA).
While rational criminal justice planning and the "social justice" it was
intended to foster remain elusive, those lofty goals remain as relevant as
ever. Reflecting on the positive contributions of the President's Commission report, Moore notes that: "The authorization to experiment has

been spread widely, and that turns out to be a very good thing for society" (176-177). At the same time, the goals of rationality and social justice have proven far more difficult to achieve than originally expected.[18]

We present our model here with a program approach in mind, but we have generalized it to include the development of policies. That is, the stages are described with the assumption that a program or policy is being developed or analyzed. Because projects differ from programs and policies mainly in terms of their shorter duration and more focused intervention approach, this seven-stage model can also be applied to the project approach to problem solving. The seven stages of the program model are briefly described here; each is dealt with in more detail in separate chapters. A summary of the seven stages is provided in Table 1.1.

Stage 1. Analyzing the Problem

The first step is to analyze the problem, carefully collecting information about dimensions of the problem, the history of the problem, who is affected by the problem, and potential causes of the problem. For example, we ask the following questions: What and where is the problem? How big is it? How long has the problem existed? Do different groups of people have different definitions of the problem? Who is affected by the problem? What causes the problem? What theories do we have about causes of the problem? What kinds of interventions have been tried elsewhere? Who is likely to support a certain course of action, and who is likely to resist it?

The pitfalls of faulty problem analysis are enormous, and can completely subvert effective intervention. Many interventions fail not necessarily because the intervention itself is flawed, but because it addresses the wrong problem (or an inadequately defined problem). Major activities at this stage include the following:

- Document the need for change: collect and analyze data about the problem.

- Describe the history of the problem.

- Examine potential causes of the problem.

- Examine previous interventions that have tried to change this problem.

- Identify relevant stakeholders (those who have a legitimate interest in the problem and/or the intervention).

- Identify barriers to change and supports for change.

- Conduct a system analysis.

Table 1.1
A Systematic Approach to Program and Policy Development and Analysis

Stage 1. Analyzing the Problem	Stage 2. Setting Goals and Objectives	Stage 3. Designing the Program or Policy	Stage 4. Developing an Action Plan
Document the need for change	Write goal statements	Choose from different intervention options	Identify resources needed
Describe the history of the problem	Write specific outcome objectives for each goal	Program design: • Define the target population	Plan to acquire or reallocate resources
Examine potential causes	Seek participation in goal setting	• Define target selection procedures	Specify dates to complete implementation tasks
Examine previous interventions	Specify an impact model	• Define program components and activities	Develop mechanisms of self-regulation
Identify relevant stakeholders	Identify compatible and incompatible goals in the larger system	• Write job descriptions of staff and specify skills required	Specify a plan to build support
Conduct a systems analysis	Identify needs for interagency collaboration	Policy design: • Define the target population of the policy	
Identify barriers and supports		• Identify the responsible authority	
		• Define the provisions and procedures of the policy	

Reassessment and Review

This last step, the system analysis, involves conducting research on the system within which the problem exists. Most problems are produced by more than one source, and most solutions affect more than one part of a system. It is important, then, to learn as much as possible about how different decisions interact to produce the problem. For example, prison crowding is not simply the result of judges sending

Stage 5. Developing a Plan for Monitoring Program/ Policy Implementation	Stage 6. Developing a Plan for Evaluating Outcomes	Stage 7. Initiating the Program or Policy Design
Design instruments to collect monitoring data	Develop outcome measures based on objectives	Planning for failure: avoid exaggerated claims.
Designate responsibility to collect, store, and analyze data	Specify the research design to be used	Planning for success: ongoing reassessment, learning, and revision are crucial.
Develop information system capacities	Identify potential confounding factors	Learning and adapting: successful interventions must adapt to change.
Develop mechanisms to provide feedback to stakeholders	Identify users and uses of evaluation results	Initiate the program or policy design from Stage 3.
	Reassess the entire program/policy plan	Initiate the action plan from Stage 4.
		Initiate monitoring of program/policy (Stage 5 plan).
		Collect and analyze evaluation data; provide feedback to stakeholders (Stage 6 plan).
		Reassess the entire program/policy plan and make necessary modifications to increase fit with environment.

more people to prison: changes in laws pertaining to drug crimes, increases in drug-related violence, and the development of sentencing guidelines for judges all contributed to increasing prison populations.[19] Unless we understand *how* these changes affect the prison population, we stand little chance of constructing an effective solution.

Example 1.1

Prostitution as a Problem

After a series of well-publicized police sweeps and arrests, a community identifies prostitution as a serious *problem* in need of change. The presumed *cause*, determined by intuition rather than careful analysis, is that police have simply not taken the problem seriously enough. The proposed *intervention*, then, is a police crackdown, with intensive law enforcement targeted in areas frequented by prostitutes and their customers. However, what if these causal assumptions were wrong or left out something important? What if it turns out that the problem is mainly limited to the summer months, and the majority of prostitutes are teenage runaways trying to make money to survive? Such information might lead to a very different type of intervention—perhaps shelters, crisis counseling, or job training and assistance.

Stage 2. Setting Goals and Objectives

Every intervention attempts to achieve some kind of outcome (i.e., some change in the problem), but sometimes it is difficult to figure out what it is. "*Goals*" are broad aims of the intervention (e.g., reduce drug abuse); *objectives* specify explicit and measurable outcomes. It is amazing how many expensive and otherwise well-designed interventions fail to define adequately the desired outcomes of the intervention. Without specific, agreed-upon criteria for success, it would be impossible to determine whether any intervention worked. If you don't know where you are going, as the saying goes, don't be surprised when you don't get there. Major activities at this stage include the following:

- Seek participation from different individuals and agencies in goal setting.

- Write goal statements specifying the general outcome to be obtained.

- Write specific outcome objectives for each goal: These should include a time frame for measuring impact and a specific measure of impact.

- Specify an impact model: this is a description of how the intervention will act upon a specific cause so as to bring about a change in the problem.

- Identify compatible and incompatible goals in the larger system: Where do values of different stakeholders overlap or conflict?

- Identify needs and opportunities for interagency collaboration. For example, police and prosecutors may need to collaborate to make a new drunk driving law work. Prosecutors could clarify the evidence needed to obtain convictions; police officers could strategize about the likelihood of obtaining different kinds of evidence.

Example 1.2

The Goals of Drunk Driving Laws

A new state law is passed that provides tougher sentences for drunk drivers. A mandatory 48-hour jail sentence is imposed on second-time offenders; a mandatory three-month jail term is imposed on third-time offenders. The goal is obvious: to reduce drunk driving. Six months after the law is passed, there is widespread disagreement about whether the law is working. Advocates of the law point to a 10 percent reduction in drunk driving arrests. Critics point to insurance statistics that indicate an increase in traffic accidents involving alcohol. Who is right? Does the law work or not? After much discussion, both sides realize that they lack an agreed-upon criterion for judging the outcome of the intervention. Eventually, they agree that a desirable outcome (change in the problem) is the following: one year after the law was passed, there should be a 30 percent reduction in auto fatalities due to drunk driving. The difficulty, it turns out, is that no specific objective was defined before the law was passed, and without such an objective, multiple and conflicting criteria for deciding "outcome" could be debated endlessly.

Stage 3. Designing the Program or Policy

This is one of the most crucial and time-consuming stages in the planning process. It is much more detailed than often realized, and it often requires considerable review of information collected during the first two stages of planning. It involves specifying, in as much detail as possible, who does what to whom, in what order, and how much? It is the "guts" of the program or policy, including its staff, its services, and its clients. While the planning steps for programs and policies are generally similar, at the design stage we find it best to distinguish activities for programs and policies separately. Major activities for program design include:

- *Define the target population*: Who is to be served or changed? This often involves specifying some level of need (e.g., level of drug involvement) and characteristics of intended clients (e.g., age, gender, geographic residence).

- *Define client selection and intake procedures*: How are clients selected and recruited for the intervention? For example, boot camp programs are often intended for first-time, nonviolent offenders. A list of eligible clients might be obtained from court records; an application from the client may be required; an interview and screening process may be required to determine the client's suitability for the program.

- *Define program components*: The precise nature, amount, and sequence of services provided must be specified. Who does what to whom, in what order, and how much? Boot camp programs, for example, might contain several components: military-style drills and physical training, academic or vocational education, life skills or problem-solving training, drug awareness education, and social skills training.

- *Write job descriptions of staff, and define the skills and training required.* How many and what kind of staff are required to operate the program? What specific duties will they carry out? What kind of qualifications do they need, and what further training will be necessary? How much money is needed for staff salaries and training?

Major activities for policy design include:

- *Define the target population of the policy*: Which persons or groups are included and which are not? For example, legislators in various states had to write specific requirements for inclusion and exclusion under new three-strikes laws. Which offenders (e.g., felony vs. misdemeanor) and offenses (e.g., violent vs. property) should be included?

- *Identify the responsible authority*: Who is required to carry out the policy, and what will their responsibilities be? For example, what roles will judges, prosecutors, defense attorneys, and others play in any case, and how can we ensure that each understands three-strikes policy correctly? Will each party understand his or her individual responsibilities and options? Will they need special training or orientation? Are additional court or prison resources required?

- *Define the provisions of the policy*: A policy should identify the sanctions, services, opportunities, or interventions that will be delivered, as well as the conditions that must be met in order for the policy to be carried out. Under a new three-strikes policy, for example, state legislators had to write specific rules for how case-processing and sentencing decisions were to be made: When and how would the District Attorney's office make charging decisions under the new law? How would pretrial motions be handled? Would trials be conducted in private or in public? What are the appropriate terms of incarceration?

- *Delineate the procedures that must be followed*: Individuals responsible for implementing a specific set of rules must clearly understand the specific actions to be taken to ensure that the policy is carried out consistently. For example, three-strikes laws specify decisions regarding the charging, processing, and sentencing of repeat offenders. These might include the court's procedures for notifying a suspect and his or her attorney that the suspect is about to be charged under three-strikes law, including delivery of written notice, and clearly specifying the suspect's legal rights and options under the new law. Procedures may also specify who signs such forms, other individuals or agencies that need to be notified, and records that must be maintained.

Example 1.3

The Design of a Boot Camp Program

Boot camps proliferated in the late 1980s and early 1990s.[20] By 1995, state correctional agencies operated 75 boot camps for adults, state and local agencies operated 30 juvenile boot camps, and larger counties operated 18 boot camps in local jails. Many different kinds of boot camp programs evolved. Earlier camps stressed military discipline, physical training, and hard work; "second-generation" boot camps emphasized rehabilitation by adding components including alcohol and drug treatment and prosocial skills training.[21] Some added intensive post-release supervision, including electronic monitoring, home confinement, and random urine tests. Some, particularly camps for juveniles, emphasized educational and vocational skills instead of military discipline.

For example, the Massachusetts Boot Camp Program offered a mix of rigid military discipline with treatment approaches.[22] This boot camp was an intensive 16-week modified therapeutic community program. The camp provided a balance of military-style discipline, community service, and programming (substance abuse, adult basic education, wellness, and life skills), focusing on accountability.[23] Inmates received approximately 30 hours of programming per week. All sessions began and ended with positive, upbeat music to stimulate motivation. During classes, classical music was used to produce a calming effect. Instructors focused attention on recovery-based themes (e.g., give 110 percent, be all you can be, participate, take the first step, see the situation clearly). Classrooms and barracks were filled with visual symbols including decision-making techniques; the 12 steps of recovery; tools of recovery; being honest, open, and willing; and following an orderly direction.

There are many more questions we could ask about program services, as well as staff and clients, but knowing simply that a program is a "boot camp" would not tell us very much at all. In a review of studies of boot camps published over a period of 10 years, Parent found that each boot camp had a different design. This lack of uniformity made it difficult to assess which components were and were not successful, and it made comparisons of one boot camp to another extremely difficult.

Stage 4. Developing an Action Plan

Once the design is complete, the next stage is to develop an "action plan" that specifies the sequence of tasks that need to be completed in order to successfully launch or implement the program or policy. These include technical and interpersonal tasks (e.g., identifying and acquiring the necessary resources for the program; locating office space and/or meeting space; hiring and training staff; designing client intake and reporting forms; purchasing equipment and supplies; setting dates and assigning responsibility for the completion of specific tasks). Major activities at this stage include the following:

- Identify resources needed and make cost projections: How much funding is needed?

- Plan to acquire or reallocate resources: How will funding be acquired?

- Specify dates by which implementation tasks will be accomplished. Assign responsibilities to staff members for carrying out tasks.

- Develop mechanisms of self-regulation (create mechanisms to monitor staff performance and enhance communication).

- Specify a plan to maintain and build support.

- Anticipate sources of resistance and develop responses.

Example 1.4

Action Planning for a Delinquency Prevention Program

This example is adapted from a funding proposal submitted by a community-based delinquency prevention program.[24] Major program components include: a seven-day challenge course in which juveniles are encouraged to examine their lives and set goals; one-to-one mentoring of youths by adult partners; and weekly follow-through meetings of all mentors and clients. The proposal spells out in necessary detail a myriad of tasks, responsibilities, and costs required in order to launch the program. For example:

Project Coordinator Training and Development. Through structured workshops and meetings, the *Consultant* will train and support the development of the applicant's staff person designated to be responsible for the successful management of the year-long project. The Consultant will train this *Program Coordinator* to enroll and manage community volunteers to function on-site as: *Facilitators, Committed Partners, Course Production Team, Coaches, Situation Intervention Team, and Security.* The Program Coordinator will also be trained to target and enroll *Youth Participants* through presentations to appropriate youth-serving agencies, and to ensure maximum

---

Example 1.4, *continued*

benefit from their participation in the program. The Consultant will also train and support the Project Coordinator in successfully managing the year-long follow-through program (training hours by quarter: 1st Qtr. = 260 hours, 2nd Qtr. = 195 hours, 3rd Qtr. = 195 hours, 4th Qtr. = 130 hours. Total training hours = 780 x 40.00 per hr. = $31,200).

Facilitator Workshop. This three-day session trains and empowers prospective Facilitators to ensure the success of the youths participating in the program (1 Workshop Leader x 3 days x $350 per day = $1,050).

Youth Enrollment Workshops. These workshops are designed to train the requisite teams of volunteers to successfully enroll 30 youths into the program and enable them to support youths in maintaining their commitments through Departure (2 Youth Enrollment Coaches x 5 days apiece x $350 per day = $3,500).

Mentor Training. Adult mentors are trained to support youths to participate fully in the seven-day course and the Follow-through Program (1 Workshop Leader x 3 days x $350 per day = $1,050).

Volunteer Enrollment Training (Course Production Team, Coaches, Situation Intervention Team, and Security). Over the course of three days this segment will prepare the Course Production Team to execute the seven-day Course. The Team learns what they can expect to encounter in the process of conducting a seven-day course and what will be expected of them. This training also empowers the Coaches and Situation Intervention Team to support the Facilitators and Youth Participants in participating fully in all seven-day course activities, including keeping their agreements and responding to breakdowns (3 Trainers x 3 days apiece x $350 per day = $3,150).

Stage 5. Developing a Plan for Monitoring Program/Policy Implementation

At this stage, we attempt to find out if the program or policy *was* implemented properly. Sometimes referred to as "process evaluation," "monitoring" refers to the collection of information to determine to what degree the program/policy design or blueprint (Stage 3) is being carried out as planned. Data is collected to find out what is actually being delivered to clients (e.g., observations, surveys, interviews). The purpose is to identify gaps between the "program on paper" (design) and the "program in action." Adjustments then need to be made to revise either the design of the program or policy (e.g., program components) or to make what is being done conform to the intended design. We ask the following types of questions at this stage: Are program/policy activities actually being carried out as planned? Is the intended target population being reached? Are staff carrying out their assigned responsibilities? Major activities at this stage include the following:

- Design monitoring instruments to collect data.

- Designate responsibility for data collection, storage, and analysis.

- Develop information system capacities.

- Develop mechanisms to provide feedback to staff, clients, and stakeholders.

Example 1.5

Monitoring Implementation of Prison-Based Therapeutic Community (TC) Drug Treatment Programs

In recent years, modified therapeutic community (TC) drug treatment programs have been widely implemented in prison settings. The aim of the TC is total lifestyle change, including abstinence from drugs, elimination of antisocial behavior, and development of prosocial attitudes and values. Individual and group counseling, encounter groups, peer pressure, role models, and a system of incentives and sanctions form the core of these programs. Inmate residents of the TC live together, participate in self-help groups, and take responsibility for their own recovery. A strong sense of community is a critical treatment component. TC participants help one another to recognize, confront, and change the negative values and behaviors that led them to substance abuse and criminal behavior.

In spite of the pervasiveness of the prison TC model, surprisingly little information is available about the *variety* (e.g., intensity, duration, and quality) of prison-based drug treatment programs in local and state correctional systems.[25] Comprehensive assessments of treatment processes within these programs is necessary in order to determine *how* TC programs are implemented across different sites, *which* treatment components of the TC model are most effective, and *the degree* to which newly developed programs actually implement services in a manner consistent with professionally accepted standards of TC treatment.[26]

Taxman and Bouffard developed a monitoring technique that emphasizes structured observations conducted by well-trained researchers, in addition to structured interviews, examination of official program documents, and collection of client-based data (e.g., drug testing, infractions, disciplinary actions).[27] Structured observations examine the degree to which certain treatment components typically associated with the TC model are present. The instrument yields narrative data for qualitative analysis, as well as quantitative scores (e.g., using five-point Likert scales, researchers rate the degree to which a particular program component was used in a treatment session). The instrument assesses five components: (1) program emphasis, (2) treatment topics, (3) treatment activities, (4) treatment style, and (5) view of the residential community.

Example 1.5, *continued*

Researchers examined six TC programs in short-term jails.[28] One or two full-time staff members typically staffed each program. The programs typically offered two to three scheduled treatment activities each weekday during regular business hours. On average, the programs served five to 12 clients at a time, with four sites providing services to both men's and women's groups (five to 12 members each). Clients volunteered to enter these programs after having been screened for eligibility based primarily on a history of drug abuse. Results on five major dimensions are briefly summarized below.

- *Program emphasis*: Few of the programs implemented the overall TC philosophy. Interviews with staff members indicated that they did not use a particular program model, formal curriculum, or structured treatment phases.

- *Treatment topics*: Programs tended to focus on members' cognitive processes, emotional reactions, and behavior, but infrequently dealt with issues related to the development of a prosocial value orientation and a strong working group of peers.

- *Treatment process*: Researchers observed a focus on awareness training, emotional growth training, and peer encounter techniques. The most commonly used activities, however, emphasized individual rather than group work, underutilizing activities intended to facilitate community cohesion.

- *Treatment style*: The programs relied heavily upon formal group meetings. In contrast to the TC model, however, informal (unscheduled and client-initiated) meetings were relatively rare, as indicated by observational data and interviews with both counselors and group members.

- *View of the community*: Five sites utilized high levels of membership feedback and participation. However, only three sites used highly structured systems (e.g., clearly defined roles for group members). Four sites relied heavily upon individual relationships rather than role models and relationships within the group, an approach inconsistent with the community-oriented goals of the traditional TC approach.

Overall, monitoring illustrated a lack of correspondence between the prototypical TC model and the implementation of these six programs. Given such slippage from the intended program design, treatment effectiveness is likely to be impaired. Although several studies have suggested reduced recidivism due to prison-based TC treatment, a given TC must first demonstrate treatment integrity before positive effects can be expected.

Stage 6. Developing a Plan for Evaluating Outcomes

The goal of this stage is to develop a research design for measuring program or policy outcome (a specific, intended change in the problem, as defined by objectives). Did the program or policy achieve its intended objectives? Why or why not? Note that all planning including the formulation of an evaluation plan should precede the actual start-up of the program or policy (Stage 7). Major activities at this stage include the following:

- Develop outcome measures based on objectives.

- Specify the research design to be used.

- Identify potential confounding factors (factors other than the program that may have influenced measured outcomes).

- Identify users and uses of evaluation results.

- Reassess the entire program or policy plan.

Example 1.6

The Kansas City Gun Experiment

If police could get more guns off the street, would there be fewer gun crimes? This was the question posed by the Kansas City Gun Experiment.[29] The experiment developed out of a federal grant awarded to the Kansas City (Missouri) Police Department (KCPD) under the federal "Weed and Seed" program. The intervention was based on the theory that additional, proactive police patrols to detect gun violations would increase gun seizures, which, in turn, would reduce gun crime either by deterring potential offenders or by incapacitating greater numbers of gun-using criminals.[30]

The target beat was an 80-by-10-block area with a 1991 homicide rate of 177 per 100,000 persons, about 20 times the national average. The population was mostly nonwhite; the area had very low property values and consisted predominantly of single-family detached homes. A comparison beat with very similar population demographics and similar crime rates (e.g., total firearm-related crimes, shots fired per incident, drive by shootings, and homicides) was chosen.

For 29 weeks, from July 7, 1992, to January 27, 1993, the Kansas City Police Department focused extra patrol attention on gun crime "hot spots" in the target area. Techniques included stop-and-search frisks based upon reasonable suspicion, searches incident to an arrest on other charges (i.e., the basis for a legitimate arrest has already been established), and safety frisks associated with car stops for traffic violations. Officer overtime was paid for by

Example 1.6, *continued*

the federal grant. While no special efforts were made to limit police activities in the comparison beat, there were no special funds available for extra patrol time in that area. The "hot spot" locations were identified by a computer analysis of all gun crimes in the area.

Because the extra patrol hours were federally funded, separate bookkeeping was required to document the time. In addition, an evaluator accompanied the officers on 300 hours of "hot spots" patrol and coded every shift activity narrative for patrol time and enforcement in and out of the area. Property room data on guns seized, computerized crime reports, calls for service data, and arrest records were analyzed for both areas under the study.

The primary data analyses compared all 29 weeks of the Phase 1 patrol program to the 29 weeks preceding phase 1. Other analyses added all of 1991 and 1993. The 1993 data included six months with no overtime patrols and Phase 2 overtime patrols for six months in the second half of 1993. Analyses thus covered six six-month periods, two of which had the program and four of which did not.

The officers generated a lot of activity. Both in and out of the target beat, the directed patrols issued 1,090 traffic citations, conducted 948 car checks and 532 pedestrian checks, and made 170 state or federal arrests and 446 city arrests, for an average of one police intervention for every 40 minutes per patrol car.

Evaluation results indicated that directed police patrols in gun crime "hot spots" reduced gun crimes by increasing the seizures of illegally carried guns. Gun seizures by police in the target area increased significantly from 46 before the intervention to 76 afterward (an increase of 65 percent), while gun crimes declined significantly from 169 to 86 (a decrease of 49 percent). The numbers of guns found during car checks tripled. During the same time period, neither gun crimes nor guns seized changed significantly in the comparison beat several miles away. If anything, the number of guns seized in the comparison beat dropped slightly from 85 to 72, and the number of gun crimes increased very slightly from 184 to 192. Further, drive-by shootings dropped from seven to one in the target area, doubled from six to 12 in the comparison area, and showed no displacement to adjoining beats. Homicides decreased significantly in the target area but not in the comparison area.

Several alternative hypotheses were ruled out. First, only gun crimes were affected by the directed patrols, with no changes in the number of calls for service or in the total number of violent or nonviolent crimes reported. Second, there was no measurable displacement of gun crimes to patrol beats surrounding the target area, as gun crimes remained stable in the seven contiguous beats. Before and after surveys of citizens showed that respondents in the target area became less fearful of crime and more positive about their neighborhood than respondents in the comparison area.

While the before-after study of the target beat and the comparison beat could not eliminate ail possible competing explanations for the results, the inverse correlation between gun seizures and gun crime suggests that proactive policing of gun crimes in high-risk places is a promising strategy deserving of further research.

Stage 7. Initiating the Program or Policy Plan

Only after planning has addressed the previous six stages is the program or policy actually ready to be launched. None of the prior six stages, including monitoring and evaluation, should come as afterthoughts. To increase the likelihood of success, all six stages of planning should ideally be completed prior to the initial start date. If a review of the planning process uncovers any discrepancies at any of the six prior stages, these gaps should be carefully addressed before proceeding. Stage 7, then, involves putting into motion the program or policy *design* and *action plan* (Stages 3 and 4), *monitoring* program or policy implementation (Stage 5), and, if appropriate, *evaluating* outcomes (Stage 6). Once evaluation data is analyzed, feedback is provided to all stakeholders, and the program/policy design should be thoroughly reassessed to determine where revisions are necessary. At the end of the process, the change agent asks whether further adjustments are necessary to meet objectives. What are the strengths and weaknesses of the program or policy? Decisions may have to be made about whether a program should be launched (or continued) and whether it should receive funding. Major activities at this stage include the following:

- Initiate the program/policy design and action plan.
- Begin monitoring program/policy implementation.
- Make adjustments to the program/policy plan as gaps are found.
- Decide whether the program/policy is ready to be evaluated.
- Collect and analyze evaluation data.
- Provide feedback to users and stakeholders.
- Review and reassess the entire program/policy plan and make modifications where needed.

This last point is extremely important. Several writers have commented on the importance of mutual adaptation: both the intervention and the environment must change if the new program or policy is going to work.[31] Lots of changes are made in the criminal justice system, but few of them stick. One important reason is that the intervention and the organizational environment didn't fit well enough.

Imagine a family adopting a 12-year-old child. The family system has to make room for this new member and shift some of its time, attention, and emotional resources to meet the child's needs. At the same time, the child needs to make changes. She must learn the family's rules, routines, and norms, and learn the idiosyncrasies of each family member. Both the child and the family adapt interactively in response to each other's actions and reactions.

In much the same way, successful implementation of a new program requires mutual adaptation. In New York City, for example, staff at the Center for Alternative Sentencing and Employment Services (CASES) wanted to make sure that their clients fit the target population: jail-bound, not probation-bound, offenders.[32] The program was designed to provide intensive community services that would enable offenders to stay in the community. The system analysis showed, however, that judges in the different boroughs of New York used different criteria for placing offenders in jail. In Queens, for example, judges required fewer jail sentences for offenders than did judges in Manhattan. In order to prevent the CASES program from being used for probation-bound cases, staff adjusted the criteria for accepting clients to the sentencing patterns in each borough. Adaptation of the program increased its chances of achieving its objective (keeping offenders in the community).

Conclusion

We need a systematic *plan* for any change effort. Good intentions are rarely sufficient to bring about successful change. We must beware of the "activist bias,"[33] by which well-intentioned advocates of change assume that they already know what the problem is and what is needed. Such advocates may insist that we desist all this prolonged planning and simply "get on with it." The perils of unplanned or poorly planned change should by now be obvious: expensive, poorly articulated, poorly implemented, ineffective programs and policies that are unable to successfully compete for scarce funds. There are *four key points* to remember about this seven-stage, systematic model of planned change that you are about to explore:

1. *Program and policy planning is an interactive and ongoing process.* It is crucial to review and modify planning (where needed) at each stage of the analysis. This takes time, but it is time well spent.

2. *A rational planning approach provides a framework for developing logical and effective programs and policies.* The default (too often) is to use unarticulated and untested assumptions to guide planning.

3. *Key to success are participation and communication with all stakeholders (e.g., program staff, clients, individuals or agencies whose cooperation is needed, funding sources, citizens affected by the intervention, elected representatives) throughout the change process.*

4. *Rarely does planning go smoothly.* We strongly believe that the advantages of systematically attending to the elements of planning discussed in this book can greatly improve the chances of devel-

oping effective policies and programs. We also recognize that the environments in which this planning occurs are messy and unpredictable. Willpower, a clear vision of what you want to accomplish, and lots of communication are required in order to remain rooted in the planning process. Planned change increases the likelihood of successful intervention; it cannot guarantee it.

In the next seven chapters, we provide detailed discussions of the seven stages of planning and the major concepts and terms associated with each stage. We have much emphasis on providing case studies that illustrate these concepts and help the reader discover how these concepts can be applied in a variety of criminal justice contexts.

What's to Come?

Chapter 2: This chapter discusses one of the most critical and most overlooked stages of planning—defining and understanding the problem or issue that is driving the planning process.

Chapter 3: Once we have an understanding of the problem or issue, then we can identify what we want to achieve. Chapter 3 discusses the ways in which goals and objectives are framed so that we can communicate around the direction in which we want our change effort to move and can know when we are heading in the right direction.

Chapter 4: In this chapter, we focus on how to design effective policies and programs. Design involves a number of critical decisions, such as who specifically will benefit from the intervention, that will affect greatly our ability to achieve our goals.

Chapter 5: Next we will learn about some of the more pragmatic aspects of planning that are essential to the real world of planning, including budgeting and cost projections, orienting staff, and assigning responsibility for completion of specific implementation tasks.

Chapter 6: This chapter gets us into the area of accountability. We decided what we wanted to do and who would do what. Now we need to make sure that we do it. We need to monitor our activities and learn about when and why we drift away from what we set out to do.

Chapter 7: How can we learn about what's working and what's not? How can we improve upon our past performance? These are questions that we discuss in the context of evaluation. The methods of evaluation are important to understand in order to draw valid conclusions.

Chapter 8: Finally, Chapter 8 brings us into the arena of experience. As we carry out our plans, new information is created that requires a response. A program or policy may have looked good on paper, but it must adapt to the real world of people, organizations, and competing goals. The results of evaluation data should be used to guide a continuous process of reassessment and improvement.

DISCUSSION QUESTIONS

1. Describe three trends that have increased the need for planned change.

2. Define *planned change* and give an example.

3. Define *unplanned change* and give an example.

4. Define and describe an example of each of the following: (1) policy, (2) program, and (3) project.

5. Why are collaborative strategies of change preferable to conflict strategies? Explain.

6. Briefly describe the first six stages of planned change (analyzing the problem, setting goals and objectives, designing the program, developing an action plan, monitoring program implementation, and evaluating outcomes). What are the major questions we need to ask at each stage?

7. How did the 1968 President's Commission Report influence thinking about criminal justice planning?

8. Give an example of *mutual adaptation*.

EXERCISE 1.1

Describe briefly, in three paragraphs: (a) Some *problem* in criminal justice. Why is it a problem? What makes it a problem? (b) What is one possible *cause* of this problem? (c) What is one possible *intervention* (a program or policy, as defined earlier in this chapter) that might change this problem?

EXERCISE 1.2

Review the example described in the preface ("The Pitfalls of Poor Planning: Three-Strikes Legislation"). Briefly illustrate how the seven-stage model of planned change can be used to *analyze an existing policy*. Give one example for each of the seven stages.

Endnotes

[1]   Kettner, Peter M., John M. Daley, and Ann Weaver Nichols (1985). *Initiating Change in Organizations and Communities*. Monterey, CA: Brooks/Cole.

[2]   Ibid, note 1.

[3]   Rossi, Peter (1991). *Down and Out in America: The Origins of Homelessness* (2nd ed.). Chicago: University of Chicago Press.

[4]   Buzawa, Eve S., and Carl G. Buzawa (2003). *Domestic Violence: The Criminal Justice Response*, 3rd ed. Newbury Park, CA: Sage.

[5]   Welsh, Wayne N., and Gary Zajac (2004). "Building an Effective Research Partnership Between a University and a State Correctional Agency: Assessment of Drug Treatment in Pennsylvania Prisons." *The Prison Journal*, 84 (2):1-28.

[6]   Zajac, Gary (1997). "Reinventing Government and Reaffirming Ethics: Implications for Organizational Development in the Public Sector." *Public Administration Quarterly*, 20(4), 385-404.

[7]   Sherman, L.W., D. Gottfredson, D. MacKenzie, J. Eck, P. Reute, and S. Bushway, (eds.) (1998). *Preventing Crime: What Works, What Doesn't, What's Promising*. Washington, DC: U.S. Department of Justice, National Institute of Justice.

[8]   Weick, K.E. (1995). *Sensemaking in Organizations*. Thousand Oaks, CA: Sage.

[9]   Tonry, Michael (1995). *Malign Neglect: Race, Crime, and Punishment in America*. New York: Oxford University Press.

[10] Lovrich, Nicholas P., Travis C. Pratt, Michael J. Gaffney, and Charles J. Johnson (2003). *National Forensic DNA Study Report* (NCJ 203970). Washington, DC: U.S. Department of Justice, National Institute of Justice. Available at: *http://www.ncjrs.org/pdffiles1/nij/grants/203970.pdf*

[11] Petersilia, Joan (2003). *When Prisoners Come Home: Parole and Prisoner Reentry*. New York: Oxford University Press.

[12] Stambaugh, Hollis, David Beaupre, David J. Icove, Richard Baker, Wayne Cassaday, and Wayne P. Williams (2000). *State and Local Law Enforcement Needs to Combat Electronic Crime*. (NCJ 183451) Washington, DC: U.S. Department of Justice, Office of Justice Programs. Available at: *http://www.ncjrs.org/pdf files1/nij/183451.pdf* (retrieved March 5, 2004).

[13] Ibid, note 1.

[14] Welsh, Wayne N. (1995). *Counties in Court: Jail Overcrowding and Court-Ordered Reform*. Philadelphia: Temple University Press.

[15] President's Commission on Law Enforcement and Administration of Justice (1968). *The Challenge of Crime in a Free Society*. New York: Avon Books.

[16] Walker, Samuel (1992). "Origins of the Contemporary Criminal Justice Paradigm: The American Bar Foundation Survey, 1953-1969." *Justice Quarterly*, 9:47-76.; see also Chapter 2 of this book.

[17] Moore, Mark (1998). "Synthesis of Symposium." In U.S. Department of Justice, *The Challenge of Crime in a Free Society: Looking Back, Looking Forward* (pp. 167-178). Symposium on the 30th Anniversary of the President's Commission on Law Enforcement and Administration of Justice. (NCJ 170029) Washington, DC: U.S. Department of Justice, Office of Justice Programs.

[18] U.S. Department of Justice (1998). *The Challenge of Crime in a Free Society: Looking Back, Looking Forward*. Symposium on the 30th Anniversary of the President's Commission on Law Enforcement and Administration of Justice. (NCJ 170029) Washington, DC: U.S. Department of Justice, Office of Justice Programs.

[19] Blumstein, Alfred, and Allen J. Beck (1999). "Population Growth in U.S. Prisons, 1980-1996" (pp. 17-61). In M. Tonry and J. Petersilia (eds.), *Prisons, Crime and Justice, v. 26*. Chicago: University of Chicago Press.

[20] Parent, Dale G. (2003). *Correctional Boot Camps: Lessons From a Decade of Research* (NCJ 197018). Washington, DC: U.S. Department of Justice, Office of Justice Programs, National Institute of Justice. Available at: *http://www.ncjrs.org/ pdffiles1/nij/197018.pdf*

[21] Ibid, note 21.

[22] Ransom, George, and Mary Ellen Mastrorilli (1993). "The Massachusetts Boot Camp: Inmate Anecdotes." *The Prison Journal*, 73:307-318.

[23] Valle, S. (1989) "Accountability for Addicted Inmates." *The Counselor*, March/April:7-8.

[24] Welsh, Wayne N., Philip Harris, and Patricia Jenkins (1996). "Reducing Overrepresentation of Minorities in Juvenile Justice: Development of Community-Based Programs in Pennsylvania." *Crime & Delinquency*, 42(1):76-98.

[25] Welsh, Wayne N., and Gary Zajac (2004). "A Census of Prison-Based Drug Treatment Programs: Implications for Programming, Policy, and Evaluation." *Crime & Delinquency*, 50(1):108-133.

26   Office of National Drug Control Policy (ONDCP). (1999). *Therapeutic Communities in Correctional Wettings: The Prison Based TC Standards Development Project. Final Report of Phase II* (NCJ-179365). Washington, DC: Executive Office of the President, Office of National Drug Control Policy.

27   Taxman, Faye, and Jeffery A. Bouffard (2002). "Assessing Therapeutic Integrity in Modified Therapeutic Communities for Drug-Involved Offenders." *The Prison Journal* 82, 189-212.

28   Ibid, note 28.

29   Sherman, L.W., J.W. Shaw, and D.P. Rogan (1995). *The Kansas City Gun Experiment* (NCJ-150855). Washington, DC: U.S. Department of Justice, Office of Justice Programs, National Institute of Justice.

30   Sherman, L.W., and D. Rogan (1995). "Effects of Gun Seizures on Gun Violence: Hot Spots, Patrol in Kansas City." *Justice Quarterly*, 12, 673-693

31   Berman, P. (1981). "Thinking about Programmed and Adaptive Implementation: Matching Strategies to Situations." In H. Ingram and D. Mann (eds.), *Why Policies Succeed or Fail*. Beverly Hills, CA: Sage; Harris, P., and S. Smith (1996). "Developing Community Corrections: An Implementation Perspective." In A.T. Harland (ed.), *Choosing Correctional Options that Work: Defining the Demand and Evaluating the Supply*. Thousand Oaks, CA: Sage; McLaughlin, M. (1976). "Implementation as Mutual Adaptation: Change in Classroom Organization." In W. Williams and R.F. Elmore (eds.), *Social Program Evaluation*. San Diego: Academic Press.

32   Schall, E., and E. Neises (1998). "Managing the Risk of Innovation: Strategies for Leadership." *Corrections Management Quarterly*, 2(4):46-55; see also Clear, Todd R., Eric Cadora, Sarah Byer, and Charles Swartz (2003). *Community Justice*. Belmont, CA: Wadsworth.

33   Sieber, Sam D. (1981). *Fatal Remedies*. New York: Plenum.

CHAPTER 2

Analyzing the Problem

CHAPTER OUTLINE

▶ *Document the need for change*: Collect and analyze data to define what the problem is, where it is, how big it is, and who is affected by it. What evidence of the problem exists?

▶ *Describe the history of the problem*: How long has the problem existed? How has it changed over time?

▶ *Examine potential causes of the problem:* What causes the problem? What theories do we have? The intervention to be chosen *must* target one or more specific causes supported by research.

▶ *Examine previous interventions* that have tried to change this problem, identify the most promising interventions, and choose a preferred intervention approach. We need to analyze available information to direct decisions about a possible course of action.

▶ *Identify relevant stakeholders*: Do different groups of people have different definitions of the problem? Who is affected by the problem?

▶ *Conduct a systems analysis*: Conduct research on the system within which the problem exists, and determine how the system may create, contribute to, or maintain the problem.

▶ *Identify barriers to change and supports for change*: Who is likely to support a certain course of action, and who is likely to resist it?

Some preliminary analysis is needed to identify the issues involved with trying to change a particular problem. This important analysis sets the stage for all subsequent planning activities. Beware of the *activist bias*: the notion that we already know what to do, so let's get on with it. In almost all cases, the person who expresses such a view has a vague definition of the problem and its causes, and little knowledge of successful interventions. Without intending it, he or she is advocating a process of unplanned change that maximizes the likelihood of a poorly planned, poorly implemented, and ineffective intervention. The many hours of hard work and the motivation that must surely guide any successful change effort should not be wasted on unplanned change. How we analyze the problem guides what kind of interventions we initiate. If problem analysis is flawed, subsequent program or policy planning is also likely to be faulty.

Document the Need for Change

We begin analysis of a problem by examining information about the problem. We are interested in questions like the following: How do we define the problem? How big is it, and where is it? Is there a potential for change? We especially want to provide evidence for the existence of a need or problem. We need to be very careful here. The media, politicians, or even criminal justice officials socially construct many problems. By *social constructions*, we mean that certain problems are perceived, and decisions are made to focus attention and resources on a particular problem.[1] However, *perceptions* of a problem and *reactions* to it may be quite different than the actual size or distribution of a problem. We need methods to document, describe, and analyze problems. At minimum, we need to be sure that a problem actually exists before taking any specific action, but we also need to know about the size and distribution of a problem in order to plan effective solutions.

Although the distinction is somewhat arbitrary, it is often worthwhile to differentiate a *need* from a *problem*. Students often point out that many "conditions" could be stated either way: for example, if victims of domestic violence lack access to shelters, then is there not only a need but also a problem, such as repeat incidents of abuse of this population? However arbitrary the distinction might appear at first glance, it might make a large difference in the problem analysis (what kind of information we collect), analysis of causes (explanations of why certain conditions are lacking

Need

A need is a *lack* of something that contributes to the discomfort or suffering of a particular group of people. For example, we might argue that there is a need for drug treatment programs for convicted offenders, or that there is a need for shelters for abused women. In each case, an existing lack of services perpetuates the difficulties experienced by the target population.

Example 2.1

School Violence: A Problem Out of Control?

Shootings in and around schools have fueled a national debate about school disorder, largely in response to tragic incidents such as the Columbine High School massacre in Littleton, Colorado, on April 20, 1999, and the Jonesboro, Arkansas, schoolyard shootings on March 24, 1998. Following several other widely publicized shootings on school properties, hundreds of school districts across the United States announced tougher disciplinary policies and security measures. While dramatic incidents fuel perceptions that school violence is out of control, available data suggest a more modest interpretation. The primary source of national data about victimization in schools, for example, is the School Crime Supplement (SCS), added to the National Crime Victimization Survey (NCVS) in 1989 and repeated in 1995, 1999, and 2001.[2] Results showed that the percentage of students ages 12 through 18 reporting one or more criminal victimizations (including either theft or violent crimes) at school during the previous six months decreased from 9.5 percent in 1995 to 7.6 percent in 1999 to 5.5 percent in 2001. The percentage of students reporting violent victimization also decreased from 3.0 percent in 1995 to 2.3 percent in 1999 to 1.8 percent in 2001. Juveniles historically commit only a small proportion of all homicides.[3] In 2002, juveniles committed only 848 (5.4 percent) of 15,813 known homicides.[4] Fortunately, tragedies such as that at Columbine are rare. Based upon current evidence, it is neither clear that school violence is out of control, nor that revision of school discipline and security policies is the proper solution. Thorough and localized problem analysis should precede the revision or development of school policies in any district.

---

versus why other conditions are present), and identification of relevant interventions (do we attempt to provide services that fill an important gap, or do we attempt to apply some intervention to change a problem?). Needs and problems are clearly related, but not identical.

Next, we attempt to apply some *boundaries* to the problem. For example, we might begin by stating a concern with juvenile violence. However, we are quickly overwhelmed with information not only about the problem, but about different causal explanations and various interventions. Are we really concerned with all types of juvenile violence, or just with more specific settings? Are we really interested in specific

Problem

A problem is the *presence* of something that contributes to the discomfort or suffering of a specific group. For example, we might argue that a specific community experiences a high rate of robberies committed by addicts to buy drugs, or that there is a high rate of repeat incidents of abuse of women applying to courts for protection orders. In each case, there is a clearly defined condition present that perpetuates the suffering of a particular group of people.

types of violence, such as gang violence, school violence, gun-related violence, drug-related violence, interpersonal conflicts versus violence committed against strangers, or instrumental (goal-oriented) versus affective (emotional) violence? This is an important point. We need to do some research first to narrow our definition of the problem. It is entirely possible that we might decide to focus not only on a specific type of violence, but upon a specific age group (say, middle-school children), a specific jurisdiction (e.g., a community with a high rate of violence, or a specific city, county, or state), or a particular demographic group (e.g., poor children living in inner-city slums). Whatever our reasons for choosing to set boundaries in particular ways (perhaps personal reasons, or perhaps political or theoretical interests), identifying boundaries involves making judgments about how widely or narrowly to define a problem. How specific versus comprehensive should the change be? Where are potential causes and potential interventions located (e.g., at the individual level, group level, community level, organizational level, or social structural level)?

We first attempt to document the need for change through an analysis of existing conditions. Is there a problem? How big is it? What is the level of "need"? What is the evidence for a problem? One way of documenting a problem is to look at its incidence versus prevalence.

Incidence

Incidence is the number of *new* cases of a problem within a specific time period (e.g., the number of new cases of AIDS diagnosed in a specific calendar year). According to the Joint United Nations Programme on HIV/AIDS, an estimated 5 million people worldwide acquired the human immunodeficiency virus (HIV) in 2003.[5]

Prevalence

Prevalance is the *existing* number of cases of a particular problem as of a specific date (e.g., the *total* number of people in the U.S. with AIDS as of a specific date). As of December 31, 2003, 40 million people worldwide were estimated to be living with HIV/AIDS.[6]

Where do we find this kind of statistical information, as well as more descriptive information about the problem? We usually need to look at some kind of data to estimate the degree and seriousness of a problem. There are several techniques available; we'll briefly review four of them for now. Wherever time and resources allow, it is always desirable to use as many techniques as possible to converge upon a specific problem.

Social indicators are perhaps the most accessible and widely used type of data for analyzing criminal justice problems. For example, the Uniform Crime Reports (UCR), collected by the FBI, contain all crimes reported to the police, as well as all police arrests for specific crimes. These figures are available for each state and for the nation as a whole. These figures are widely used to calculate changes in the homicide rate, for example, from year to year. Another widely used indicator is the National Crime Victimization Survey (NCVS), which is a survey administered to a national probability sample, asking respondents to report whether they have been a victim of specific crimes within a specific time period (e.g., the previous six months), as well as other information about any victimization, such as degree of injury suffered, and characteristics of the offender (if known).

Figure 2.1

Data Collection Techniques: Documenting the Need for Change

- **Key informant approach:** We could conduct interviews with local "experts" to assess level of need or seriousness of a problem (e.g., community leaders, police officers, social service agents, clergy, etc.). One problem with this technique is that people to be interviewed need to be selected carefully for their expertise. We need to be aware that their views may be biased or inaccurate.

- **Community forum:** We could bring together a wide variety of people interested in a particular problem. Through discussion and exchange of ideas, we attempt to identify major problems or needs to be addressed. One common difficulty is that the most vocal groups may not necessarily be representative of a given community (e.g., special interest groups).

- **Community survey:** We may decide to conduct a survey by sampling part of a community or specific areas in a city. We might ask people, for example, "How serious would you rate the following problems in your community . . .?" A common problem with this technique is that it requires skilled researchers, and it can be very expensive and time-consuming.

- **Social indicators:** Social indicators are statistics reflecting some set of social conditions in a particular area over time. For example, the U.S. Bureau of Census collects and reports extensive data on unemployment, housing, education, and crime. Common problems include difficulty in collecting data on certain questions (e.g., underreporting of illiteracy due to embarrassment), samples that are unrepresentative of the population (e.g., the census undercounts a large segment of transient urban dwellers), and questions about the accuracy (reliability and validity) of some data.

Examination of social indicators often leads to the definition of a problem and attempts at change. For example, as part of a Community Corrections Program Development Project, the National Institute of Corrections entered into a contract with researchers at Temple University to provide consultation to agencies developing specific community corrections programs. Orange County and Los Angeles Probation Departments filed a joint application that was selected for assistance under this project. Their analyses identified a small group of juveniles (about 8% of the juveniles in their study) who accounted for the great majority of repeat referrals to juvenile court. Program planning efforts for this targeted "high-risk" population became known as the "8% Solution."[7] Various county agencies (probation, health care, mental health, social services, and the schools) participated in a multiagency task force to address program planning.

Figure 2.2

Examples of Social Indicators for Criminal Justice Problems

One extremely valuable source of criminal justice data is the *Sourcebook of Criminal Justice Statistics*, an annual publication by the U.S. Department of Justice. It is available in the Government Documents section of most libraries, and on the Internet.[8] Here are two examples.

- *Drug use by high school seniors.* In 2002, in response to the question "On how many occasions, if any, have you used marihuana/hashish during the past 12 months?" 36.2 percent of high school seniors reported using these drugs at least once. This figure was up from 27.0 percent in 1990, but down from 38.5 percent reporting such use in 1997.[9]

- *Domestic violence.* In 2002, a "nonstranger" (i.e., an acquaintance, spouse, ex-spouse, parent, child, brother/sister, other relative, boyfriend/girlfriend) committed fully 67 percent of all non-fatal violent crimes against females.[10]

Social indicators are extremely useful for identifying the seriousness of a problem, how it varies across groups (e.g., income), and how it is changing over time (is it getting better or worse?). Such data are not without biases, however, and the potential user needs to be aware of these.[11] For example, crime victimization measures may be biased by numerous factors (e.g., respondent misunderstanding of questions or crime definitions; faulty recall of incidents and time periods; deliberate underreporting due to fear, embarrassment, or the respondent's participation in illegal activities). Police-reported crime rates such as the UCR also carry potential biases, including police errors in recording and coding crime incidents. Many crimes are never even reported to the police for various reasons (e.g., victim or witness fear, embarrassment, or mistrust of the legal system). Social indicators, like the problems they measure, can be viewed as social constructions rather than objective indicators of reality. As Reiss and Roth suggest: "Any set of crime statistics, therefore, is not based on some objectively observable universe of behavior. Rather, violent crime statistics are based on the events that are defined, captured, and processed as such by some institutional means of collecting and counting crimes. . . ."[12]

Example 2.2

The New York Crime Story: Fact or Fiction?

The following example demonstrates some of the difficulties involved in analyzing problems and potential causes. How does this example illustrate the points discussed so far in this chapter?

Should we hesitate before praising public officials for observed decreases in crime rates (or blaming them for increases)? Former New York Mayor Rudolph Giuliani and former Police Commissioner William Bratton claimed that reductions in police-recorded crime rates from 1991 to 1996 (including a 55% decrease in homicide rates) were due to improved crime-fighting strategies and a "zero tolerance" for crime. There are reasons to be skeptical.[13]

- The decline in the murder rate began in 1991, three years before either Giuliani or Bratton took office.

- Murder and violent crime rates dropped nationwide for the same time period: New York was not unique.

- Public officials assumed that police policies and resources are the major influences on crime statistics. Much criminological research over the past 30 years suggests otherwise.

- Many different factors influence crime rates, including changes in illegal drug markets, weapon availability, social and economic conditions, incarceration rates, age distribution of the population, and youth involvement in legitimate labor markets. It is extremely difficult to parcel out specific causes for crime decreases.[14]

Describe the History of the Problem

As part of a problem analysis, we need to know something about the history of the problem: How long has a given problem existed, and how has it changed over time? Some of this information will have been gathered through research methods such as "key person" interviews, community forums, surveys, or examination of social indicators. Most likely, however, we will need to look further in published literature for specific, important historical events that shaped the definition of something as a social problem in need of attention, and how responses to the problem changed over time. What significant event or events helped shape the perception of certain conditions as a social problem in need of change? Such historical events often include lawsuits, legislation, dramatic public events, or specific social indicators such as crime statistics.

Lawsuits often fuel the perception of a problem, as they did with domestic violence. Liability issues led police to seriously consider calls for reform. The first of several major cases was *Thurman et al. v. City of Torrington, Conn.*[15] After the defense successfully demonstrated that police showed deliberate indifference to continued pleas for help from Tracey Thurman, the court awarded Thurman $2.3 million in damages. This case not only raised awareness of the problem of domestic violence but also led many police departments to favor a presumption of arrest.

Legislation may also create an important push for change. For example, changes in the federal Juvenile Justice and Delinquency Prevention (JJDP) Act led to enormous state initiatives to reduce minority overrepresentation in juvenile justice (see Example 2.3 below).

Dramatic, violent, well-publicized events often demand the recognition of a problem, as did the prison riots at New York's Attica prison in September of 1971, which resulted in enormous damages and the deaths of 32 inmates and 11 guards. Attica riots led to the most intensive investigation of prison violence in U.S. history to date, and drove prison management policies for years to come.[16]

One useful technique for summarizing the history of responses to a problem is to construct a *"critical incidents" list*: a chronology of specific events explaining how a problem was recognized as such and how a specific type of intervention has developed. Once again, we caution readers that reactions to a problem are social constructions, not objective indicators of the problem. An example is given below.

Example 2.3

A Critical Incidents List: Reducing Disproportionate Minority Confinement (DMC) in Juvenile Justice

Here is a brief "critical incidents" list specifying major historical events and milestones in a national policy initiative. The efforts of one "model" state are included as an example.

- **1985-1988**: Intensive lobbying by various groups at the federal level raised awareness of the problem of minority overrepresentation in juvenile justice. Advocates documented the problem by pointing to various reports indicating that minority youths made up a majority of juveniles housed in secure detention facilities, even though they constituted only a small proportion of the overall juvenile population in each state.[17]

- **1988**: The Juvenile Justice and Delinquency Prevention (JJDP) Act was amended to require states that receive Formula Grants program funding to determine whether the proportion of juvenile minorities in confinement exceeded their proportion of the population and, if so, to develop cor-

---

Example 2.3, *continued*

---

rective strategies. In order to qualify for federal block grants, states were required to comply with the new Act.[18]

- **1989-1990:** States began to address provisions of the JJDP Act. Many states commissioned research studies to assess the problem.

- **1990:** The Juvenile Advisory Committee established the Minority Confinement Subcommittee to focus on the DMC issue in Pennsylvania. Analysis of 1988 and 1989 juvenile justice data revealed that all counties showed minority overrepresentation, which was amplified as cases moved through the system. In response to these analyses, the subcommittee funded outside research to identify causes and develop options to address the problem while simultaneously implementing prevention and intervention programs. This two-pronged approach guided the subsequent state DMC strategy.[19]

- **Spring of 1991:** Pennsylvania Commission on Crime and Delinquency (PCCD) held an informational session for various groups active in community-based programming for minority youths in Harrisburg and solicited proposals from various agencies interested in obtaining state funding to address the problem. Five programs were funded.

- **Fall of 1991:** PCCD commissioned an evaluation of the Harrisburg programs by a team of researchers at Shippensburg University.

- **1992:** The U.S. Congress strengthened the national commitment to addressing disproportionate confinement of minority youths in secure facilities by elevating this issue to a "core requirement" of the JJDP Act. Noncompliance with the core requirements results in the loss of 25 percent of the state's annual Formula Grants program allocation.

- **April of 1992:** Pennsylvania extended its initiative to Philadelphia, once again inviting various groups active in community-based programming to an informational session, and solicited proposals from agencies interested in obtaining state funding to address the problem. Four programs were funded.

- **1993:** PCCD commissioned an evaluation study of nine funded programs (five in Harrisburg and four in Philadelphia) by Temple University. The evaluation consisted of three parts: a community assessment of the target areas, including social, economic, and crime indicators; an evaluability assessment (i.e., ability to be evaluated) and process evaluation, which included clarification of program goals, activities, and objectives and an examination of service delivery; and an outcome evaluation of client performance both during and after participation in the programs through a review of police, juvenile justice, and school records from 1992 to 1995.

Example 2.3, *continued*

- **1993-1997.** The first DMC-related conference, "Crisis of Minority Over-representation," was held in Philadelphia in January 1993. A second conference, "Promising Approaches: Prevention and Intervention Services for Minority Youth," was held in Harrisburg in May 1997. This was followed by a third conference, "Promising Approaches II: Building Blocks for Prevention and Intervention Services for Minority Youth," in Pittsburgh in May 1998.

- **1995:** Program implementation problems were noted as impeding successful intervention and valid evaluation. Recommendations to rectify these issues, rendering the programs more effective and more evaluable, were suggested.[20]

- **1995-1996:** A process to address DMC issues began in Allegheny County, the third target area in Pennsylvania. A local analysis of minority crime and an identification of community-based youth and family programs were completed in 1995. Minority neighborhoods in and adjacent to the east end of Pittsburgh were identified as having high numbers of minority juvenile arrests and were targeted. Three DMC programs began in Allegheny County in April 1996.

- **1997:** Diverse strategies employed by other states included programmatic, legislative, administrative, and policy changes in juvenile justice system processing.[21]

- **1997:** Significant racial and ethnic disparity in the confinement of juvenile offenders remained. In 1997, minorities made up about one-third of the juvenile population nationwide but accounted for nearly two-thirds of the detained and committed population in secure juvenile facilities.[22]

- **1998:** Positive outcomes were reported for the Harrisburg site in Pennsylvania. The rate of recidivism over a three-year period for the high-attendance group (25.8%) was impressive, considering that nearly one-half of the clients had arrests prior to their referral. In contrast, the low-attendance control group had a recidivism rate of 53 percent for the same period.[23]

- **1998:** As of 1998, 55 of 57 eligible states and territories were participating in the Formula Grants program. The vast majority was in compliance with the core requirements, although this means only that efforts were undertaken to reduce the problem, not that the problem was ameliorated.[24]

- **2002:** The majority of empirical studies over the past three decades reported race effects in juvenile processing, and race effects remain. The state of knowledge is far from complete. More precise research-based information is needed, as are additional efforts to identify gaps in the knowledge base, encourage targeted research to fill these gaps, conduct well-focused efforts to address DMC-related issues, and build sustained partnerships between DMC researchers and practitioners at both the national and the local levels.[25]

Examine Potential Causes of the Problem

This is a critical stage of the problem analysis: Different causes imply different solutions. If you choose a solution before you examine causes, it is likely that your intervention will be ineffective. Any intervention should be aimed at a specific cause or causes. By attempting to change one or more causes, the goal is to bring about a specific change in the problem. Causes mediate the effect of an intervention on a problem.

When we talk about examining causes, we are analyzing the *etiology* of a problem: the factors that cause or contribute significantly to a specific problem or need. A theory attempts to describe and explain relationships between cause and effect (e.g., a specific problem). A theory will describe causes of a specific problem, and it will outline proposed relationships between different causes. A theory may also suggest solutions to a problem: it provides a logical rationale for using one intervention over another.

Causes may be identified at different levels of analysis ranging from individual to social structural:

- **Individual**: Presumed causes lie within individuals (e.g., personality traits such as "aggressiveness").

- **Group**: Presumed causes lie within the dynamics of particular groups to which a person belongs (e.g., patterns of roles and relationships within a family).

- **Organizational**: Presumed causes lie within the particular culture and procedures of a specific organization such as the police, courts, or prisons (e.g., how police are recruited, selected, or trained).

- **Community**: Presumed causes lie within the behavioral patterns and dynamics existing within a specific community (e.g., community "cohesiveness": degree of involvement in community organizations such as churches and community associations; attitudes toward deviance; supervision of juveniles).[26]

- **Social structural**: Presumed causes lie within the underlying social structure of society (e.g., the unequal distribution of wealth and power engendered by the economic system of capitalism) or its cultural attitudes regarding behaviors such as drug use, sexuality, education, crime, and so on. Factors commonly examined at this level of analysis include poverty, unemployment, and discrimination.[27]

We argue that any individual or agency who proposes an intervention always has some theory about what causes what, and at least a "hunch" about what kind of strategy would solve a specific problem and why (even if they haven't clearly thought about it or articulated it). In planned change, one very carefully thinks about such theories and articulates them before intervention is begun. In other words, in planned change, one must explicitly tell the rest of the world what the causal assumptions about a specific problem are, and then support these assumptions before proposing a specific type of change.

Where do you find causes and theories? One method is by reading published material and performing library research on your problem. One should look at journal articles, books, and government and agency reports (e.g., numerous branches of the U.S. Department of Justice, including the National Institute of Justice). There are many different theories of different kinds of social behavior, including criminal behavior. While some theories are very general, and most theories are constantly refined and applied to different problems, we highly recommend that anyone proposing a criminal justice intervention acquire at least a basic knowledge of criminological and criminal justice theories, either through a course on criminological theory, or by reading one of several excellent books on criminological theory.[28] As we investigate causes, we should be guided by two major questions:

- What is the *evidence* for competing theories? No intervention should be aimed at causes that are not supported by empirical evidence of some sort.

- What kind of *intervention* is suggested by a particular causal theory? How can a specific cause be affected by an intervention?

Example 2.4

Causes and Correlates of Domestic Violence

There are at least four general categories of causes (theories) or correlates of domestic violence.[29]

- Individual
- Family structure
- Organizational
- Social structural

Individual-oriented theories: Researchers often examine characteristics of offenders and victims that increase the likelihood of domestic violence. Causes or contributing factors that lie within offenders, according to researchers, have included poor self-control, low self-esteem, immaturity, depression, stress, poor communication skills, and substance abuse. Characteristics of victims contributing to domestic violence have included low self-esteem, psychological dependence, and passivity.

Example 2.4, *continued*

Family-oriented theories: Certain kinds of family structures or roles may create high potential for violence. For example, *social isolation* of families neutralizes potential support and increases risk of abuse. The best family-centered predictors of spouse abuse are: family conflict over male substance abuse and conflicts over control in the relationship. Such conflicts tend to escalate over time. In addition, children who have been victimized themselves or who have witnessed domestic violence in the home may be at higher risk for domestic violence (the "violence begets violence" thesis).

Organizational theories: Processes within criminal justice agencies may unintentionally contribute to domestic violence. In particular, reluctance by police to arrest suspected abusers received much criticism in the 1970s. Research pointed to at least five reasons for the "hands-off" police response to domestic violence:

- *Police culture and training*: Police are socialized into a "crime-fighting" culture; they dislike tasks that imply a "social worker" role.

- Disincentives: Police performance is often evaluated on the basis of numbers such as arrest rate and clearance rate, not "mediation skills."

- *Perception of danger in domestic assault cases*: Although widely perceived among police officers, it is a myth that domestic violence calls are the most likely to result in officer deaths.

- *Perceived futility*: Police perceive, often accurately, that few arrests for domestic violence actually result in successful prosecution (e.g., victims drop charges; prosecutors decline to proceed).

- *Fatalistic attitudes*: Police have lamented legal restraints (e.g., search and seizure) on their own use of power. They are sensitive to the potential liability involved in domestic violence cases.

Social structural perspectives: Broad-based patterns of gender inequality in Western society are seen by many researchers as significant contributors to high rates of domestic violence. For example, patriarchal (male-dominated) religions have been said to affirm a family structure dominated by the authority and power of males. Economic patterns have also discriminated against women: women's traditional role as housewife was not as highly valued as men's "breadwinner" role, and women have historically been more economically dependent on men as a result. Other researchers point to the influence of a class-based social system: men have traditionally exerted domination over women in all areas of private and public life. According to this view, culturally sanctioned sexism is the problem to be addressed, not deviant individuals or dysfunctional families. We live in a stratified society, it is suggested, where men retain more power and social advantage than women.

Examine Previous Interventions

As in documenting the need for change, and in analyses of causes, some thorough research is needed to discover what types of interventions have been attempted to change a specific problem. Often, a single study will report both causal factors and the intervention that was designed to address those causes, but this is not always the case. The planner or analyst must attempt to find out what major interventions have addressed the problem of interest, and they should identify which specific causes the intervention was attempting to modify.

Excellent sources of information about interventions include key persons working in justice-related positions, criminal justice journals and books, and (especially) government reports. Numerous databases can be searched by key words and terms. Excellent criminal justice literature searches can be conducted online, via computer software (disk or CD-ROM), and in printed index format. These include the National Criminal Justice Reference Service (NCJRS) sponsored by the U.S. Department of Justice.[30] It is necessary to familiarize oneself with the various search instruments and techniques available, preferably at a well-equipped university library. A good reference librarian can be an invaluable source of assistance.

Identify Relevant Stakeholders

Next in the process is the identification of the stakeholders in the change process. A *stakeholder* is any person, group, or agency who has a legitimate interest in the problem and/or the proposed intervention. We need to decide whose views should be considered in the planning process. Some stakeholders will provide essential cooperation; others may provide potentially fatal opposition. If the intervention is to be successful, it is important that the right individuals, groups, and organizations are involved in the planning process. Otherwise, the project may run into insurmountable difficulties stemming from a lack of adequate information, resources, or cooperation. Who, then, should be included in the planning phase?

- Experts?
- Agency heads?
- Agency staff?
- Clients?
- Community groups?
- Business people in the neighborhood?
- Other community organizations (e.g., church, school)?

Before we can answer these questions, we need to review the information we have already collected, and answer some key questions. For example, what expectations do various individuals and groups have for change? What results are expected? Are there differences of opinion? We can think of potential stakeholders in terms of several key roles that participants may play in the change process.[31] Major roles include the following.

Change Agent System

Who begins the planning process to design an intervention? Who actually gets the ball rolling to address the problem? The change agent system usually includes the change agent and his or her sanctioning institution (e.g., the State Department of Corrections announces plans for developing offender-reentry programs). Change agents, as noted previously, come from many different backgrounds, for example, legislators, criminal justice policymakers, professional planners, administrators, and service professionals.

Initiator System

This includes those who bring the problem to the attention of the change agent. Initiators raise awareness about a specific problem. Examples include professional lobbyists, including national groups such as the ACLU, National Organization of Women, the Urban League, and so on.

Client System

This includes the specific individuals, groups, organizations, or communities that are expected to benefit from the change. For example, juveniles, families, and their community might be expected to benefit from a delinquency prevention program that requires performance of community service.

Target System

This includes the persons, group, or organization that needs to be changed in order to reach objectives. For example, to reduce domestic violence, do we need to change abused women? Their spouses? The police response? The court response?

Action System

This includes all those who, in some way, assist in carrying out the change plan, including program planning, implementation, monitoring, and evaluation. Particularly important, however, is the actual agency responsible for providing programming (i.e., service delivery). Primarily, then, the action system includes the actual service providers who implement the change.

Sometimes, overlapping roles are possible: For example, the change agent may be part of both the target system and the action system. For example, a police commissioner orders sweeping changes in police policy for dealing with domestic assault complaints. In such a case, the change agent, by virtue of overlapping roles, enjoys a degree of credibility or authority with both patrol officers (the target system) and their supervisors who are responsible for implementing the new policies (action system). Overlapping roles may also enhance continuity, for example, in casese where the same person who initiates change (initiator system) carries it out (action system) with the cooperation of other participants. On the other hand, there are clearly instances in which overlapping roles are undesirable. For example, the person or agency actually carrying out the intervention should never be held responsible for program or policy monitoring and evaluation, because of their potential subjectivity or bias.

Conducting a Systems Analysis

Current thinking about criminal justice as a "system" was largely influenced by the 1967 President's Commission report.[32] Criminal justice problems and policies, the Commission concluded, are shaped by the *interactive* actions and decisions of various actors and agencies in any jurisdiction (e.g., a particular city, township, county, or state). At the same time, criminal justice projects, programs, and policies are shaped in a volatile political environment. Diverse interest groups and agencies compete for attention, and fragmented decisionmaking is common. Because criminal justice officials and agencies often act without consideration of how their decisions might affect those elsewhere in the system, the criminal justice system has often been called a "nonsystem." While the past 20 years have occasionally witnessed increased coordination among criminal justice units, there is still a long road to travel.[33]

A *system* can be defined as "all aspects of criminal justice case processing that relate to punishment or sanctions from the time of arrest—including decisions about pre-trial custody—through the execution and completion of a sentence—whether that sentence is served in the community and/or in a correctional institution."[34] All individuals, groups, and organizations that play a role in such decisions in a specific jurisdiction are part of the relevant system.

The change agent, whether a consultant, a criminal justice or government official, or an academic, must identify relevant individuals and agencies in the policy environment: those whose decisions potentially have shaped the problem and those whose decisions may potentially shape the development and implementation of change (i.e., new or modified policies, programs, or projects). Once identified, the change agent must consider how various officials and agencies have impacted the problem and solutions in the past, and how they might do so in the future. Many of the problems we seek to address in criminal justice are "systems" problems. Consider the following examples:

Example 2.5

Examples of "Systems" Problems

Jail Overcrowding. Jails interact extensively with law enforcement agencies, courts, probation, and local government. Local police decide whether to arrest and book accused offenders, and thus control the major intake into the jails. Local courts influence jail populations through pretrial release decisions and sanctions for convicted offenders. Charging decisions by district attorneys influence the efficiency with which pretrial suspects are processed. Probation may administer both pretrial release programs, such as "ROR" (release on own recognizance), and intermediate sanctions for sentenced offenders, such as electronic surveillance, intensive supervision probation, and work release. County government is responsible for financial and personnel allocations to each of these agencies. In turn, county government decisions are affected by financial allocations and legislation determined at the state level.[35]

Sentencing Disparities. Concerns about disparities in sentencing (i.e., individuals who commit similar offenses receiving different penalties), the use of judicial discretion (wide variations in sentences across different judges and jurisdictions), and perceptions of excessive leniency or harshness have led to the development and revision of state and federal sentencing guidelines. However, actual "sentencing" policy in any jurisdiction is an outcome resulting from the input of numerous individuals and agencies. Judges obviously impose criminal sanctions, but they must do so within the limits of state criminal statutes, which are set by the state legislature. Prosecutors make decisions about charging, which depend upon the strength and quality of evidence supplied by police, the ability and willingness of witnesses to testify, and so on. Prosecutors' charging decisions determine which criminal statutes apply to a case, and thus influence legal procedures and outcomes. Pretrial service providers make decisions about which defendants are eligible for release pending trial, which in turn affect a defendant's ability to assist in the preparation of his or her defense. Defense attorneys participate in negotiations with prosecutors regarding admissible evidence, appropriate charges, potential plea bargains, and so on. Probation personnel usually prepares a pre-sentencing report on convicted offenders, and their recommendations influence judicial options for sanctioning. At the time of sentencing, elected judges also consider the values of their constituents, their colleagues, and local justice officials. Judges must be at least to some degree aware of and responsive to their local political environment.[36]

Guidelines for Systems Analysis

While the methods for analyzing systems tend to be complex, we offer 11 basic guidelines for conducting a systems analysis. A model developed by the Center for Effective Public Policy assumes that in order to understand the criminal justice system in any jurisdiction, it is essential to examine the full range of sanctions that are imposed upon offenders. A criminal justice system assessment involves gathering and analyzing information that may exist in the experiences of individual decisionmakers, in agency information systems and databases, and in agency reports and communications. In general, "a system assessment is a collaborative effort to synthesize individuals' experiences with the criminal justice system into a shared understanding of how things work now. This provides a common base upon which to evaluate the present, to shape a common vision for the future, and to make that vision a reality." [37]

This model assumes the presence of two key elements: (1) a set of policymakers committed to understanding and shaping their system of sanctions to operate in a more collaborative manner (i.e., a "policy team"); and (2) a team of outside consultants committed to working with the jurisdiction to complete the assessment. It prescribes a set of assessment activities that constitute information collection, analysis, and vision building. Eleven steps are described below; sources of information for systems analysis are summarized in Table 2.1. Restorative justice, an approach ripe for systems analysis, is presented in Case Study 2.3.

1. Describe the problem. What is the problem, issue, crisis, or impending disaster that has suggested a systems analysis might be helpful? What has brought certain officials to the table to discuss some problem, such as child sexual abuse or drug-related violence? Special attention should be devoted to assessing the problem as it exists throughout an entire *system* (e.g., consider diverse perspectives, definitions, and stakeholders).

2. Describe the roles and responsibilities of different levels, branches, and agencies of government. There is enormous variety in how justice functions are distributed across jurisdictions. At the state level, for example, typical actors and agencies include a Commissioner and Department of Corrections, the Attorney General, the Probation and Parole Department, officials in the State Planning Agency and/or the Governor's Office of Criminal Justice, a Senate Judiciary Committee, and so on. Often, a state Sentencing Commission or other state body sets policy and makes decisions about the distribution of justice funds. The actual structure and operation of policing, courts, and corrections vary substantially by state and locality. At the county level, various public and private agencies may provide pretrial assessment and services, prevention and treatment programs, halfway houses, and so on. We want to find out what agencies have responsibility for different elements of the sanctioning system, and how they relate to each other.

Table 2.1
Information Sources for Criminal Justice Systems Analysis

Stakeholders (Interviews/Forums)	Documents/Social Indicators
Local and state policymakers involved in justice activities: judges, prosecutors, public defenders, corrections officials, police, sheriff, jail administrator, community corrections personnel, probation officers, bail bondsmen.	• Annual reports of local and state justice agencies • City and state budgets; agency budgets • Criteria for various sanctions as expressed in agency policies, mission statements, etc. • Any agency and committee reports on the problem • Community corrections plans • Newspaper accounts • Minutes of criminal justice policy committees
Key legislators (state and local) and committee staff involved in criminal justice legislation; county commissioners.	• Reviews of past and pending litigation • Legislative Study Commission Reports
Sentencing Commission staff.	• State sentencing guidelines
Staff of agencies involved in the sanctioning process, especially those who have responsibility for data collection, reports, or research (e.g., court clerk, booking staff of the jail, research staff in justice agencies, information system managers, criminal justice coordinators).	• Jail booking records • Court data systems • Presentence investigation reports • Information system documentation and codebooks • Court and probation files
Citizens, service organizations, business organizations, churches, neighborhood organizations, and community groups.	• Records of any public opinion polls or community forums on criminal justice issues • Newspaper accounts
Private business groups; board members of large private and nonprofit organizations that fund or supervise justice-related activities.	• Minutes of meetings • Newspaper accounts
Association or union representatives for police, corrections, or court staff.	• Union contracts
Private-sector service providers that work with police, courts, and corrections (e.g., drug, alcohol, sex offender, educational, job training, and mental health treatment providers who accept criminal justice referrals).	• Internal agency documents and listings of referral sources and treatment providers • Service directories • Standards and audits for private care providers
Faculty in local law schools and universities who have conducted policy analyses and research on the problem.	• Research reports

3. Describe the funding environment. Who pays for what in a specific jurisdiction? To what degree are agencies and programs funded by local, state, or federal funds? Private-sector funds? Nonprofit agencies? There is often tension between state and local governments over budget responsibility for public services such as criminal justice, education, and health. For example, state law requires cities and counties to enforce the criminal code of the state, but usually provides only about one-third of the funding needed for local courts. Community corrections programs are likely to be funded by a variety of sources—public, private, and nonprofit. We need to understand, then, how funding is provided for various elements of sanctioning, the level of funding provided for each, whether the funding is likely to decrease or increase, and what conflicts or changes are likely in the near future.

4. Describe the role of the private sector (if any). Private-sector agencies have been involved in criminal justice for many years, through treatment programs, halfway houses, and so on. Their role has increased tremendously in recent years to include pretrial services, urine screening, electronic monitoring, offender assessments, residential programming, and even secure detention. We want to answer questions such as the following: What proportion of what types of sanctions are provided by private and public-sector agencies? What are the criteria for contracting with private providers? How do resources influence program availability, targeting, funding, use, and offender performance? Are unique incentives (e.g., profitability) associated with the use of particular sanctions? What effects do these incentives have on criminal justice processing and outcomes?

5. Describe how discretion is distributed throughout the system. Responsibility for different sanctions varies greatly among different agencies in different jurisdictions. As such, we need to find out who has discretion over particular decisions in the sanctioning process. Note that this task is distinct from the "roles" question; we want to determine not only *which* decisions different agencies and individuals exert discretion over, but *how* they use that discretion. For example, what are the typical options available to prosecutors in charging and dismissal decisions? What discretion do Parole, Probation, and the Department of Corrections have regarding the timing of release and the use of pre-release programs such as furlough and halfway house placements? How often does the judge follow the recommendations in a presentence investigation? In general, we seek to determine answers to the following questions: Where does discretion exist in case processing and dispositions? What discretion does each individual and agency possess in relation to a specific type of sanction?

6. Describe the existing continuum of sanctions. Here, we seek to formally identify all possible sanctions available in a particular jurisdiction, through both the public and private sectors. Sanctions may be punitive, incapacitative, or rehabilitative in nature. In addition to jail or prison beds, we want to record treatment beds, educational programming slots, and community service placements. We want to know the number of slots available, average length of stay, per-day costs, and methods of referral or access.

7. Describe the offender population. We need to know about the volume and characteristics of offenders who move through each stage of criminal justice processing and sanctioning. We need to understand what types of offenders are receiving what types of sanctions. Ideally, sanctions should be appropriate to individual offenders (e.g., seriousness of offense, past record, specific needs and level of risk). For example, are scarce jail and prison beds being used for the most high-risk offenders? Are community sanctions being used for appropriate offenders?

8. Describe the policy environment. Sentencing and sanctioning policy in any jurisdiction is usually the result of formal and informal interactions between various policymakers. At the local level, formal efforts often take the form of public officials and perhaps citizens appointed to "criminal justice coordinating councils," "intermediate sanctions policy groups," "community corrections advisory boards," and similar groups. In many cases, individual actors and agencies communicate haphazardly. The key question is whether a jurisdiction exhibits the readiness to begin and engage in a more formal "systems" policy process. The Center for Effective Public Policy emphasizes building effective "policy teams" to examine systems issues. Policy teams consist of key decisionmakers in the local criminal justice system: those who have the authority to make major decisions and those who are willing to make a commitment to system-level policy analysis and development. Assumptions are made that no single individual can develop system policy, and absent any system-level policy, responses will continue to occur randomly and unpredictably. Questions to ask include the following: What pressures are there for policymakers to meet to discuss a specific problem? Is there necessary leadership and commitment to engage in a group policy-making process? What is happening in the jurisdiction that might distract policymakers from this effort?

9. Describe the historical context. We've described how to analyze the history of a problem earlier in this chapter; we emphasize here a "systems" approach. For example, we want to know: What traditions exist in the use of sanctions (e.g., little or extensive use of intermediate sanctions)? Are there traditions of coordination among different branches of the justice system? Is there any history of conflict? Are there unique political factors in the history of a jurisdiction that help us to understand current sanctioning policy?

10. Describe current uses and availability of information. A key factor influencing any jurisdiction's ability to engage in successful systems assessment is the quality of information resources at its disposal. In some systems, information about case processing and sanctioning is still stored in manual systems (e.g., files and folders, index cards). In other systems, some agencies have rudimentary computerized data systems. In other agencies, sophisticated information systems may exist, but there is still no guarantee that agencies share information or communicate effectively with one another. Key questions include the following: To what degrees do agencies currently share information? Are they willing to share information? What information is available from each source, how is it kept, and where is it?

11. Describe community involvement in the criminal justice system. Jurisdictions may vary in the degree to which community involvement has been invited or encouraged. For example, citizens may be involved in town watch and similar community policing efforts. In some cases, citizens may be appointed to local criminal justice councils, police review boards, and other policy groups. Lack of community involvement can create suspicion and resistance; positive involvement can be an asset to planning and policy development. To what degree is the community involved in aspects of criminal justice processing and sanctioning? What are community attitudes toward existing forms of sanctions? Who are active and vocal community leaders on criminal justice issues?

Identify Barriers to Change and Supports for Change

We have talked only a bit so far about resistance to change. Even at this early stage, a decision must be made about whether to continue forward. Is the change attempt possible? Are the necessary resources and cooperation likely to be available? Before proceeding, we offer some techniques to identify potential barriers to change. These "barriers" or sources of resistance take many forms:

- *Physical* (e.g., the physical design of a jail prevents adequate supervision)

- *Social*: (e.g., inequalities related to class, gender, race)

- *Economic* (e.g., inequalities related to income and employment)

- *Educational* (e.g., clients don't understand or know about services)

- Legal (e.g., criminal justice agencies are often legally obligated to *do* certain things and not do other things). For example, prison industry programs that could reduce the costs of incarceration are restricted by federal prohibitions regarding the movement and sale of prisoner-made goods.

- *Political* (e.g., some groups have more power than others to make their views heard; political processes can support or block a change).

- Technological (e.g., sophisticated information and communications systems may be required to implement a specific program or policy).

Consider the following example. Under permanent provisions of the Brady Act, effective November 1998, presale firearm inquiries are made through the National Instant Criminal Background Check System (NICS). State criminal history records are provided to the FBI through each state's central repository and the Inter-State Identification Index. The index points instantly to criminal records held by states. Although the Brady Act required states to develop their criminal history record systems and improve their interface with the NICS, states complained bitterly that the federal government did not provide sufficient technical or financial resources to implement the informational requirements of the Brady Act (see Chapter 5).

Consider a second example. A county is under court orders to reduce its jail population. Everyone agrees that a new jail is needed. However, when certain locations within the county are proposed as sites for the new jail, citizens with economic and/or political power organize community opposition to oppose the construction of a jail in their own neighborhood. This "NIMBY" ("not in my back yard") response[38] may take the form of protests or even lawsuits by powerful citizens to block construction. Is it fair that some can more effectively resist unwanted change than others?

One particularly useful technique for analyzing sources of support and resistance is called *force field analysis*. Remember that participation and communication are keys to change, and that collaborative strategies are preferred to conflict strategies. This technique requires us to consider diverse views and use collaborative strategies to reduce resistance and increase support for change.

The technique of force field analysis, developed by Kurt Lewin,[39] is based upon an analogy to physics: a body will remain at rest when the sum of forces operating on it is zero. When forces pushing or pulling in one direction exceed forces pushing or pulling in the opposite one, the body will move in the direction of the greater forces. The difference is that, in planned change, we are dealing with *social* forces rather than *physical* ones. To succeed in implementing any intervention, we want to try to reduce resistance to change.

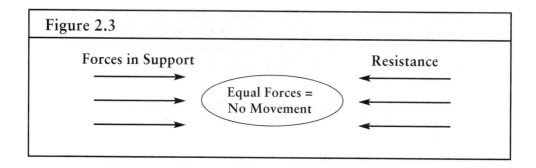

Figure 2.3

Forces in Support   Resistance

Equal Forces =
No Movement

Social change, like physical change, requires one of three options:

1. Increasing forces in support of change

2. Decreasing forces against change (usually creates less tension and leads to fewer unanticipated consequences)

3. Doing both in some combination

There is always resistance to change. At best, there is inertia that the change agent must anticipate and overcome. Force field analysis is a valuable tool for doing this. Generally, we focus on reducing, rather than overcoming, resistance. Case Studies 2.1 and 2.3 at the end of this chapter provide opportunities to apply these concepts. Three steps are involved in a force field analysis:

1. *Identify driving forces* (those supporting change) *and restraining forces* (those resisting change).

2. *Analyze the forces* identified in Step 1. Assess (for each):

    *   *Amenability to change* (How likely is it that this force can be changed?)

    *   *Potency* (How much impact would reducing this source of resistance have on moving the intervention forward?)

    *   *Consistency* (Does this force remain stable or change over time?)

3. *Identify alternative strategies* for changing each force identified in Step 1. Focus on reducing sources of resistance.

Figure 2.4

Kurt Lewin and "Action Research"

In our travels to academic conferences, we often hear complaints by researchers that policymakers ignore the results of their research. In our consultations with policymakers, we often hear complaints that researchers use excessive jargon, research results are inconsistent, and research rarely provides the timely and specific information needed to base decisions upon. Clearly, researchers and policymakers need to interact more closely to facilitate *relevant* research and *informed* policy decisions.[40] Few social scientists took this task more seriously than Kurt Lewin, who asserted: "Research that produces nothing but books will not suffice."[41]

Lewin coined the term *action research* to describe an intentional process of change whereby social science research intentionally and explicitly informs and shapes social action (including organizational and public policy decisions) and evaluates the results of that action. It involves fact-finding, planning, execution, and evaluation. Results from action research provide new information that gives planners a chance to learn and gather new insights about the strength and weaknesses of their decisions. Lewin emphasized that action research is a *dynamic* and *interactive* process. Successful action research requires attention to the "field" or system in which particular decisions are made and the identification of different "forces" (individuals, groups, or agencies) pushing for and against a particular type of change.

DISCUSSION QUESTIONS

1. Define each of the following:

   (a) *change agent* system
   (b) *initiator* system
   (c) *client* system
   (d) *target* system
   (e) *action* system

2. Define: (a) *need*, and (b) *problem*.

3. Define: (a) *incidence*, and (b) *prevalence*.

4. What techniques can we use to estimate the degree and seriousness of a problem? Describe each method of documenting the need for change: (a) *key informant approach*, (b) *community forum*, (c) *community survey*, and (d) *social indicators*.

5. What does it mean to say that a problem is "socially constructed"? Give an example.

6. (a) Define *etiology*. (b) Describe the five levels of etiology, and give an example of each.

7. Define *theory*.

8. What is a *systems analysis*? Describe four steps in a criminal justice systems analysis. Use examples to illustrate your understanding of these concepts.

9. Discuss different types of barriers to change, and give an example of each: (a) physical, (b) social, (c) economic, (d) educational, (e) political, (f) legal, and (g) technological.

10. (a) Define *force field analysis*. (b) Describe each of the three steps.

11. Define *action research*.

Case Study 2.1

Domestic Violence

Instructions: *Read the hypothetical case scenario on the next page. Then, break into groups (assigned by the instructor) and answer the questions below. Each group member should take some notes about the discussion, but the group will appoint a spokesperson to report the group's findings to the class. Plan on preparing a five-minute summary.*

A headline in a local newspaper, the *Bigtown Chronicle*, read: "Woman killed by husband in domestic dispute." Bigtown Police said that Betty Benson, age 32, died of multiple stab wounds allegedly inflicted by her husband, Bill, age 34, following a violent argument in the couple's home. Police had been called to the home four times in the previous six months in response to complaints by neighbors that "there was a lot of yelling, and she was screaming like she was being beaten." Ms. Benson had declined to press charges in each instance.

The next day, there was a noisy protest in front of city hall by a local group called WASA (Women for Action against Spouse Abuse). WASA spokesperson Sarah Smith told reporters, "This kind of nonsense has been going on far too long. The police were called to that house four times before she got murdered, and they didn't do anything to help her. The police should be arresting sick people like Bill Benson and putting them away for a long time, not just talking to them and letting them go right back to beating their wives."

Police Commissioner Frank Fine responded to the criticisms by pointing out that the police don't make the laws. "WASA can complain all they want," Fine said, "but the state legislature makes the laws regarding domestic assault, and right now, the law says that police can't make an arrest unless the victim swears out a complaint. We can't arrest people like Bill Benson just because they appear to be unsavory characters."

WASA began protesting in front of the state capital, and two days later, Rep. Alan Atkinson introduced a new bill calling for sweeping changes in the laws regarding spouse abuse. The bill called for mandatory arrest and a mandatory 48-hour detention period, pending investigation, for anyone suspected of spousal assault. According to the bill, the police would use "reasonable discretion" in enforcing the law. The local chapter of the ACLU (American Civil Liberties Union) expressed outrage, arguing that the new bill would deprive suspects of their constitutional rights of due process and give the police the power to be "judge, jury, and hangman."

Bob Bigheart, a spokesperson for the Bigtown Social Services Agency said that tough new laws were not the answer. Instead, he suggested, the police should train officers in family crisis counseling so that they can mediate domestic disputes and refer couples to community agencies to help solve their problems. Police Commissioner Frank Fine says that is what the police do any-

Case Study 2.1, *continued*

way: "We are a service-oriented police department," Fine said, "and our offi-cers are among the best-trained in the nation." Claiming that the Commissioner was "arrogant and insensitive to the rights of victims," WASA called for Fine's immediate resignation.

Questions

The governor has asked you, as members of the State Planning Agency, to study the problem of domestic assault and make preliminary recommendations about what to do, if anything, to deal with the problem. Include the following in your answer:

1. Is there a *problem* here? If so, what is it? How can you tell?

2. Identify the *participants* and the role that each plays.
    • Change agent system
    • Initiator system
    • Client system
    • Target system
    • Action system

3. Identify the specific change being proposed, and conduct a *force field analysis*.

4. Who perceives the need for what kind of change? Are there differences of opinion? Whose views need to be considered, and how do you choose among competing views?

5. Do you need any additional information before you make your report to the governor? Should some kind of change proceed?

Case Study 2.2

Club Drugs[1]

Instructions: *Read the briefing paper on the next page. Then, break into your groups (assigned by your instructor) and answer the questions that follow. Each group member should take some notes about the discussion, but the group will appoint a spokesperson to report the group's findings to the class. Plan on preparing a 5-minute summary.*

In recent years, certain drugs have emerged and become popular among teens and young adults at dance clubs and raves. These drugs, collectively termed "club drugs," include MDMA/Ecstasy (methylenedioxymethamphetamine), Rohypnol (flunitrazepam), GHB (gamma hydroxybutyrate), and ketamine (ketamine hydrochloride).

Producing both stimulant and psychedelic effects, MDMA is often used at parties because it enables partygoers to dance and remain active for long periods of time. This substance is usually ingested in tablet form, but can also be crushed and snorted, injected, or used in suppository form.[2]

The tasteless and odorless depressants Rohypnol and GHB are often used in the commission of sexual assaults due to their ability to sedate and intoxicate unsuspecting victims. Rohypnol, a sedative/tranquilizer, is legally available for prescription in more than 50 countries outside of the U.S. and is widely available in Mexico, Colombia, and Europe.[3] Although usually taken orally in pill form, reports have shown that some users grind Rohypnol into a powder and snort the drug.[4]

GHB, available in an odorless, colorless liquid form or as a white powder material, is taken orally, and is frequently combined with alcohol. In addition to being used to incapacitate individuals for the commission of sexual assault/rape, GHB is also sometimes used by body builders for its alleged anabolic effects.[5]

The abuse of ketamine, a tranquilizer most often used on animals, became popular in the 1980s, when it was realized that large doses cause reactions similar to those associated with the use of PCP, such as dream-like states and hallucinations.[6] The liquid form of ketamine can be injected, consumed in drinks, or added to smokable materials. The powder form can also be added

---

[1] Office of National Drug Control Policy (2004). *Club Drugs (MDMA/Ecstacy, Rohypnol, GHB, Ketamine).* [Online]. Available at: *http://www.whitehousedrugpolicy.gov/drugfact/club/* (retrieved March 8, 2004).

[2] National Institute on Drug Abuse, *Infofax: Club Drugs*, February 2000.

[3] Drug Enforcement Administration Web site, *Drug Descriptions: Flunitrazepam (Rohypnol).*

[4] National Institute on Drug Abuse, *Community Drug Alert Bulletin: Club Drugs*, December 1999.

[5] Drug Enforcement Administration Web site, *Drug Descriptions: Gamma Hydroxybutyric Acid (GHB).*

[6] National Institute on Drug Abuse, *Community Drug Alert Bulletin: Club Drugs*, December 1999.

Case Study 2.2, *continued*

to drinks, smoked, or dissolved and then injected.[7] In some cases, ketamine is being injected intramuscularly.[8]

Extent of Use

According to the 2002 National Survey on Drug Use and Health, an estimated 10.2 million Americans age 12 or older tried MDMA at least once in their lifetimes, representing 4.3 percent of the U.S. population in that age group. The number of past-year MDMA users in 2002 was 3.2 million (1.3% of the population age 12 and older), and the number of past-month MDMA users was 676,000 (0.3%). Among 12–17 year olds surveyed in 2002, 3.3 percent reported lifetime MDMA use, 2.2 percent reported past year MDMA use, and 0.5 percent reported past month MDMA use. Among 18–25 year olds surveyed in 2002, 15.1 percent reported lifetime MDMA use, 5.8 percent reported past year MDMA use, and 1.1 percent reported past-month MDMA use.[9]

According to the 2003 Monitoring the Future Study, 3.2 percent of eighth graders, 5.4 percent of tenth graders, and 8.3 percent of twelfth graders reported using MDMA at least once during their lifetimes. One percent of eighth graders and tenth graders reported using Rohypnol at least once during their lifetimes (twelfth-grade data are not available). Lifetime use of GHB and ketamine was not captured in the survey.[10]

Percent of Students Reporting MDMA and Rohypnol Use, 2003

Student Club Drug Use	8th Grade		10th Grade		12th Grade	
	MDMA	Rohypnol	MDMA	Rohypnol	MDMA	Rohypnol
Past month use	0.7%	0.1%	1.1%	0.2%	1.3%	—
Past year use	2.1	0.5	3.0	0.6	4.5	1.3
Lifetime use	3.2	1.0	5.4	1.0	8.3	—

Data showing past year use of GHB and ketamine are captured in the Monitoring the Future Study. In 2003, 0.9 percent of eighth graders, 1.4 percent of tenth graders, and 1.4 percent of twelfth graders reported using GHB at least once in the past year.[11]

---

[7]   Drug Enforcement Administration, *Club Drugs: An Update*, September 2001.

[8]   National Institute on Drug Abuse, *Community Drug Alert Bulletin: Club Drugs*, December 1999.

[9]   Substance Abuse and Mental Health Services Administration, *Results from the 2002 National Survey on Drug Use and Health: National Findings*, September 2003.

[10] National Institute on Drug Abuse and University of Michigan, *Monitoring the Future 2003 Data from In-School Surveys of 8th-, 10th-, and 12th- Grade Students*, December 2003.

[11] Ibid.

Case Study 2.2, *continued*

Percent of Students Reporting Past Year Use of GHB & Ketamine, 2003

Past Year Use	8th Grade	10th Grade	12th Grade
GHB	0.9%	1.4%	1.4%
Ketamine	1.1	1.9	2.1

Approximately 42 percent of eighth graders and nearly 50 percent of tenth graders surveyed in 2003 reported that using MDMA once or twice was a "great risk."[12]

Percent of Students Reporting Risk of Using MDMA, 2003

Percent Saying "Great Risk"	8th Grade	10th Grade	12th Grade
Try MDMA once or twice	41.9%	49.7%	56.3%
Use MDMA occasionally	65.8	71.7	Not available

During 2002, 12.7 percent of college students and 14.6 percent of young adults (ages 19-28) reported using MDMA at least once during their lifetimes.[13]

Percent of College Students and Young Adults Using MDMA, 2002

Past Use of MDMA	College Students	Young Adults
Past month use	0.7%	1.3%
Past year use	6.8	6.2
Lifetime use	12.7	14.6

Health Effects

Using MDMA can cause serious psychological and physical damage. The possible psychological effects include confusion, depression, anxiety, and paranoia and may last weeks after ingesting the substance. Physically, a user may experience nausea, faintness, and significant increases in heart rate and blood pressure. MDMA use can cause hyperthermia, muscle breakdown, seizures, stroke, kidney and cardiovascular system failure, and may lead to death. In addition, chronic use of MDMA has been found to produce long-lasting, possibly permanent, damage to the sections of the brain critical to thought and memory.[14]

Rohypnol, GHB, and ketamine are all central nervous system depressants. Lower doses of Rohypnol can cause muscle relaxation and can produce general sedative and hypnotic effects. In higher doses, Rohypnol causes a loss of

---

[12] Ibid.
[13] National Institute on Drug Abuse and University of Michigan, *Monitoring the Future National Survey Results on Drug Use, 1975-2002, Volume II: College Students & Adults Ages 19-40* (PDF), 2003.
[14] National Institute on Drug Abuse, *Infofax: MDMA (Ecstasy)*.

Case Study 2.2, *continued*

muscle control, loss of consciousness, and partial amnesia. When combined with alcohol, the toxic effects of Rohypnol can be aggravated.[15] The sedative effects of Rohypnol begin to appear approximately 15–20 minutes after the drug is ingested. The effects typically last from four to six hours after administration of the drug, but some cases have been reported in which the effects were experienced 12 or more hours after administration.[16]

GHB has been shown to produce drowsiness, nausea, unconsciousness, seizures, severe respiratory depression, and coma. Additionally, GHB has increasingly become involved in poisonings, overdoses, date rapes, and fatalities.[17]

The use of ketamine produces effects similar to PCP and LSD, causing distorted perceptions of sight and sound and making the user feel disconnected and out of control.[18] The overt hallucinatory effects of ketamine are relatively short-acting, lasting approximately one hour or less. However, the user's senses, judgment, and coordination may be affected for up to 24 hours after the initial use of the drug.[19] Use of this drug can also bring about respiratory depression, heart rate abnormalities, and a withdrawal syndrome.[20]

The number of emergency department (ED) MDMA mentions reported to the Drug Abuse Warning Network (DAWN) has increased from 421 in 1995 to 4,026 in 2002. During this same time period, the number of GHB mentions increased from 145 to 3,330. The number of ketamine ED mentions has increased from 81 in 1996 to 260 in 2002.[21]

Arrests and Sentencing

In response to the Ecstasy Anti-Proliferation Act of 2000, the U.S. Sentencing Commission increased the guideline sentence for trafficking MDMA. The new amendment, enacted on November 1, 2001, increases the sentence for trafficking 800 MDMA pills by 300 percent, from 15 months to five years. It also increases the penalty for trafficking 8,000 pills by nearly 200 percent, from 41 months to 10 years.[22]

---

[15] National Institute on Drug Abuse, *Community Drug Alert Bulletin: Club Drugs*, December 1999.

[16] Drug Enforcement Administration Web site, *Drug Descriptions: Flunitrazepam (Rohypnol)*.

[17] National Institute on Drug Abuse, *Infofax: Club Drugs*, February 2000.

[18] National Institute on Drug Abuse, *Research Report: Hallucinogens and Dissociative Drugs*, March 2001.

[19] Drug Enforcement Administration Web site, *Drug Descriptions: Ketamine*.

[20] National Institute on Drug Abuse, *Research Report: Hallucinogens and Dissociative Drugs*, March 2001.

[21] Substance Abuse and Mental Health Services Administration, *Emergency Department Trends from the Drug Abuse Warning Network, Final Estimates 1995-2002*, July 2003.

[22] U.S. Sentencing Commission, Congressional Testimony, *Statement of Diana E. Murphy, Chair of the U.S. Sentence Commission, before the Senate Caucus on International Narcotics Control* (PDF), March 21, 2001.

Case Study 2.2, *continued*

Production and Trafficking

MDMA is primarily manufactured in clandestine laboratories located in Europe, particularly the Netherlands and Belgium. From these labs, MDMA is transported to the United States and other countries using a variety of means, including commercial airlines, express mail services, and sea cargo. Currently, Los Angeles, Miami, and New York are the major gateway cities for the influx of MDMA from abroad.[23]

Although most of the MDMA available in the United States is produced in Europe, a small number of MDMA clandestine laboratories operate in the United States. In 2000, U.S. law enforcement seized seven labs. In 2001, the number of MDMA clandestine labs seized in the United States increased to 17.[24]

The Drug Enforcement Administration (DEA) and the U.S. Customs Service have seen increases in the number of seizures involving MDMA. Domestically, the DEA seized more than 1 million MDMA tablets in 1999, 3.3 million in 2000, and more than 5.5 million in 2001.[25] The amount of seizures made by Customs has increased from 400,000 in FY 1997 to 7.2 million in FY 2001.[26]

GHB, GHB kits, and recipes for making GHB can be found on the Internet.[27] In 2001, the DEA, along with state and local law enforcement, seized 13 labs used to produce GHB. This is down from 20 GHB labs seized in 2000.[28]

Rohypnol, legally produced and sold in Latin America and Europe, is typically smuggled into the United States using mail or delivery services. States along the U.S. border with Mexico have the most significant activity related to Rohypnol being mailed or brought into the United States via couriers from Mexico.[29] Since the mid-1990s, the numbers of Rohypnol seizures in the United States has decreased. In 1995, a high of 164,534 dosage units of Rohypnol were seized, while in 2000, less than 5,000 dosage units were seized.[30]

Legitimately used by veterinarians, ketamine is sometimes stolen from animal hospitals and veterinary clinics. DEA reporting also indicates that some of the ketamine available in the United States has been diverted from pharmacies in Mexico.[31] Since first recorded in 1999, the number of ketamine seizures reported by the DEA has increased each year. Seizures of this drug have increased from 4,551 dosage units in 1999 to 1,154,463 in 2000. DEA data also indicate that 581,677 dosage units were seized from January to June 2001.[32]

---

[23] Drug Enforcement Administration, *Ecstasy: Rolling Across Europe*, August 2001.
[24] Drug Enforcement Administration Web site, *Drug Trafficking in the United States*.
[25] Drug Enforcement Administration, Ecstasy and Predatory Drugs, February 2003.
[26] Drug Enforcement Administration Web site, *Drug Trafficking in the United States*.
[27] Drug Enforcement Administration, *Club Drugs: An Update*, September 2001.
[28] Drug Enforcement Administration Web site, *Drug Trafficking in the United States*.
[29] Drug Enforcement Administration, *Club Drugs: An Update*, September 2001.
[30] National Drug Intelligence Center, *National Drug Threat Assessment 2002*, December 2001.
[31] Drug Enforcement Administration, *Club Drugs: An Update*, September 2001.
[32] National Drug Intelligence Center, *National Drug Threat Assessment 2002*, December 2001.

Case Study 2.2, *continued*

Legislation[33]

MDMA, GHB, Rohypnol, and ketamine have all been scheduled under the Controlled Substance Act (CSA), Title II of the Comprehensive Drug Abuse Prevention and Control Act of 1970. The Schedules of the club drugs are as follows:[34]

- MDMA—Schedule I as of 1998

- GHB—Schedule I as of 2000

- Rohypnol—Schedule IV as of 1984

- Ketamine—Schedule III as of 1999

Street Terms[35]

GHB	Ketamine	MDMA	Rohypnol
Goop	Cat valium	Disco biscuit	Forget-me drug
Grievous bodily harm	K	Hug drug	Mexican valium
Max	Jet	Go	Roaches
Soap	Super acid	XTC	Roofies

Other Links

http://www.ncjrs.org/club_drugs/summary.html
A comprehensive online resource providing data, publications, events, and other information related to club drugs.

http://www.clubdrugs.org/
This NIDA site provides club drugs resources including publications, news, and data.

http://www.whitehousedrugpolicy.gov/publications/factsht/gamma/index.html
This fact sheet provides an overview of GHB abuse, effects, scheduling, street terms, and its use in drug-facilitated rape.

---

[33] Drug Enforcement Administration, *Club Drugs: An Update*, September 2001.

[34] Schedule I drugs have the most restrictions. They may not be possessed by anyone except for the purposes of research that has been licensed by the government. Schedules II through V are considered to have successively less abuse potential, but are still controlled by the government.

[35] Office of National Drug Control Policy, Drug Policy Information Clearinghouse, *Street Terms: Drugs and the Drug Trade*.

Case Study 2.2, *continued*

http://www.whitehousedrugpolicy.gov/publications/factsht/mdma/index.html
This fact sheet provides a summary of data related to the club drug Ecstasy.
It includes information on ecstasy use, health effects, and related enforcement
initiatives.

http://www.whitehousedrugpolicy.gov/publications/drugfact/pulsechk/midyear
2000/clubdrugs.html
From the Mid-Year 2000 Pulse Check, this special report provides an overview
club drugs abuse in U.S. cities.

http://www.whitehousedrugpolicy.gov/publications/asp/subtopics.asp?sub=
Club%20Drugs&topic=Justice%20System&language=All
A listing of club drug-related publications from various sources.

Questions

Assume that you are part of a task force appointed by the White House to
address the growing problem of club drugs in the United States. Your committee has just been given a briefing by top White House staff (i.e., the article you just read). Your committee has been asked to answer the following
questions:

1. Describe the need for change. What is the extent of the problem, and what
   kind of data documents the need for change?

2. What kinds of causes does the report suggest or imply? Give examples.

3. What kinds of interventions might be suggested by this brief analysis? Give
   examples.

4. What further information is needed to inform efforts to develop effective
   interventions? Be specific.

Case Study 2.3

Incorporating Restorative and Community Justice into American Sentencing and Corrections[1]

Instructions: *Read the National Institute of Justice report below and answer the questions that follow.*

Directors' Message

It is by now a commonplace that the number of people under criminal justice supervision in this country has reached a record high. As a result, the sentencing policies driving that number, and the field of corrections, where the consequences are felt, have acquired an unprecedented salience. It is a salience defined more by issues of magnitude, complexity, and expense than by any consensus about future directions.

Are sentencing policies, as implemented through correctional programs and practices, achieving their intended purposes? As expressed in the movement to eliminate indeterminate sentencing and limit judicial discretion, on the one hand, and to radically restructure our retributive system of justice, on the other, the purposes seem contradictory, rooted in conflicting values. The lack of consensus on where sentencing and corrections should be headed is thus no surprise.

Because sentencing and corrections policies have such major consequences—for the allocation of government resources and, more fundamentally and profoundly, for the quality of justice in this country and the safety of its citizens—the National Institute of Justice and the Corrections Program Office (CPO) of the Office of Justice Programs felt it opportune to explore them in depth. Through a series of Executive Sessions on Sentencing and Corrections, begun in 1998 and continuing through the year 2000, practitioners and scholars foremost in their field, representing a broad cross-section of points of view, are being brought together to find out if there is a better way to think about the purposes, functions, and interdependence of sentencing and corrections policies.

We are fortunate in having secured the assistance of Michael Tonry, Sonosky Professor of Law and Public Policy at the University of Minnesota Law School, as project director.

---

[1]   Kurki, Leena (1999). "Incorporating Restorative and Community Justice Into American Sentencing and Corrections." *Sentencing & Corrections: Issues for the 21st Century.* Papers From The Executive Sessions on Sentencing snd Corrections, No. 3 (NCJ 175723). Washington, DC: U.S. Department of Justice, Office of Justice Programs, National Institute of Justice. Available at: *http://www.ncjrs.org/pdffiles1/nij/175723.pdf* (retrieved March 17, 2004).

Case Study 2.3, *continued*

One product of the sessions is this series of papers, commissioned by NIJ and the CPO as the basis for the discussions. Drawing on the research and experience of the session participants, the papers are intended to distill their judgments about the strengths and weaknesses of current practices and about the most promising ideas for future developments.

The sessions were modeled on the executive sessions on policing held in the 1980s and 1990s under the sponsorship of NIJ and Harvard's Kennedy School of Government. Those sessions played a role in conceptualizing community policing and spreading it. Whether the current sessions and the papers based on them will be instrumental in developing a new paradigm for sentencing and corrections, or even whether they will generate broad-based support for a particular model or strategy for change, remains to be seen. It is our hope that in the current environment of openness to new ideas, the session papers will provoke comment, promote further discussion and, taken together, will constitute a basic resource document on sentencing and corrections policy issues that will prove useful to State and local policymakers.

Jeremy Travis
Director, National Institute
 of Justice
U.S. Department of Justice

Larry Meachum
Director, Corrections
 Program Office
U.S. Department of Justice

Programs based on restorative and community justice principles have proliferated in the United States over the past decade, simultaneously with tough-on-crime initiatives like three-strikes, truth-in-sentencing, and mandatory minimum sentence laws. Restorative justice and community justice represent new ways of thinking about crime. The theories underlying restorative justice suggest that government should surrender its monopoly over responses to crime to those most directly affected—the victim, the offender, and the community. Community justice redefines the roles and goals of criminal justice agencies to include a broader mission—to prevent crime, address local social problems and conflicts, and involve neighborhood residents in planning and decisionmaking. Both restorative and community justice are based on the premise that communities will be strengthened if local citizens participate in responding to crime, and both envision responses tailored to the preferences and needs of victims, communities, and offenders.

In contrast to this bottom-up approach, recent changes in sentencing law are premised on retributive ideas about punishing wrongdoers and on the desir-

Case Study 2.3, *continued*

ability of controlling risk, increasing public safety, and reducing sentencing disparities. Restorative and community justice goals of achieving appropriate, individualized dispositions often conflict with the retributive goal of imposing certain, consistent, proportionate sentences.

There are many ways to resolve this normative conflict. Restorative and community justice initiatives could continue to confine their efforts to juvenile offenders and people who commit minor crimes. This seems unlikely, as these approaches are expanding rapidly and winning many new supporters who want to extend their application. Alternatively, retributive sentencing laws could be revised or narrowed. But this too seems unlikely in the near term. How precisely the two divergent trends will be reconciled remains to be seen. Nevertheless, it seems likely that restorative and community justice values will to some extent become more institutionalized in criminal justice processes.[2]

What is Restorative Justice?

Restorative justice has evolved from a little-known concept into a term used widely but in divergent ways. There is no doubt about its appeal, although the varied uses of the term cause some confusion. The umbrella term *restorative justice* has been applied to initiatives identified as restorative by some but not by others. Examples are sex-offender notification laws, victim impact statements, and murder victim survivors' "right" to be present at executions. Most advocates of restorative justice agree that it involves five basic principles:

- Crime consists of more than violation of the criminal law and defiance of government authority.

- Crime involves disruptions in a three-dimensional relationship of victim, community, and offender.

- Because crime harms the victim and the community, the primary goals should be to repair the harm and heal the victim and the community.

- The victim, the community, and the offender should all participate in determining the response to crime; government should surrender its monopoly over that process.

---

[2]   This paper is one of four in the first "round" of publications from the Executive Sessions on Sentencing and Corrections. Together the four constitute a framework for understanding the issues raised in the sessions. The other three are *Fragmentation of Sentencing and Corrections in America*, by Michael Tonry (NCJ 175721; *Reconsidering Indeterminate and Structured Sentencing*, by Michael Tonry (NCJ 175722); and *Reforming Sentencing and Corrections for Just Punishment and Public Safety*, by Michael E. Smith and Walter J. Dickey (NCJ 175724). All: *Research in Brief—Sentencing & Corrections: Issues for the 21st Century*, Washington, DC: U.S. Department of Justice, National Institute of Justice/Corrections Program Office, September 1999.

Case Study 2.3, *continued*

- Case disposition should be based primarily on the victim's and the community's needs—not solely on the offender's needs or culpability, the dangers he or she presents, or his or her criminal history.

The original goal of restorative justice was to restore harmony between victims and offenders. For victims, this meant restitution for tangible losses and emotional losses. For offenders, it meant taking responsibility, confronting shame, and regaining dignity.

This notion has evolved, with the major recent conceptual development the incorporation of a role for the community. Many people still associate restorative justice primarily with victim-offender mediation or, more broadly (but mistakenly), with any victim-oriented services. The more recent conceptualization—that offenses occur within a three-dimensional relationship—may change the movement.

All three parties should be able to participate in rebuilding the relationship and in deciding on responses to the crime. The distinctive characteristic is direct, face-to-face dialogue among victim, offender, and increasingly, the community.

What is Community Justice?

The concept of community justice is less clear. It can be portrayed as a set of new organizational strategies that change the focus of criminal justice from a narrow, case-processing orientation: operations are moved to neighborhood locations that offer flexible working hours and services, neighborhoods are assigned their own officers and are provided with more information than is standard practice, and residents may identify crime problems and define priorities for neighborhood revitalization. Most experience with community justice is in the context of community policing, but prosecutors, judges, and correctional officers are increasingly rethinking their roles and goals.

The most frequently cited standpoints for community justice are problem solving and community empowerment. Problem solving is understood broadly: first, as an effort to build partnerships between criminal justice and other government agencies and between government agencies and neighborhoods; and, second, as an attempt to address some of the complex social problems underlying crime.

Community justice proponents suggest that criminal justice agencies change the way they interact with the public, learn to listen to citizens, and work together with local people to prevent crime and solve crime-related problems.[3]

---

[3] Barajas, Eduardo, "Moving Toward Community Justice," in *Community Justice: Striving for Safe, Secure, and Just Communities*, Washington, DC: U.S. Department of Justice, National Institute of Corrections, 1996.

Case Study 2.3, *continued*

Advocates of community justice believe that to maximize public safety and optimize crime prevention, residents must work on an equal basis with government agency representatives and elected officials. Dennis Maloney, Director of the Deschutes County, Oregon, Department of Community Justice, has described the connection between citizen involvement and crime prevention: "In a community justice framework, the goal is to engage as many citizens as possible in building a better community . . . . People who share a strong sense of community are far less likely to violate the trust of others. Their stake in and bond with the community is the strongest force of guardianship to prevent crime from flourishing."

Should Restorative and Community Justice be Incorporated into the Criminal Justice System?

Advocates of restorative justice and community justice often differ over the desirability of becoming part of the official criminal justice system. Restorative justice proponents believe in the efficacy of grassroots citizen efforts and thus many want to keep restorative justice initiatives separate from the criminal justice system. Community justice advocates often support a total, systemwide transformation that would incorporate the new principles. Both groups are concerned about the role of government in these approaches and their growing popularity. They emphasize that restorative and community justice represent fundamental change: comprehensive philosophies or theories, not "silver bullets" or fads.

Proponents are also concerned that criminal justice agencies will add new community or restorative justice programs to appear "fashionable" or to solve a particular problem, but will do so without fundamentally rethinking their missions. Ronald Earle, District Attorney in Travis County, Texas, summarized this concern: "The question is how to focus the criminal justice system and fashion programs on a new way of thinking, not just another way of doing." Some advocates are skeptical about whether the new goals and principles can be meaningfully adopted by criminal justice agencies, which like many other government agencies tend to value passionless, specialized, professionalized, and routinized operations.

Another worry is that government agencies or experts will establish guidelines, standards, and requirements for programs reflecting these values, thereby bureaucratizing them and once again "stealing the conflicts" from communities. As Ronald Earle put it, the "unstructured lack of standardization is the genius of the movement," but, at the same time, he added, "there is a great temptation to create a national template for community justice programs." The challenge for government will be to encourage and support the new initiatives without stifling the spontaneity, creativity, and grassroots ties that are their strengths.

Case Study 2.3, *continued*

What is Happening Now

A fundamental difficulty in documenting or estimating the impact of restorative or community justice in the United States is the lack of systematic data. No one knows how many or what kinds of programs there are; how many offenders, victims, and volunteers participate; the amounts of restitution paid or community service performed; or the effects on victims, communities, and offenders. It is nearly impossible to monitor what is happening in different states or regions.

Little evaluation research is available, and there is no consensus on how to measure "success." Most advocates contend that recidivism is not the correct or only measure. Evaluations might also consider such measures as victim and offender satisfaction, amounts of restitution or community service, rates at which reparative agreements are fulfilled, levels of volunteer participation and community action, and victims' and offenders' quality of life.

Some advocates do not want to encourage rigorous evaluation because that might create pressure to standardize and "expertize" the movements. However, because the varied programs and practices are what make restorative and community justice visible, concrete, and distinctive, it is important to document their types, analyze their characteristics, and evaluate outcomes.

The dearth of information affects the writings of practitioners and academics. There is, however, a sizable literature on the principles and goals of restorative justice, how it differs from traditional criminal justice approaches, and its processes and terminology.[4] Other works describe programs or present details of local projects.[5] Most of the literature on community justice focuses on community policing, with little information on community prosecution, courts, or corrections.

Restorative Justice Practices

Although something akin to restorative justice has long been observed in premodern and indigenous societies, restorative justice principles, in the form of victim-offender reconciliation programs, appeared in Western industrialized countries only in the 1970s. The first program was established in 1974 in Kitchener, Ontario. By the 1990s, such programs had spread to all Western countries—at least 700 in Europe and 300 in the United States.

---

[4] Examples are Braithwaite, John, "Restorative Justice: Assessing Optimistic and Pessimistic Accounts," in *Crime and Justice: A Review of Research*, vol. 25, ed. Michael Tonry, Chicago: University of Chicago Press, 1999; and Van Ness, Daniel, and Karen Heetderks Strong, *Restoring Justice*, Cincinnati: Anderson, 1997.

[5] Galaway, Burt, and Joe Hudson, eds., *Restorative Justice: International Perspectives*, Amsterdam: Kugler Publications, 1996; and Messmer, Heinz, and Hans-Uwe Otto, *Restorative Justice on Trial: Pitfalls and Potentials of Victim-Offender Mediation*, Dordrecht, Netherlands: Kluwer, 1992.

Case Study 2.3, *continued*

Victim-offender mediation. Victim-offender mediation is the most widespread and evaluated type of restorative program. Offenders and victims meet with volunteer mediators to discuss the effects of the crime on their lives, express their concerns and feelings, and work out a restitution agreement. The agreement is often seen as secondary to emotional healing and growth. Victims consistently report that the most important element of mediation is being able to talk with the offender and express their feelings, and offenders also emphasize the importance of face-to-face communication. Advocates believe that developing an offender's empathy for the victim has preventive effects.

In many countries, victim-offender mediation is widely used. In Austria, for example, it became an official part of the juvenile justice system as early as 1989. Public prosecutors refer juveniles to mediation, probation officers coordinate cases, and social workers serve as mediators. If an agreement is reached and completed, the case is dismissed.[6] In the United States, most programs are operated by private, nonprofit organizations; handle largely juvenile cases; and function as diversion programs for minor, nonviolent crimes. However, there is a movement to develop programs established and operated (or at least initiated) by corrections departments, police, or prosecutors and used as a condition of either probation or dropping charges. Most studies of mediation programs report high rates of success.[7]

Advocates are beginning to challenge the assumption that mediation is not suitable for violent or sexual crimes. Increasingly, in the United States and Canada, for example, victims and offenders meet in prisons. These meetings are not oriented to a tangible goal such as a restitution agreement, nor does the offender obtain benefits like early release or parole consideration. Usually the meetings are held because the victim wants to meet the offender and learn more about what happened to reach beyond fear and anger and facilitate healing. The results of a Canadian survey indicated that 89 percent of victims of serious, violent crimes wanted to meet the offender.[8]

Serious violent crimes are usually mediated on a case-by-case basis, but the need for permanent programs is growing. Such programs are offered, for example, by the Correctional Service of Canada in British Columbia and the Yukon Territory and by the Texas Department of Criminal Justice.

---

[6]   Lösching-Gspandl, Marianne, and Michael Kilchling, "Victim/Offender Mediation and Victim Compensation in Austria and Germany—Stock-taking and Perspectives for Future Research," *European Journal of Crime, Criminal Law and Criminal Justice* 5 (1997):58-78.

[7]   Umbreit, Mark, *Victim Meets the Offender: The Impact of Restorative Justice and Mediation,* Monsey, NY: Criminal Justice Press, 1994. It should be noted that evaluations of restorative justice conducted in the United States are usually not based on experimental and control groups, do not often measure recidivism rates, and seldom use sophisticated research designs.

[8]   Gustafson, Dave, "Facilitating Communication between Victims and Offenders in Cases of Serious and Violent Crime," *The International Community Corrections Association Journal on Community Corrections,* 8 (1997):4-49.

Case Study 2.3, *continued*

Family group conferencing. Family group conferencing is based on the same rationales as victim-offender mediation, with two main differences. Conferencing involves a broader range of people (family, friends, coworkers, and teachers), and family members and other supporters tend to take collective responsibility for the offender and for carrying out his or her agreement. The other difference is that conferencing often relies on police, probation, or social service agencies for organization and facilitation.

Family group conferences originated in New Zealand, where they became part of the juvenile justice system in 1989. There, the new juvenile justice model, which incorporates Maori traditions of involving the family and the community in addressing wrongdoing, has four dispositional options:

- An immediate warning by the police.

- "Youth Aid Section" dispositions in which a special police unit may require, for example, an apology to the victim or community service.

- Family group conferencing.

- Traditional youth court sentencing.

About 60 percent of juvenile offenders receive a warning or go to the Youth Aid Section, 30 percent go to conferencing, and 10 percent go to youth court.[9]

By the mid-1990s, family group conferencing had been adopted in every state and territory of Australia. In South Australia, it is used statewide as a component of the juvenile justice system and resembles the New Zealand approach. In Wagga Wagga, New South Wales, conferences (originally part of a police diversion program) were organized and facilitated by police officers who were often in uniform.[10] Responsibility was transferred to juvenile justice agencies in 1998, and trained community members now facilitate conferences. In Canberra, the Federal Police set up a program called the Reintegrative Shaming Experiment, which involved more than 100 trained police officers.

There is evidence that conferencing can be successful. A recent evaluation of the Bethlehem, Pennsylvania, Police Family Group Conferencing program revealed that typical police officers were able to conduct conferences in conformity with restorative justice and due process principles if adequately

---

[9] Maxwell, Gabrielle, and Allison Morris, *Family, Victims, and Culture: Youth Justice in New Zealand*, Wellington, New Zealand: Social Policy Agency and Institute of Criminology, Victoria University of Wellington, 1993.

[10] Wundersitz, Joy, and Sue Hetzel, "Family Conferencing for Young Offenders: The South Australian Experience." In John Hudson et al. (ed.), *Family Group Conferences: Perspectives on Policy and Practice*. Monsey, NY: Criminal Justice Press, 1996.

Case Study 2.3, *continued*

trained and supervised, and that very high percentages of offenders, victims, and other participants were pleased with the process.[11] Evaluation of Canberra's Reintegrative Shaming Experiment showed similar results.[12]

Sentencing circles. Sentencing circles originated in traditional Native Canadian and Native American peacemaking. They involve the victim and the offender, their supporters, and key community members, and they are open to everyone in the community. They attempt to address the underlying causes of crime, seek responses, and agree on offenders' responsibilities. The process is based on peacemaking, negotiation, and consensus, and each circle member must agree on the outcomes.

Sentencing circles are so named because participants sit in a circle, and a "talking piece" (a feather, for example) is passed from person to person. When participants take the talking piece, they explain their feelings about the crime and express support for the victim and the offender. Separate circles often are held for the offender and the victim before they join in a shared circle.

In Minnesota, sentencing circles are used not only in Native American communities but also in rural white, suburban, and inner-city black communities (see "Minnesota—A Pioneer in Restorative Justice"). Community Justice Committees, established by citizen volunteers, handle organizational and administrative tasks and provide "keepers" who lead the discussions. Judges refer cases, and the committees make the final decision on acceptance. The agreements reached are presented to the judge as sentencing recommendations. In some cases, the judge, prosecutor, and defense attorney participate in the circle, and then the agreement becomes the final sentence.

Reparative probation and other citizen boards. Reparative probation in Vermont involves a probation sentence ordered by a judge, followed by a meeting between the offender and volunteer citizen members of a Reparative Citizen Board. Together they draw up a contract, based on restorative principles, which the offender agrees to carry out. Fulfilling the contract is the only condition of probation (see "Vermont—Statewide Reparative Probation").

Vermont's program is different from most other restorative justice initiatives in the United States. Designed by the state's Department of Corrections, it operates statewide, handles adult cases, and involves a sizable number of citizen volunteers. Compared with family group conferencing or

---

[11] McCold, Paul, and Benjamin Wachtel, *Restorative Policing Experiment: The Bethlehem Pennsylvania Police Family Group Conferencing Project*, Pipersville, PA: Community Service Foundation, 1998. This evaluation was sponsored by the National Institute of Justice.

[12] Sherman, Lawrence, Heather Strang, Geoffrey Barnes, John Braithwaite, Nova Ipken, and Min-Mee The, *Experiments in Restorative Policing: A Progress Report to the National Police Research Unit in the Canberra Reintegrative Shaming Experiments (RISE)*, Canberra: Australian Federal Police and Australian National University, 1998.

Case Study 2.3, *continued*

sentencing circles, the Reparative Citizen Boards work faster, require less preparation, and can process more cases; however, they involve fewer community
members. For example, offenders' and victims' families and supporters usually are not present.

Citizen boards also may be established to adjudicate minor crimes. For example, a Merchant Accountability Board in Deschutes County, Oregon, consists
of local business owners who adjudicate thefts of property valued at $50 or less,
and some more serious cases involving property valued at between $51 and $750.
Under an agreement with the district attorney, the police refer all minor
shoplifting cases directly to the program. If offenders decide to participate, they
are typically ordered by the board to pay fines, make restitution, or both.

Minnesota—A Pioneer in Restorative Justice

Minnesota has been a groundbreaker in restorative justice. Its Department of Corrections created the Restorative Justice Initiative in 1992, hiring
Kay Pranis as a full-time Restorative Justice Planner in 1994—the first such
position in the country. The initiative offers training in restorative justice principles and practices, provides technical assistance to communities in designing and implementing practices, and creates networks of professionals and
activists to share knowledge and provide support.

Sentencing Circles

Besides promoting victim-offender mediation, family group conferencing, and neighborhood conferencing, the department has introduced sentencing
circles. Citizen volunteers and criminal justice officials from Minnesota
have participated in training in the Yukon Territory, where peacemaking circles have been held since the late 1980s. In Minnesota, the circle process is
used by the Mille Lacs Indian Reservation and in other communities in several counties.

The Circle Process

The circle process usually has several phases. First, the Community Justice Committee conducts an intake interview with offenders who want to participate. Then, separate healing circles are held for the victim (and others who
feel harmed) and the offender. The committee tries to cultivate a close personal relationship with victims and offenders and to create support networks for them. In the end, a sentencing circle, open to the community, meets
to work out a sentencing plan. In the towns of Milaca and Princeton, follow-
up circles monitor and discuss the offender's progress.

Manitoba's Restorative Resolutions Project offers an alternative to cus-
todial sentences for offenders who otherwise are likely to face a minimum
prison sentence of six months. Offenders and project staff develop sentenc-

Case Study 2.3, *continued*

ing plans, and victims are encouraged to participate. The plans are presented to judges as nonbinding recommendations. Most plans require restitution, community service, and counseling or therapy. A recent evaluation revealed that offenders who participate have significantly fewer supervision violations and slightly fewer new convictions than those in comparison groups.[13]

Community Justice Practices

People who have no personal experience with community justice are often preoccupied with what "community" means and who is involved. Explanations vary. Reginald Wilkinson, Director of Ohio's Department of Rehabilitation and Correction, says: "In a community, there would exist a sense of hope, belonging, and caring . . . . A sense of commitment, responsibility, and sacrifice would be basic tenets of a communitarian." For Minnesota Department of Corrections Restorative Justice Planner Kay Pranis, "Community self-defines around the issue that surfaces, so everybody who sees themselves as a stakeholder in a particular issue [makes up the community]." Vermont Department of Corrections Commissioner John Gorczyk says: "Beyond place, community is defined by relationships and the amount of interaction. In my community, the quality of those interactions, doing favors for one another, is what builds community."

Although in "practicing" community justice, it is essential to identify the community and consider possible definitions, it is at least as important to think about the community's role. While many new approaches in criminal justice have improved access to and satisfaction with justice services, often they have not transformed the role of citizens from service recipient to participant and decisionmaker.[14] For many community justice advocates, the ultimate goal is for communities to feel ownership of programs, but that can be achieved only if citizens participate. Even then the question remains whether government genuinely shares power or simply allows communities to supplement its power and exercise it only in certain types of cases.

---

[13] Bonta, James, Jennifer Rooney, and Suzanne Wallace-Capretta, *Restorative Justice: An Evaluation of the Restorative Resolutions Project*, Ottawa: Solicitor General of Canada, 1998.

[14] Bazemore, Gordon, "The 'Community' in Community Justice: Issues, Themes, and Questions for the New Neighborhood Sanctioning Models," *Justice System Journal*, 19 (1997): 193-228.

Case Study 2.3, *continued*

Vermont—Statewide Reparative Probation

A pilot reparative probation program began in Vermont in 1994, and the first cases were heard by a Reparative Citizen Board the following year. Three features distinguish this restorative justice initiative from most others in the United States: (1) The Department of Corrections, headed by John Gorczyk, designed the program; (2) it is implemented statewide; and (3) it involves a sizable number of volunteer citizens. In 1998, the program was named a winner in the prestigious Innovations in American Government competition.

The Process

The concept is straightforward. Following an adjudication of guilt, the judge sentences the offender to probation, with the sentence suspended and only two conditions imposed: the offender will commit no more crimes and will complete the reparative program. The volunteer board members meet with the offender and the victim and together discuss the offense, its effects on victim and community, and the life situations of victim and offender. All participants must agree on a contract, to be fulfilled by the offender. It is based on five goals: (1) the victim is restored and healed, (2) the community is restored, (3) the offender understands the effects of the crime, (4) the offender learns ways to avoid reoffending, and (5) the community offers reintegration to the offender. Because reparative probation targets minor crimes, it is not meant as a prison diversion program.

The Numbers

In 1998, the 44 boards handled 1,200 cases, accounting for more than one-third of the probation caseload. More than 300 trained volunteers serve as board members. Ten coordinators handle case management and organization for the boards. The goal is to have the boards handle about 70 percent of the targeted probation cases. That only about 17 percent of offenders fail to complete their agreements or attend followup board meetings is a measure of the program's success. These offenders are referred back to court.

Related Initiatives

Other practices based on restorative justice are under way. More than 150 volunteers or Department of Corrections staff have been trained in family group conferencing. A Community Justice Center is operating in Burlington, and others are being developed elsewhere. The department is also looking into sentencing circles and ways to become more active in crime prevention and early intervention.

Community policing and prosecution. Experiences with community policing show there is no shared understanding of the community's role, and that it is difficult to generate citizen participation. Priorities and routines vary; for example, some efforts rely on heavy street-level enforcement, while

Case Study 2.3, *continued*

others emphasize citizen involvement, better quality public services, delivery of community-based treatment, or diversionary policing that withholds enforcement as a way to build relationships with communities.

Few studies have attempted to measure the extent to which the rhetoric of community empowerment, involvement, and partnership building becomes reality, and the results are not particularly encouraging. Community input is often limited to assisting law enforcement. Many evaluations have not shown positive results, and implementation is often incomplete or partial.[15]

Many applications of community policing and prosecution are not fundamentally different from traditional approaches, although they may shift control to local levels and include the community in law enforcement efforts. They often promote tougher responses to crime than do traditional approaches because the emphasis is on a broader view of crime control that takes seriously minor, nuisance, and quality-of-life offenses. Some approaches, such as the one taken by the District Attorney of Travis County, Texas, however, clearly identify themselves as restorative (see "Travis County, Texas—Community Justice as the Prosecutorial Response").

Applications in courts and corrections. The first community court in the United States, New York City's Midtown Community Court, is based on the idea of partnership with the neighborhood and focuses on quality-of-life crimes. Several restorative elements are evident:

- Offenders are sentenced to work on projects in local neighborhoods.

- Court staff try to link offenders with drug treatment, health care, education, and other social services and thus combine punishment with help.

- The community is encouraged to participate in shaping restorative, community-based sanctions.[16]

Nearly 70 percent of those convicted are ordered to perform community work, and of these nearly 70 percent complete it without violations. By fall 1996, almost 33,000 defendants had been arraigned.[17] The court houses health care and drug treatment providers, organizes education and job training, maintains mediation services for community-level conflicts, and provides counseling rooms and space to perform community service.

---

[15] Skogan, Wesley G., and Susan M. Hartnett, *Community Policing, Chicago Style*, New York: Oxford University Press, 1997.

[16] Feinblatt, John, and Greg Berman, *Responding to the Community: Principles for Planning and Creating a Community Court*, Washington, DC: U.S. Department of Justice, Bureau of Justice Assistance, 1997.

[17] Midtown Community Court, *The Midtown Community Court Experiment: A Progress Report*, New York: Midtown Community Court, 1997.

Case Study 2.3, *continued*

The Manhattan Court opened in 1993 and was followed by several others. The Portland (Oregon) Community Court began operations in 1998, and plans for community courts are under way in Baltimore, Hartford (Connecticut), Hempstead (New York), Indianapolis, Minneapolis, St. Louis, and no doubt elsewhere.

Deschutes County, Oregon, has made a comprehensive effort to implement community justice in corrections (as distinct from traditional community corrections), reinventing its Community Corrections Department as the Department of Community Justice. Committed to principles of both community and restorative justice, the department differs in this respect from most current community policing and prosecution initiatives.

The Deschutes approach is especially ambitious (see "Deschutes County, Oregon—Reinventing Community Corrections"). A true paradigm shift would combine operational strategies and the crime prevention and citizen involvement goals of community justice with the values and practices of restorative justice.

Travis County, Texas—Community Justice as the Prosecutorial Response

Ronald Earle, who has been District Attorney of Travis County (Austin), Texas, for more than 20 years, is a strong advocate of restorative and community justice. Recognizing that people's natural reaction to crime is anger and fear, particularly if they lack power to influence responses, he believes this wasted energy can fuel positive change. This can be done if citizens are empowered and can participate in planning and deciding on the response to crime.

To promote such participation, he drafted the Texas law that authorizes in each county a Community Justice Council and Community Justice Task Force. The task force includes representatives of criminal justice agencies, social and health services, and community organizations. With task force assistance, the council, consisting of elected officials, handles planning and policymaking and prepares a "Community Justice Plan."

Many efforts are directed at juvenile offenses. In Austin, the Juvenile Probation Office offers victim-offender mediation for young people in trouble. For misdemeanors, juveniles may be diverted from court to Neighborhood Conference Committees. These consist of panels of trained adult citizens who meet with the juvenile offenders and their parents and together develop contracts tailored to the case.

The Travis County Children's Advocacy Center provides support and help to abused children through collaboration among social and criminal justice agencies, medical professionals, and private citizens. The Child Protection Team brings together police officers, social workers, and prosecutors to improve responses to child abuse and to reduce traumatization when cases are investigated and prosecuted.

Case Study 2.3, *continued*

Can the Justice System Incorporate Restorative Principles?

Although many activists would prefer that restorative justice remain an unofficial alternative to the criminal justice system, others contend that there are reasons for a systemwide shift to incorporate its values.

Why Not the Best?

If restorative justice is a significantly better way to deal with crime, proponents ask why not implement it systemwide? If it really is a better idea, why should it not become the governing principle of the whole criminal justice system rather than be confined to small-scale, grassroots activities? Minnesota Restorative Justice Planner Kay Pranis emphasized the need to focus on community when she said, "It is very important for us to recognize that our current criminal justice interventions actually destroy community. So even to get neutral would be a huge step for this system."

No Significant or Lasting Effects on Values and Practices

Advocates contend that restorative justice is unlikely to have significant or lasting effects on the official criminal justice system if it continues to operate primarily as local, unorganized grassroots activities. It is doubtful whether any program can be truly restorative in a system based on retributive values. Even if restorative justice principles cannot completely transform the justice system, they may turn criminal justice policy and values in another, arguably better, direction.

Increased Control and Punishment

Advocates argue that if crime is seen in both traditional and restorative ways—as an offense against the state and as harm to the victim and the community—a double system of punishment may be created. Offenders will first be processed through the traditional system and receive punishment and then move to the informal restorative programs to agree to a reparative contract. As a consequence, they often will be subjected to greater social control and more sanctions.

> ### Deschutes County, Oregon—
> ### Reinventing Community Corrections
>
> Deschutes County, Oregon, is attempting to apply community justice principles throughout its correctional system. In 1996 the County Board of Commissioners passed a "Community Justice Resolution," which recognizes community justice as "the central mission and purpose of the county's community corrections effort." It calls for incorporating community justice principles into corrections by striking a balance among prevention, early inter-

Case Study 2.3, *continued*

vention, and correctional efforts; ensuring participation by and restoration of victims; including community decisionmaking in crime prevention and reduction; and fostering offender accountability. In recognition of this major change, the Community Corrections Department, headed by Dennis Maloney, was renamed the Department of Community Justice.

Basic Principles

The Commission on Children and Families, a lay citizen body, was assigned authority over the department's budget. In 1998, it set budget principles that for the first time included:

- Enhancing public safety.

- Paying particular attention to offender accountability, responsibility, and skill development.

- Incorporating the findings of research on cost-effective interventions.

- Focusing on restoration and defining offenders' accountability as meeting their obligations to victims and the community.

- Encouraging volunteer involvement and reducing dependence on service delivery by professionals.

- Managing crime problems as cost effectively as possible.

- Directing reallocated resources to crime prevention.

- Viewing investment in prevention as the first order of business.

State law permits the county to apply any savings in juvenile detention to crime prevention.

Community Action and Other Initiatives

A number of former juvenile probation officers constitute a Community Action Team, which devotes most of its time and resources to neighborhood crime prevention. The new Community Justice Center contains space for juvenile custody facilities, houses a number of criminal justice agencies as well as victim service and other nonprofit organizations, and has a meeting room available for community groups.

Deschutes County also offers victim-offender mediation in criminal cases and dispute resolution in other conflicts. Merchant Accountability Boards, consisting of local business owners, adjudicate minor shoplifting cases. Reparative community service projects are operated through the collaboration of business owners, neighborhood residents, and community leaders. As part of these projects, offenders have built houses for Habitat for Humanity, cut and distributed firewood for elderly citizens, and built and maintained parks.

Case Study 2.3, *continued*

Trivialization of Restorative Programs

If the criminal justice system endorses restorative justice principles but does not participate in designing, implementing, and monitoring programs based on them, it is not likely to refer cases other than those considered trivial. Criminal justice agencies and officials understandably do not want to rely heavily on practices whose outcomes they cannot comprehend, influence, predict, or trust. For the same reason, judges often are reluctant to divert offenders to these programs.

No Resource Savings

Although restorative justice advocates emphasize that the goal is not decreased criminal justice caseloads or costs, it is unrealistic not to consider resource savings in the current climate of exploding correctional costs. Few resources will be saved if restorative solutions only supplement traditional punishments or are used only for minor crimes.

Inconsistent Practices and Outcomes

The most common argument against restorative justice is that practices and outcomes vary with the particular program, and that fairness requires comparable crimes and criminals to be punished equally. Restorative justice involves individualized responses to crimes.

Proportionality and equality in punishment are often understood narrowly as calling for the same sentence for people who have committed similar crimes. However, they could just as well be interpreted as requiring comparable sentences for comparable offenses. This would mean punishment or responses may vary as long as they are meaningfully related to the nature and effects of the crime. Thus, in principle, there is no reason restorative justice cannot respect the tenets of proportionality and equality.

In practice, responses to crime will be different and inconsistent as long as restorative justice is not implemented systemwide. Many people are concerned that assigning substantial punishment power to lay volunteers will mean random, inequitable, and capriciously severe sanctions. Restorative justice, with its positive, constructive goals, attempts to move in the opposite direction. If participants, including the offender, understand and accept restorative justice principles, the requirements of fairness will not be circumvented and there will be no extreme consequences.

If there is no systemwide shift, programs based on restorative justice will probably continue to handle only minor offenses, and problems of inequity will likely not become serious. It will not much matter whether one offender is sentenced to 10 hours of community service and $50 in restitution and another, who commits a similar crime, to 20 hours of service and $100 in resti-

Case Study 2.3, *continued*

tution. However, the more serious the crimes, the more unjust the differences could become and the greater the need for consistent practices.

Other matters of equity relate to socioeconomic considerations. Without official encouragement and support, restorative justice initiatives are likely to be concentrated in middle-class white neighborhoods or rural areas, and volunteers will disproportionately be white, middle-class, and middle-aged and older individuals, as these are the demographic groups from which activists tend to emerge. Moreover, if citizen activists work on their own, new practices may be concentrated in areas with relatively minor crime problems. By contrast, disadvantaged urban neighborhoods with large proportions of minority group members and immigrants—who are disproportionately affected by serious crime—would be unlikely to benefit.

The Future of Restorative and Community Justice

How deeply restorative and community justice ideas will penetrate the traditional justice system remains to be seen. So far, restorative justice approaches are used much more for juveniles than for adults, and for minor offenses rather than for serious crimes. Experience with community justice has consistently shown that generating citizen involvement and building relationships with the community is a challenge. Both movements have spread rapidly, however, and both are increasingly reaching out to encompass adult offenders, more serious crimes, and disadvantaged urban communities where, arguably, the need is greatest.

Leena Kurki, who holds law degrees from the University of Turku, Finland, and the University of Minnesota, is a Research Associate at the University of Minnesota Law School and the Project Association of the Executive Sessions on Sentencing and Corrections.

This study was supported by cooperative agreement 97-MUMU-K006 between the National Institute of Justice and the University of Minnesota.

Findings and conclusions of the research reported here are those of the author and do not necessarily reflect the official position or policies of the U.S. Department of Justice.

The National Institute of Justice is a component of the Office of Justice Programs, which also includes the Bureau of Justice Assistance, the Bureau of Justice Statistics, the Office of Juvenile Justice and Delinquency Prevention, and the Office for Victims of Crime.

This and other NIJ publications can be found at and downloaded from the NIJ Web site (http://www.ojp.usdoj.gov/nij).

NCJ 175723

Case Study 2.3, *continued*

Questions

1. Describe how the case study illustrates the need for criminal justice system assessment. Give an example of at least *two* of the following:

    *   Describe the roles and responsibilities of different levels, branches and agencies of government.

    *   Describe how discretion is distributed throughout the system.

    *   Describe the existing continuum of sanctions.

    *   Describe the offender population.

    *   Describe the policy environment.

    *   Describe the historical context.

    *   Describe community involvement in the criminal justice system.

2. Assume now that the following hypothetical circumstances occur:

    > The governor makes an announcement that restorative and community justice is about to become the preferred practice in your state. The governor states that a new law will require all counties within the state to reduce the number of their court commitments to state prison by 50 percent within two years. There will be substantial financial incentives for compliance and substantial financial penalties for noncompliance. Assume you have been assigned to a county planning committee that has been asked to respond to this change in law.

    Now, using force field analysis, do the following:

    (a) *Identify "driving forces" and "restraining forces."* Try to identify at least two of each.

    (b) *Analyze one* of the restraining forces in part (a) in terms of its: amenability, potency, and consistency.

    (c) Describe two possible strategies to reduce this source of resistance.

Endnotes

[1] Spector, Malcolm, and John Kitsuse (2001). *Constructing Social Problems.* Transaction Publishers; Walker, Samuel (2001). *Sense and Nonsense About Crime and Drugs*, 5th ed. Belmont, CA: Wadsworth.

[2] Bastian, L.D., and B.M. Taylor (1991). *School Crime* (NCJ-131645). Washington, DC: U.S. Department of Justice, Office of Justice Programs, Bureau of Justice Statistics; Chandler, K.A., C.D. Chapman, M.R. Rand, and B.M. Taylor (1998). *Students' Reports of School Crime: 1989 and 1995* (NCES 98-241/NCJ-169607). Washington, DC: U.S. Department of Education and U.S. Department of Justice; Kaufman, P., X. Chen, S.P. Choy, S.A. Ruddy, A.K. Miller, J.K. Fleury, K.A. Chandler, M.R. Rand, P. Klaus, and M.G. Planty (2000). *Indicators of School Crime and Safety, 2000.* Washington, DC: U.S. Department of Education and U.S. Department of Justice; DeVoe, J.F., K. Peter, P. Kaufman, S.A. Ruddy, A.K. Miller, M. Planty, D.T. Snyder, D.T. Duhart, and M.R. Rand (2002). *Indicators of School Crime and Safety, 2002.* NCES 2003-009/NCJ 196753.Washington, DC: U.S. Department of Education and Justice.

[3] Harris, P.W., W.N. Welsh, and F. Butler. "A Century of Juvenile Justice." In G. LaFree (ed.), *Criminal Justice 2000, Volume 1*, pp. 359-426. Washington, DC: U.S. Department of Justice, Office of Justice Programs, National Institute of Justice (NCJ-182408). Available at: *http://www.ojp.usdoj.gov/nij/criminal_justice 2000/vol1_2000.html* (retrieved March 12, 2004).

[4] Federal Bureau of Investigation (2002). *Crime in the United States – 2002.* Washington, DC: U.S. Department of Justice. Available at: *http://www.fbi.gov/ucr/ucr.htm* (retrieved March 8, 2004).

[5] Center for Disease Control, National Center for HIV, STD and TB Prevention, Divisions of HIV/AIDS Prevention (2004). *International Statistics.* Available at: *http://www.cdc.gov/hiv/* (retrieved March 8, 2004).

[6] Ibid, note 5.

[7] Kurz, G., and M. Schumacher (1999). *The 8% Solution: Preventing Serious, Repeat Juvenile Crime.* Thousand Oaks, CA: Sage.

[8] Maguire, Kathleen, and Ann L. Pastore (eds.) (2002). *Sourcebook of Criminal Justice Statistics* [Online]. Available at: *http://www.albany.edu/sourcebook/* [retrieved March 8, 2004].

[9] Maguire, Kathleen, and Ann L. Pastore (eds.) (2002). *Sourcebook of Criminal Justice Statistics* [Online] (p. 249). Available at: *http://www.albany.edu/sourcebook/* [retrieved March 8, 2004].

[10] Maguire, Kathleen, and Ann L. Pastore (eds.) (2002). *Sourcebook of Criminal Justice Statistics* [Online] (p. 200). Available at: *http://www.albany.edu/sourcebook/* [retrieved March 8, 2004].

[11] Biderman, Albert D., and James P. Lynch (1991) *Understanding Crime Incidence Statistics.* New York: Springer-Verlag.

[12] Reiss, Albert J., and Jeffrey A. Roth (eds.) (1993). "Appendix B: Measuring and Counting Violent Crimes and Their Consequences." *Understanding and Preventing Violence (Vol. 1).* Washington, DC: National Academy Press, p. 404.

[13]   Moran, Richard (1997). "New York Story: More Luck Than Policing." *The Washington Post*, February 9, 1997, p. C03.

[14]   Blumstein, A., J. Wallman, and D. Farrington (eds.) (2000). *The Crime Drop in America*. New York: Cambridge University Press.

[15]   *Thurman v. City of Torrington*, 595 F. Supp. 1521 (1984); *Thurman v. City of Torrington*, USDC. No. H-84120 (June 25, 1985).

[16]   Riveland, C. (1999). "Prison Management Trends, 1975-2025." In M. Tonry and J. Petersilia (eds.), *Prisons. Crime and Justice, A Review of Research, Vol. 26*, pp. 163-203. Chicago: University of Chicago Press.

[17]   Welsh, Wayne N., Philip Harris, and Patricia Jenkins (1996) "Reducing Overrepresentation of Minorities in Juvenile Justice: Development of Community-Based Programs in Pennsylvania." *Crime & Delinquency*, 42(1):76-98.

[18]   OJJDP (1999). *Minorities in the Juvenile Justice System*. [Online]. Available at: *http://www.ncjrs.org/html/ojjdp/9912_1/contents.html* (retrieved March 8, 2004).

[19]   OJJDP (1997). Disproportionate Minority Confinement: 1997 Update [Online]. Available at: *http://www.ojjdp.ncjrs.org/jjbulletin/9809/contents.html* (retrieved March 8, 2004).

[20]   Welsh, W.N., P.W. Harris, and P.H. Jenkins (1996). "Reducing Overrepresentation of Minorities in Juvenile Justice: Development of Community-Based Programs in Pennsylvania." *Crime & Delinquency*, 42:76-98.

[21]   OJJDP (1997). *Disproportionate Minority Confinement: 1997 Update* [Online]. Available at: *http://www.ojjdp.ncjrs.org/jjbulletin/9809/contents.html* (retrieved March 8, 2004); OJJDP (1998). *DMC: Lessons Learned from Five States*. [Online]. Available at: *http://www.ncjrs.org/94612.pdf* (retrieved March 8, 2004).

[22]   OJJDP (1999). Minorities in the Juvenile Justice System. [Online]. Available at: *http://www.ncjrs.org/html/ojjdp/9912_1/contents.html* (retrieved March 8, 2004).

[23]   Welsh, W.N., P.H. Jenkins, and P.W. Harris (1998). *Reducing Minority Over-Representation in Juvenile Justice: Results of Community-Based Intervention in Pennsylvania, 1992-1995*. Philadelphia: Temple University, Department of Criminal Justice; Welsh, W.N., P.H. Jenkins, and P.W. Harris (1999). "Reducing Minority Over-Representation in Juvenile Justice: Results of Community-Based Delinquency Prevention in Harrisburg." *Journal of Research in Crime and Delinquency,* 36:87-110.

[24]   Ibid, note 23.

[25]   Pope, C.E., R. Lovell, and H.M. Hsia (2002). " Disproportionate Minority Confinement: A Review of the Research Literature From 1989 Through 2001." [Online]. Available at: *http://ojjdp.ncjrs.org/dmc/pdf/dmc89_01.pdf* (retrieved March 8, 2004).

[26]   Definitions of "community" vary considerably. Should it refer to a small number of street blocks where regular, face-to-face interaction among residents occurs? Larger clusters of homes, businesses, and places that are still recognized by residents as distinct "communities"? City-designated wards or districts? Census tracts? Areas that are demarcated by physical boundaries such as busy streets, rivers, rail-

road tracks, parks? We do not attempt to resolve such debates here. The change agent should be explicit, however, about which definition of "community" he/she decides to adopt and why. For more detailed discussion, see: Bursik, Robert J., Jr., and Harold Grasmick (1993). *Neighborhoods and Crime: The Dimensions of Effective Community Control.* New York: Lexington Books; Reiss, Albert J., Jr. and Michael Tonry (eds.) (1986). "Communities and Crime." *Crime and Justice* (Vol. 8). Chicago: University of Chicago Press; and Sampson, R.J., S.W. Raudenbush, and F. Earls. (1997). "Neighborhoods and Violent Crime: A Multi-Level Study of Collective Efficacy." *Science*, 277:918-924.

27   For examples, see LaFree, G. (1998). *Losing Legitimacy: Street Crime and the Decline of Social Institutions in America.* Boulder, CO: Westview; and Messner, S., and Richard Rosenfeld (2001) *Crime and the American Dream*, 3rd ed. Belmont, CA: Wadsworth.

28   See, for example: Akers, Ronald L. (2004). *Criminological Theories: Introduction and Evaluation*, 4th ed. Los Angeles, CA: Roxbury; Vold, George B., Thomas J. Bernard, and J.B. Snipes (2001) *Theoretical Criminology*, 5th ed. New York: Oxford University Press.

29   Adapted from: Buzawa, Eve S., and Carl G. Buzawa (2003). *Domestic Violence: The Criminal Justice Response*, 3rd ed. Newbury Park, CA: Sage.

30   See *http://www.ncjrs.org*

31   Kettner, Peter, John M. Daley, and Ann Weaver Nichols (1985). *Initiating Change in Organizations and Communities: A Macro Practice Model.* Monterey, CA: Brooks/Cole; Kettner, Peter M., Robert K. Moroney, and Lawrence L. Martin (1999). *Designing and Managing Programs: An Effectiveness-Based Approach*, 2nd ed. Thousand Oaks, CA: Sage.

32   President's Commission on Law Enforcement and Administration of Justice (1968). *The Challenge of Crime in a Free Society.* New York: Avon Books; Rossum, Ralph A. (1978). *The Politics of the Criminal Justice System. An Organizational Analysis.* New York: Marcel Dekker.

33   Wellford, Charles (1998) "Changing Nature of Criminal Justice System Responses and Its Professions." In U.S. Department of Justice, *The Challenge of Crime in a Free Society: Looking Back, Looking Forward*, pp. 58-71. Symposium on the 30th Anniversary of the President's Commission on Law Enforcement and Administration of Justice. (NCJ-170029) Washington, DC: U.S. Department of Justice, Office of Justice Programs.

34   Burke, Peggy, Robert Cushman, and Becki Ney (1996). *Guide to a Criminal Justice System Assessment: A Work in Progress.* Washington, DC: National Institute of Corrections, p. 7.

35   Welsh, Wayne N. (1995). *Counties in Court: Jail Overcrowding and Court-Ordered Reform.* Philadelphia: Temple University Press; Welsh, Wayne N., and Henry N. Pontell (1991). "Counties In Court: Inter-Organizational Adaptations to Jail Litigation in California." *Law and Society Review*, 25:73-101.

36   Eisenstein, James, Roy B. Flemming, and Peter F. Nardulli (1999). *The Contours of Justice.* New York: Rowan and Littlefield.

37   Ibid, note 35, p. 8.

38   Welsh, Wayne N., Matthew C. Leone, Patrick T. Kinkade, and Henry N. Pontell (1991). "The Politics of Jail Overcrowding: Public Attitudes and Official Policies." In Joel A. Thompson and G. Larry Mays (eds.), *American Jails: Public Policy Issues*. Chicago: Nelson-Hall.

39   Lewin, Kurt (1951). *Field Theory in Social Science*. New York: Harper and Row.

40   Petersilia, Joan (1991). "Policy Relevance and the Future of Criminology—The American Society of Criminology 1990 Presidential Address." *Criminology*, 29:1-15; see also Welsh, Wayne N., and Gary Zajac (2004). "Building an Effective Research Partnership between a University and a State Correctional Agency: Assessment of Drug Treatment in Pennsylvania Prisons." *The Prison Journal*, 84(2):1-28.

41   Lewin, Kurt (1947). "Group Decision and Social Change." In T.M. Newcomb and E.L. Hartley et al. (eds.), *Readings in Social Psychology*. New York: Holt and Company, pp. 202-203.

CHAPTER *3*

Setting Goals and Objectives

CHAPTER OUTLINE

▶ *Write goal statements* specifying the general outcomes to be obtained. Consider the goals of criminal sanctions and normative values driving desired outcomes.

▶ *Write specific outcome objectives for each goal*: These should include a time frame for measuring impact, a target population, a key result intended, and a specific criterion or measure of impact.

▶ *Seek participation* from different individuals and agencies in goal setting. Consider "top-down" vs. "bottom-up" approaches.

▶ *Specify an impact model*: This is a description of how the intervention will act upon a specific cause so as to bring about a change in the problem.

▶ *Identify compatible and incompatible goals in the larger system*: Where do values of different stakeholders overlap or conflict?

▶ *Identify needs and opportunities for interagency collaboration.* Whose cooperation and participation is needed to achieve the goals of this program or policy?

Many interventions fail not because they lack good ideas, but because of vague goals or disagreement about goals. Every program or policy needs a precise definition of what outcome is expected if we are to know whether the intervention is effective. Defining goals and objectives is crucial to the rest of the planning process. It is amazing how many expensive and otherwise well-designed interventions fail to define adequately the desired outcomes of the intervention. Without specific, agreed-upon criteria for success, it is impossible to measure whether any intervention works. It is also likely that without agreed-upon goals, program staff, directors, and various stakeholders will frequently disagree on the mission of the program and the type of intervention approach to use.

Every intervention attempts to achieve some kind of outcome—some desired change in the problem. Both goals and objectives refer to desired outcomes, but objectives are much more specific. *Goals* are broad aims of the intervention (e.g., to reduce drug abuse); *objectives* specify explicit and measurable outcomes (e.g., in a one-year follow-up of ex-offenders who participated in a drug treatment program while in prison, researchers predict that participants will have a lower re-arrest rate than nonparticipants).

Identifying Goals and Values

Goals describe desired future states, some intended change in the problem. Generally, goals are broad statements intended to provide direction for change. While goals lack the specificity needed to measure actual outcomes of the intervention, they provide some sense of mission that may be crucial to gaining political support for the intervention. For example, the goals of a shelter for abused women might be "to provide temporary shelter for victims of domestic violence and reduce spouse abuse"; the goals of a drug treatment program might be "to reduce drug dependency and help clients lead productive, drug-free lives." Goal statements should be relatively brief (one or two sentences), but at the same time they should accurately capture the intent of a particular program or policy and explain the rationale (reasons) for its creation and its particular structure.

Writing goal statements can be difficult, particularly where relevant stakeholders (individuals, groups, and organizations) have widely differing viewpoints about the desired results of a proposed change. Formulating goal statements requires disclosure and discussion of personal beliefs and values. It requires officials to be clear about what they are doing and why there are doing it.

We present below a few brief examples of the most common goals of criminal sanctions, and the some of the most common normative values guiding the formulation of criminal justice programs and policies. Case studies at the end of this chapter ask students to further consider these issues and apply their understanding of concepts to specific examples. The change agent and relevant stakeholders involved should seek to explicitly identify and acknowledge the goals and values that underlie any specific program or policy being considered.

The Goals of Criminal Sanctions

Often referred to as purposes of sanctioning, five different goals (retribution, rehabilitation, deterrence, incapacitation, and restoration) are commonly asserted as reasons for punishing particular offenders and offenses in particular ways. Some authors[1] have suggested that our society alternates or cycles through punitive and rehabilitative extremes over history, while others[2] have argued that a more discrete progression from one set of goals (e.g., rehabilitation in the 1950s and 1960s) to another (e.g., incapacitation in the later 1980s and early 1990s) has occurred. Regardless of the historical perspective that one adopts, the dominance of any one goal at any one time in history is never complete. The five goals below are currently relevant and are likely to be hotly debated for some time.

Retribution

According to advocates of this position, the rightful purpose of punishment is to assign blame and punishment to the wrongdoer. No future good for society is intended, only that the balance of justice be restored by making the offender pay for his or her transgression against society. Advocates of the death penalty often justify its use on such grounds.

Rehabilitation

The purpose of punishment, according to this view, is to reduce the likelihood of future offending by diagnosing and treating its causes within the individual. Implicit are theoretical notions that criminal behavior is learned and can be unlearned, and that individual deficits can be corrected. Programs may attempt to alter educational deficits or psychological factors such as anger control, social skills, and problem-solving skills.

Deterrence

According to *general deterrence*, the purpose of punishment is to send a message to other potential lawbreakers that the specific offense being punished will not be tolerated. Potential lawbreakers, as a result of fearing the punishment they see inflicted on others, should be "deterred" from committing similar acts. This approach assumes that people make a rational calculation of costs and benefits associated with specific actions, and its advocates intend that the "pain" (of apprehension, prosecution, and punishment) outweigh the "gain" (the benefits of criminal behavior). For *specific deterrence*, the message is to the specific individual being punished, not to others who might be deterred. The individual is expected to learn his or her lesson and refrain from future criminal acts. Many "shock incarceration" programs such as Scared Straight and juvenile boot camps have been based on such premises.

Incapacitation

The simple purpose of incapacitation is to physically restrain the offender from committing further crimes. The logic is simple: a person cannot commit further crimes against society during the time they are locked up or incapacitated. Long prison sentences for certain offenses are often based, at least in part, upon such notions. Less severe forms of incapacitation might include curfews, house arrest, intensive supervision probation, and day reporting centers. Advocates often believe that crime rates can be reduced by incarcerating (incapacitating) the worst offenders ("career criminals") for long periods of time.[3]

Restoration

More recent than the other four types of goals, restoration or reparation attempts to restore the victim and or the community to his or her (its) prior state before the crime occurred. It is similar to retribution in the sense that crime is viewed as a disruption of the peace. However, restoration seeks to repair the harm that resulted from the offense, where retribution seeks only to apply blame and punishment. Many current programs are exploring options such as financial restitution to victims, as well as requiring offenders to perform community service work. Still others involve the offender, the victim, and family members and friends of both parties in face-to-face encounters during which reparation steps are negotiated and empathy is encouraged.[4]

Normative Values

Normative values are guiding assumptions held by individuals about how the justice system *should* work. For example, Packer[5] discusses two very broad, competing value orientations of the criminal justice system. To some officials, criminal case processing is like an "assembly line," in which cases should be processed and disposed of as quickly as possible. Proponents of this view, the *crime control model*, believe that for the most part, police, prosecutors, judges, and juries make correct decisions, and the system effectively ferrets out the guilty from the innocent. In contrast, those who lean more toward the *due process model* view believe that the system is imperfect, and that individual officials frequently make hasty and incorrect decisions. As a result, many safeguards are needed to protect the interests of the accused against the much greater power of the state. Criminal case processing, according to this view, is more like an "obstacle course" than an assembly line. We warn the reader that neither model truly represents reality. No individual should completely adopt one or the other orientations. In Packer's own words, "A person who subscribed to all of the values underlying one model to the exclusion of all of the values underlying the other would be rightly viewed as a fanatic."[6]

Criminal justice officials hold normative values about what type of change should be pursued and why, how important specific goals are, and what results should be expected from a specific program or policy. For example, the discussion of restorative justice at the end of Chapter 2 illustrated that a value orientation toward handling criminal cases was dramatically at odds with the orientation of using traditional law enforcement strategies to protect public safety. Any potential solution had to account for at least the values and interests of police and court personnel. Four very broad value orientations common to criminal justice are described below.

Proportionality

Proportionality is a principle that punishment for criminal behavior should not be any more onerous, intrusive, or painful than warranted by the severity of the crime. At least in theory, this principle holds that there is some logical hierarchy of crimes, and a corresponding ("proportional") hierarchy of appropriate punishments. One does not give the death penalty to jaywalkers, for example.

Equity

Equity is the principle that similarly situated offenders should be treated similarly. For example, those accused of committing the same criminal offense should receive similar punishments, unrelated to their personal or demographic characteristics (e.g., age, race, gender, or income).

Parsimony

Parsimony is the principle of using the least drastic and expensive measure needed to produce a specific objective. For example, if a one-year driver's license suspension and probation term is sufficient to motivate a first-time offender to abstain from drunk driving, a three-year suspension and probation term would be overly harsh and wasteful.

Humane Treatment

Humane treatment is a principle meaning that the decision about appropriate punishment is guided by a preference to seek the most humane method to achieve specific objectives. One attempts to avoid unnecessary humiliation, pain, and discomfort. For example, incarceration and its associated deprivations of liberty can be considered appropriate punishment in and of itself. Only considerations of appropriate sentence length, security classification, and perhaps rehabilitation opportunities should guide the decision about where and how the offender serves his or her sentence, and for how long. Under this principle, one would not impose additional punishment by making prison conditions as unbearable as possible (e.g., by denying inmates a heated facility in cold weather).

What Are the "Right" Goals and Values?

We do not advocate any particular set of punishment goals or values in this book; we attempt to give readers the tools they need to make such decisions feasible and explicit. We also caution that different goals and values are not necessarily mutually exclusive: it is possible that a specific program or policy could attempt to address more than one goal or value simultaneously. A considerable amount of research has been conducted to test assumptions and expectations that underlie the goals of policies and programs. Excellent discussions of competing views and related research evidence are provided elsewhere.[7] Do rehabilitation programs work sufficiently well to serve as a basis for correctional policy? Does retributive justice result in satisfaction of the victim that justice was done? Does the threat of punishment deter others from committing crimes? Consulting the body of research that addresses these questions will help to avoid unrealistic expectations and increase our capacity to clearly identify and evaluate the intended outcomes of our programs and policies.

It is important to understand that the pursuit of specific goals may be driven by values, in spite of past failures to achieve these goals. The goal of rehabilitation, for example, has been challenged consistently over the past two decades, and yet many continue to believe that people can change and that positive change can be supported by well-designed interventions.[8] Similarly, in spite of consistent evidence that capital punishment does not deter others from committing murder, death penalty statutes continue to be supported because of the *perceived* deterrent effect of executions.[9]

Write Specific Outcome Objectives for Each Goal

Objectives are much more specific than goals. Objectives should define clearly and concisely exactly what outcome is to be achieved by the intervention. Objectives precisely describe the intended results of the intervention in measurable terms.

An intervention should have at least one specific goal, and each goal should be accompanied by at least one specific objective. It is possible, therefore, to have more than one objective for each goal. Because goals are broadly defined, any program may have several specific objectives. For example, the goal of a new drug treatment program is "to help clients lead drug-free lives." Two objectives are possible:

- Objective #1: Six months after leaving the program, fewer clients will have been re-arrested on drug charges, compared to those who did not go through the program.

- Objective #2: After six months, treated clients will score higher (on average) on a "personal and family responsibility" scale.

Objectives, therefore, must always be *measurable* and *specific*. Objectives should include four major components:

1. A *time frame*: a date by which objectives will be completed.

2. A *target population*: who will evidence the intended change?

3. A *result*: the key outcome intended; a specific change in the problem.

4. A *criterion*: a standard for measuring successful achievement of the result.

Example 3.1

Four Components of an Objective:
The Minneapolis Domestic Violence Experiment.

In the Minneapolis Domestic Violence Experiment,[10] researchers reviewed major studies of police response to domestic violence. In various jurisdictions, they found a rather low rate of arrest out of all calls reported to the police. Other more frequently used police responses included: separation (ordering the offender to leave the house for a cooling-off period, often overnight) and mediation (officers encourage a couple to resolve the conflict).

The researchers hypothesized that, due to greater deterrent effects, mandatory arrest for misdemeanor domestic assault would result in fewer repeat offenses (recidivism) than either separation (order the suspect to leave for at least eight hours) or mediation (try to restore peace, informally solve the conflict). Researchers convinced police to randomly assign all misdemeanor domestic violence cases in two precincts to one of these three interventions. Six months later, researchers predicted, there would be a lower rate of repeat incidents of domestic assault for cases where mandatory arrest was used. We can summarize the four components of the objective as follows:

1. *Time frame*: Six months.

2. *Target population*: The experiment included only misdemeanor assaults, for which police were empowered (but not required) to make arrests under a new state law. Police had to have probable cause, and felonies (e.g., obvious or serious injury) were excluded (that is, felony suspects were always arrested). Two precincts with the highest density of domestic violence were selected for the study.

3. *Result*: Fewer repeat incidents of domestic abuse.

4. *Criteria*: Two measures were used: (1) police arrest records (incident reports over a six-month period); and (2) victim self-reports (follow-up interviews were conducted with victims every two weeks for 24 weeks, which asked about frequency and seriousness of any victimization).

Note that these four components could have been quite different depending upon the results of the problem analysis. First, a different time frame could have been specified (e.g., one year? two years? three years?). Second, a different target population could have been specified (e.g., different demographic and income groups could have been studied in different neighborhoods). Third, a different result could have been specified (e.g., victim satisfaction with the police response they received). Finally, different criteria (measures) could have been used (e.g., hospital records of injuries, incidents reported to social service agencies or crisis lines). Any change agent should define the four components of an objective and explain the reasoning behind these specifications.

Another distinction is sometimes made between process and outcome objectives. *Process objectives* refer to short-term tasks that must be completed in order to implement a program (e.g., within 30 days, all police agencies will hold orientation sessions to acquaint officers with a new domestic violence policy). Strictly speaking, these are not objectives at all, because they do *not* define any specific change in the problem. We note this distinction only because it is likely to arise as one reads published reports of interventions, and one should be aware of the difference. We are concerned here with *outcome objectives*, which describe a specific, measurable change in the problem.

Seek Participation in Goal Setting

Is it necessary that everyone agree on the same goals for a specific program or policy? What are the implications if they don't? At the most basic level, the implications are that different individuals (stakeholders) perceive that they are each working toward some specific end point. They may believe, correctly or incorrectly, that they are working toward the same desired end. The problem is: if they have not articulated or discussed their own goals and values with each other, they may find out after considerable expenditure of energy and resources that they are working toward very different ends. Certainly no effective program or policy can be constructed if those responsible for designing the program or policy hold widely disparate or conflicting goals. Participants need some basic agreement about what it is they are trying to achieve, and why. Not every single stakeholder needs to agree on the final goals, but those responsible for implementing the program or policy must be held accountable for articulating what they are doing and why.

Once again, we stress the virtues of participation in program planning. Having the relevant stakeholders involved in setting program goals is crucial to gaining the support and cooperation necessary to make the intervention work. The first step, if it has not already been accomplished (see Chapter 2), is to identify relevant participants for inclusion in the goal-setting and objective-setting phase.

The change agent (e.g., the person responsible for coordinating the program planning effort) should involve various participants in the planning process, not just agency administrators. Participants might include program staff, potential clients, citizens in the surrounding community, representatives from justice and social service agencies, schools, and so on. Doing this requires patience and negotiating skills, as there are likely to be different assumptions and opinions regarding the problem, its causes, and the type of intervention needed.

Targets and clients are often overlooked at this stage: What should *they* expect to result from this planned change? A major question to ask at this point is whether goal-setting should proceed from a "top-down" or "bottom-up" approach.

Typically, change follows a top-down format. This is often the case because the change agent is likely to be working for, or contracted by, the agency that is funding the intervention, and the change agent owes some obligation to weight their definitions of goals more heavily. There may be advantages to this situation, as well as costs. It may be the case that those in the higher levels of the organization have the most experience with interventions of this type, and they might indeed be in the best position to state realistic, feasible outcomes to be expected. They might also be best equipped to formulate goals that can garner widespread political support for the program (e.g., support from other stakeholders). However, there is a very real danger in ignoring the views of program staff and clients. The danger is that the goals handed down from above may be unrealistic to program staff or irrelevant to the clients. In either case, the impact of the intervention could be severely compromised. The goals might prove unrealistic, in which case the program would be held accountable for unreachable goals; or clients and program staff might refuse to provide information to program evaluators, or might provide incomplete or inaccurate information.

Regardless of which approach is used to formulate initial goals, it is crucial that all stakeholders eventually have some input into defining program goals. These issues are examined in more detail in Case Study 3.1 at the end of this chapter.

Goal Setting: Top-Down versus Bottom-Up Approaches

Top-Down

The change agent begins by getting goal definitions from top officials at the administrative level of his or her organization (e.g., the Chief of County Probation, the Chief of Police, the Director of Social Services, etc.), and then gets responses from lower levels of the organization: perhaps from agency supervisors, then program staff, and eventually from potential clients. Thus, those at the top of the organizational hierarchy have more "say" in defining the program's goals, because their definition is the first one, and it carries more weight and more power as subordinates and clients are asked to respond to it.

Bottom-Up

The change agent begins by seeking goal definitions at the client or staff level. In contrast to the top-down approach, here the change agent first gets definitions from clients and staff about what the program goals are or should be, and then gets responses to these goal definitions from successively higher levels of the agency responsible for implementing the intervention, as well as the agency that is funding the intervention. Other stakeholders to approach may include agency supervisors, administrators, and government representatives. The views of clients and program staff are given more priority using this format; their definitions guide subsequent responses. This approach is favored when it is widely viewed that so-called "experts" are out of touch and that front-line program staff and/or clients are in a better position to state the needs and goals of the target population. Many "grassroots" organizations follow this format.

Specify an Impact Model

We discussed causes and theories in Chapter 2. Examination of theories helps us to formulate what is called an *intervention hypothesis* or an *impact model*: a prediction that a particular intervention will bring about a specific change in the problem. Formulating such a model forces us to answer several important questions: What is the intervention? Why would a proposed intervention work? Which causes will it address? In other words, through what process will change occur, and why? What outcome (a change in the problem) is expected? We can now illustrate how the impact model is made up of three key elements we have discussed: the intervention (policies and programs); the cause(s) to be addressed by the intervention (theories about what causes the problem); and some specific outcome, a desired change in the problem (goals and objectives). We can analyze an intervention by working backwards, first specifying the intervention, then the problem it addresses and the causes of that problem. Program planning proceeds from problem analysis to causal analysis to formulation of goals and objectives. Analysis of an existing program simply reverses the process, even though it requires going through the same three crucial steps.

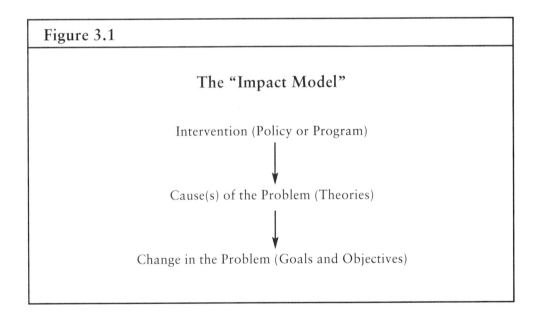

Figure 3.1

The "Impact Model"

Intervention (Policy or Program)

↓

Cause(s) of the Problem (Theories)

↓

Change in the Problem (Goals and Objectives)

Example 3.2

An Impact Model for A Reentry Program[11]

The Problem

Texas has a prison population well in excess of 162,000. As far back as 1984, researchers in Texas reported that 38 percent of parolees were reincarcerated within a period of three years. Both the huge corrections costs and the failure of parolees to succeed in the community produced a demand for solving the parole failure problem.

The Program:

Project RIO (Re-Integration of Offenders) was started as a joint effort of the Texas Department of Corrections and the Texas Workforce Commission. Originally started in two cities as a federally funded pilot project, it is now a statewide and state-funded program. Project RIO has assembled 12,000 employers who hire parolees, and every parolee in the state has access to its services. Preparatory work with parolees begins while they are still in prison. Six months prior to release, Project RIO staff conduct assessments of skills and work history and initiate job readiness training. Vocational training is made available, and many employers come to the prison to meet with inmates and to encourage them during this difficult time of transition back to the community. Once released from prison, parolees receive more preparation and help with job placement.

The Cause(s):

Several research studies have found that parolees with jobs are less likely to reoffend and be returned to prison. Those with higher incomes were found to reoffend less than those with low incomes. The lack of a job and means of support is one factor that drives parolees back into crime.

The Intended Change in the Problem:

A study of recidivism conducted by a research team from Texas A&M University found that participants in Project RIO were less likely to recidivate than nonparticipants. For example, among high-risk parolees, 48 percent of Project RIO parolees were arrested during the first year of parole, compared with 57 percent of nonparticipants. Among this same group, 23 percent of the Project RIO participants were returned to prison, compared to 38 percent of nonparticipants.

Identify Compatible and Incompatible Goals in the Larger System

As we discussed in Chapter 2, criminal justice problems and policies are shaped by the interactive actions of various decisionmakers and agencies in any jurisdiction. We argued that a "systems assessment" provides a common language to describe and evaluate the present state of affairs (i.e., "the problem"), to shape a common vision for the future, and to make that vision a reality.

It is the notion of shaping a common vision that is relevant to this chapter. Based upon information collected at Stage 1, Problem Analysis, we should be able to identify and describe the competing interests of different individuals and agencies. We try to determine where agreement and disagreement about goals exists, and we try to get stakeholders to articulate and discuss their desired goals for any specific program or policy.

In Case Study 2.3 (Incorporating Restorative and Community Justice into American Sentencing and Corrections), for example, we saw that government control over criminal justice has not resulted in safer and more closely knit communities. Proponents of restorative and community justice strategies argue that communities should exercise control over certain justice processes. On the one hand, communities feel safer when there is a significant police presence and when the courts imprison wrongdoers. However, the problems that generate crime do not go away because of these criminal justice system responses, and victims generally feel left out of the process. Community justice strategies engage members of the community in the business of solving community crime problems. Restorative justice strategies involve victims in the process of deciding on an appropriate sanction. Even members of the offender's family can have a role in efforts to restore victims to pre-offense conditions.[12]

In another example, contracting out prison operations to private companies (i.e., privatization of prison operations) is often seen by elected officials as a benefit due to assumed cost savings. Other stakeholders disagree about whether cost savings are likely, and whether cost savings should be the goal at all. Several major objections to privatization have emerged.[13]

- Correctional officers have initiated lawsuits alleging violation of their collective bargaining agreements. Privatization, they argue, is designed to drive down wages and benefits that were won through hard-fought, legitimate union negotiations.

- Inmate advocates and attorneys, concerned with civil rights, argue that turning over the power to punish from the government to the private sector is absolutely unethical. Private corporations are motivated to make profits, not to rehabilitate prisoners, protect public safety, or to provide constitutionally mandated, humane conditions of confinement.

- Private interests, many argue, will attempt to use inmates as a source of cheap labor, or worse, indentured slavery. Such conditions would mark a return to the barbaric days of inmate exploitation and abuse prior to court intervention.

- Cost-cutting motivations, it is feared, will lead to lapses in prison security that threaten public safety (e.g., higher inmate-to-guard staffing ratios).

The change agent, consultant, or analyst guiding the change effort should constantly carry a systems perspective throughout the seven-stage planned change process. A systems perspective is no less important at the goal-setting stage than any other stage, and perhaps more so because the fundamental assumptions developed at this stage will critically shape the design and structure of the entire program or policy. Case Study 3.2 at the end of this chapter further examines these issues, using mandatory sentencing as a context for analysis.

We offer six guidelines to identify compatible and incompatible goals or values in the larger system:

1. Have the appropriate stakeholders been identified via a thorough problem analysis (see Chapter 2)?

2. Review the five goals and four values described earlier in this chapter: Do different stakeholders disagree over specific goals and values? Have their assumptions about the problem, its possible causes, and possible solutions been described?

3. Do individuals within the same agency agree or disagree about the goals or values of the proposed change? Where and how?

4. Do individuals within different agencies agree or disagree about the goals or values of the proposed change? Where and how?

5. Has a systems analysis been conducted to provide stakeholders with relevant information about criminal case processing in this jurisdiction? Is all the information needed to make decisions about goals available, or does some information need to be developed?

6. Do any group mechanisms (e.g., a criminal justice cabinet) exist for bringing stakeholders together to discuss the goals of a proposed change? Is it necessary to create or further develop such a group before proceeding?

Identify Needs and Opportunities for Interagency Collaboration

It is highly likely that any criminal justice intervention will at some point require the cooperation of other agencies to achieve its goals. Many criminal justice interventions, to be successful, require the participation of police, courts, and corrections to carry out their program plans. Other public agencies such as schools or social service agencies may also be called upon, depending upon the problem to be addressed (e.g., juvenile violence) and the type of intervention to be attempted. The change agent, as part of the planning process, needs to consider his or her program's and/or agency's "external environment" when attempting any kind of change. Different types of collaboration or support may be required: political support, shared information, exchange of services, joint client intake or assessment, and perhaps even cross-referrals of clients among different agencies.[14] Such forms of cooperation must be negotiated and agreed upon. Each agency must perceive tangible benefits from undertaking such cooperation.

Interagency cooperation is not always possible or even desirable, however. Political relationships and administrative structures occasionally preclude opportunities for collaboration.

Example 3.3

Agency Politics: Roadblocks to Collaboration?

In a recent project, we found that the juvenile court, part of a state agency, was resistant to participating in the development of an information system that would benefit a group of city agencies. The purpose of the information system project was to create an integrated system that would link the databases of the juvenile court, the department of human services, the police, the district attorney, the public defender and the school district. Sharing information electronically was viewed as a primary means of supporting effective decisions and avoiding fragmented planning for individual youths and families. The juvenile court resisted involvement because pre-existing political conflicts with other agencies had not been resolved and because of its stated desire to protect confidential court data from misuse by other agencies.

Under some circumstances, planning partnerships may not be desirable. Kevin Wright, for example, argues that a complex justice system in a complex society cannot and should not have any common set of goals and values.[15] There is (and should be) a certain tension between different criminal justice agencies, because they do not (and should not) all have the same goals. For example, prosecutors tend to emphasize goals of crime control while defense attorneys emphasize goals of due process. Such goal "tension" helps protect the competing interests of victims and suspects. Moreover, distinctions need to be made between goal conflicts and agency conflicts. Opposition on specific goals does not imply that agencies cannot work together under any circumstances. There will be many situations where collaboration will serve the purposes of agencies that represent different interests. Plea bargaining between prosecutors and defense attorneys is perhaps the classic example of such exchange relations.

Example 3.4

Goal Conflict in Criminal Justice:
Roadblocks or Speedbumps for Interagency Collaboration?

According to Wright, there are at least three reasons why goal conflict within the criminal justice system is desirable: (1) reflective diversity, (2) mediation of interests and system adaptation, and (3) efficient offender processing.

1. *Reflective Diversity*: Fragmentation and lack of integration allow different interests to be incorporated into the system. Conflict may be necessary to mediate among conflicting interests in the community, including competing demands for crime prevention, public order, justice, due process, efficiency, and accountability.

2. *Mediation of Interests and System Adaptation*: Conflicting goals promote a system of checks and balances. No single component of the system can dominate others; nor can any unitary interest be overemphasized. Conflict establishes and maintains a balance of power within the structure of the system [e.g., a prosecutor gives an overly stiff sentence in reaction to public sentiment, but corrections (parole) may modify that sentence and balance out the fairness (and vice versa)].

3. *Offender Processing*: Conflict and fragmentation may actually promote and support rather than hinder the processing of offenders. Prosecution, for example, may be smoother and more efficient precisely because police officers do consider decisions about prosecution, and that tension reduces the likelihood that prosecutors will need to void illegal, improper, or weak arrests.

The concept of *loose coupling* further illustrates the need for interagency cooperation in criminal justice. Loose coupling refers to agencies that are responsive to one another and yet maintain independent identities.[16] In such systems, "structural elements are only loosely linked to one another and to activities; rules are often violated; decisions often go unimplemented, or if implemented, have uncertain consequences; and techniques are often subverted or rendered so vague as to provide little coordination."[17] In other words, the criminal justice "system" has been called a "nonsystem" due to its decentralized and fragmented nature.[18] Different agencies interact with one another, but only rarely do different agencies cooperate effectively or efficiently to process criminal cases.

For example, narcotics enforcement and white-collar crime prosecution require a departure from the loose coupling that dominates criminal justice organizations.[19] While reactive police work based on loosely coupled processes is the norm, proactive policing requires more tightly coupled interagency relations. Narcotics work involves police in using more controversial tactics to obtain evidence, including undercover work, entrapment, and informants.[20] Police officers are more dependent upon prosecutors for feedback on the legal permissibility of evidence, and prosecutors are more dependent upon police officers for extensive information and cooperation in the preparation of cases. This kind of information exchange influences charging decisions and plea bargains engineered to develop cooperation from informants and codefendants. Hagan argues that the proactive prosecution of white-collar criminals requires similar leverage to "turn witnesses." Judges must participate in these decisions as well, because their approval is necessary to implement charge reductions or negotiated sentences.

Using loose coupling as an explanatory concept, Hagan describes how sudden changes in the external environment of an organization (e.g., a riot, a murder committed by an escaped prisoner, court orders to reduce jail overcrowding) create demands for tighter coupling.[21] The distinction between proactive and reactive problem solving is critical. For example, proactive policing or prosecution implies that officials actively target certain problems for attention. Proactive problem solving, however, requires a departure from the norm of "loose coupling"; it necessitates cooperation and planning from multiple agencies and actors. In an analysis of urban riots in Los Angeles and Detroit, Balbus[22] suggested that black suspects were rounded up en masse, at least initially, to serve an ostensible order maintenance function ("clearing the streets"). This initial increase in restrictiveness was followed by "uncharacteristic leniency" as bail release became much more frequent than usual ("clearing the jails"). This shift from "normal" court operations required a tightening of the relations between the police, prosecutorial, and judicial subsystems, so that bail decisions became less variable.

Similarly, most criminal justice agencies today have computerized information systems that are used to gather, analyze, and provide reports. In many jurisdictions, the same information on offenders is collected and stored by several agencies, producing a considerable waste of resources. More critically, important information about an offender may be available inside of an agency such as a police department but may never reach the court where important decisions need to be made. The implications of this agency fragmentation perspective are illustrated in Example 3.5.

Example 3.5

Reorganizing the Federal Government to Meet the Threat of Terrorist Attacks[23]

In the aftermath of the attacks on the World Trade Center and the Pentagon on September 11, 2001, the Bush administration proposed the reorganization of those federal agencies responsible for protecting U.S. citizens and recommended the creation of a Department of Homeland Security. Those attacks demonstrated the vulnerability of our country to terrorist attacks and caused our leaders to make a quick analysis of our sources of weakness. The problems identified included an inability to share and use existing intelligence information, lack of strategic coordination of resources among those agencies responsible for our national security, and a lack of technical preparedness for the kinds of weapons likely to be used by terrorists. In fact, several federal agencies, including the FBI and CIA, had information relevant to this tragedy, but this information was not shared. Competition and administrative barriers among these agencies had created a security system that was so loosely coupled that it was incapable of adequately meeting national security needs.

The proposal to create a Department of Homeland Security was passed quickly by Congress, and former Pennsylvania Governor Tom Ridge was appointed to head the new agency. The "impact model" looks like this:

Intervention: Establishment of the Department of Homeland Security

↓

Cause(s): "Loose Coupling"

↓

Problem: Vulnerability to Terrorism and Its Consequences

The overall homeland security strategy was directed at enhancing resources that are designed: to prevent terrorist attacks, such as increased airline security; to reduce our vulnerability to attacks by doing such things as increasing border controls; and to increase our capacity to respond to attacks if and when they occur. Under the Department of Homeland Security, 22 smaller agencies were brought together under one administrative entity, thus eliminating some of the "loose coupling" that existed. The Department of Homeland Security also was made an intelligence analysis and reporting hub for all intelligence-gathering agencies, including state and local law enforcement agencies. In addition to creation of this new agency, other agencies such as the CIA and FBI were restructured in light of the mission laid out by the White House in its National Strategy for Homeland Security.

Conclusion

Failure to make a clear identification of the goals, values, and expectations guiding the development of an intervention can spell certain failure. At best, continued disagreement over intended goals and outcomes can be expected long after the program or policy is implemented. While discussion between stakeholders of competing goals and values can initially heighten conflict, it may also direct us toward eventual compromise or collaboration, more effective planning, and achievement of our intended goals.

DISCUSSION QUESTIONS

1. At the end of Chapter 1, we asked you to write a short essay describing one possible intervention to address a specific problem in criminal justice. You are also likely to be doing one of the following in this course: (a) writing about a specific problem and/or intervention as a class assignment, or (b) participating in the development of a specific program or policy within the agency for which you work. Briefly describe a specific criminal justice program or policy, and then describe one goal and one objective for this intervention.

2. Define: (a) *goal*, and (b) *objective*. (c) Describe the difference between the two.

3. Describe the four components of an objective.

4. Some argue that goal-setting should proceed from the bottom up; others argue that it should proceed from the top down. (a) Describe each of these positions. (b) Which position do you agree with? Why?

5. Describe five common goals of punishment.

6. Describe four common value orientations in criminal justice.

7. Describe an example of incompatible goals within the criminal justice system, and explain why it is important.

8. Discuss advantages nd disadvantages of interagency collaboration. Give specific examples.

9. Describe the concept of "loose coupling," and explain why it is important using a specific example.

Case Study 3.1[1]

Top-Down versus Bottom-Up Goal Setting: Responding to Negative Information about Conditions of Juvenile Confinement

Instructions: *Read the case study below, and then answer the following questions.*

1. *Was original goal setting in this example top-down or bottom-up? Explain, and give evidence to support your answer.*

2. *How are performance standards similar to and different from objectives? How were goals and objectives developed?*

3. *What kinds of resistance to the creation of performance standards did the designers of PbS face? How did they address this resistance? Be specific, using concepts discussed in this chapter.*

By the early 1990s, the juvenile justice system was declared "broken," and delinquent youths were labeled "super predators" needing the severity of criminal prosecution and adult prison. What happened within the walls and razor wire of the "kiddie prisons" was little known or cared about. The public perception of juvenile justice was formed by the media coverage of a single horrendous crime committed by a youth. Juvenile justice leaders, nationally and locally, and youth workers were highly frustrated with the inability to demonstrate the positive things they do for delinquents. The public was similarly frustrated with the inability to hold the facilities and government agencies accountable for operations and expenditures of tax dollars.

In 1994, the Office of Juvenile Justice and Delinquency Prevention (OJJDP) of the Office of Justice Programs, U.S. Department of Justice, released a report that showed deplorable conditions in the facilities housing juvenile delinquents across the country.[2] The Congressionally mandated study found that in the nearly 1,000 facilities operating at that time, there was "substantial and widespread deficiencies" in living space, security, control of suicidal behavior, and health care. The facilities were overcrowded, youths and staff were suffering high rates of injuries, suicidal behavior was frequent, and health and mental health care was inadequate and sometimes unavailable. The report also found that the conditions were no better in facilities that met correctional accreditation standards. Joining businesses and government in the movement toward standards that indicate performance rather than process, OJJDP called for the development and implementation of national performance-based standards and a new way of doing business for juvenile corrections.

---

[1] This case study material was taken from a 2004 unpublished application to the Innovations in American Government program, located at Harvard University. It was provided to us by the submitting agency, the Council of Juvenile Correctional Administrators, and is published here with the agency's permission.

[2] Parent, D., V. Leiter, S. Kennedy, L. Livens, D.Wentworth, and S. Wilcox. (1994, August). *Conditions of Confinement: Juvenile Detention and Correctional Facilities* (Research Report). Washington, DC: Office of Juvenile Justice and Delinquency Prevention, U.S. Department of Justice.

Case Study 3.1, *continued*

The Performance-based Standards (PbS) for Juvenile Correction and Detention Facilities project developed and directed by the Council of Juvenile Correctional Administrators (CJCA) directly addresses the problems cited in the COC report.[3] PbS is a system for juvenile agencies to demonstrate improvement and success in treating confined youths through national standards and performance outcome measures. The PbS data collection—analysis—improvement planning and implementation cycle provides a quality improvement structure and monitoring tools. The supporting PbS tools—the table of practices and processes that are expected to lead to better outcomes and performance, visits and support by experienced consultants, and links to other resources—provide facilities and agencies with a blueprint to move from deplorable conditions to safe, productive, and cost-effective management of youths in government care. PbS capitalized on Internet advances to build a secure national data collection and reporting system that provides easy access across the country and quick feedback to facilities.

PbS asks facilities to report data twice a year on 106 outcomes that indicate performance toward meeting 30 standards derived from seven goals, one goal for each of the following components of facility operations: safety, security, order, programming (including education), health/mental health, justice, and reintegration. In this case, standards are objectives that are defined in terms of the values of the system and best practices among facilities nationally. Facilities collect the data from administrative records, youth records, youth exit interviews, incident reports, and climate surveys of youths and staff. The information is entered into the web portal and is reported back in easy-to-read bar graph reports. Each outcome is reported for the current data collection period as well as any past data collections, allowing for comparison over time. The reports also include the average outcome of the field, indicated by a vertical line intersecting the bar graph, which provides a quick analysis of whether the facility is doing better or worse than other PbS facilities. The outcomes include critical rates such as injuries, suicidal behavior, assaults, time in isolation, percentages of youths receiving suicide and mental health screenings, changes in academic achievement from admission to release, and percentages of youths completing educational, life skills, behavior management, and other programming curriculum.

Leaders at the OJJDP conceived PbS following the release of the Conditions of Confinement Study. OJJDP at that time envisioned the development of national performance-based standards setting the highest goals for facilities and providing outcome measures (numbers such as rates, percentages) to monitor progress meeting the standards. CJCA was awarded the competitive bid September 30, 1995.

---

[3] For information on the Performance Based Standards Project, the technical web site is *http://www.pbstandards.org/*; the general web site is *http://www.cjca.net/sitecode/cjca_projects_pbs.html*

Case Study 3.1, *continued*

As part of the proposal, OJJDP required the creation of a project advisory board with members representing national organizations and relevant government entities. OJJDP believed that the major government entities and national organizations should define and guide PbS' development in order to create widely-accepted and supported national standards and encourage voluntary participation. The strategy was effective in creating a comprehensive set of standards and establishing a respected group of leaders to initiate and promote PbS. The breadth of the advisory board continues as a solid basis for PbS' unique position as the only performance-based standards for juvenile facilities. The advisory board membership included a seat for:

- CJCA, representing the juvenile correctional agencies;

- American Correctional Association (ACA), representing the adult agencies and staff of both adult and juvenile facilities;

- National Juvenile Detention Association (NJDA), representing county detention centers;

- National Association of Juvenile and Family Court Judges (NAJFCJ), representing the judicial branch;

- National Commission on Correctional Health Care (NCCHC), representing the correctional medical field;

- The National GAINS Center for People with Co-Occurring Disorders in the Justice System, representing the mental health and substance abuse field;

- American Bar Association, Juvenile Justice Center, working to improve access to counsel and the quality of representation for children in the juvenile justice system;

- Youth Law Center, representing juvenile advocates; and

- Correctional Education Association, representing corrections teachers.

OJJDP has served throughout the development and implementation of PbS as an active contributor. The federal project monitor has participated in all major meetings and project discussions since 1995. OJJDP has worked with CJCA each funding cycle to assess progress, identify expansion opportunities, and discuss priorities for resources. Additionally OJJDP separately funded the ongoing evaluation by the National Academy of Public Administration to help PbS succeed.

Case Study 3.1, *continued*

Government agencies have found tremendous benefit to PbS data. Historically, agencies feared data because it counted mistakes and poor practices without a vehicle to show how they responded. For example, if a facility screened youths for risk of suicide and the screen indicated the youth was at risk, the facility would be liable for addressing the needs of any youth and keeping him or her safe. Lacking data to demonstrate activities to keep the youths safe, too many facilities in the past opted not to collect data and relied in part on good luck to protect youths. PbS gives facilities the opportunity to show how they deal with and improve negative data. In South Dakota, a federal court judge approved the settlement agreement (*Christina A. v. Bloomberg*) giving the agency one year to abolish the use of restraints as punishment, limit the use of isolation, and increase mental health and education services for the youths—and demonstrate that the practices had changed. Under the watchful eye of the Youth Law Center, the agency implemented less punitive behavior management systems and presented to the court its PbS data demonstrating no incidences of restraints, reduced use of isolation, and increased services delivered to the youths. In December 2001, the federal court judge found the state in substantial compliance and ended its involvement.

The state agency directors (CJCA's members) have played a very significant role, beginning with letters of support for CJCA's application to OJJDP from 25 state and county governments. The juvenile correctional CEOs have served as advisors to development strategies and volunteered employees in expertise areas when needed. The juvenile CEOs also were instrumental in opening their facilities to the first PbS pilot test visits and data collection. The positive experience of those agencies opened doors and peaked interest in other states and counties so PbS could grow and learn. Continually CJCA members volunteer to participate in PbS and educate their peers, staff, legislator, and the public about its value. Because PbS is not mandated and is not attached to funding, the reason to participate was because an administrator wanted to improve. However, the risks were high —data could discover problems. It was the encouragement and belief in PbS by other juvenile CEOs that moved many agencies to join PbS. The support and leadership of CJCA members was critical to PbS' development and continues to aid PbS' goals of expansion and self-sustainability within the field.

Case Study 3.2

The Goals of Mandatory Sentencing[24]

Instructions: Read the case study below, and then answer the following questions.

1. What goals and normative values guided the creation of mandatory sentencing policies? Explain and give evidence.

2. Identify and describe any incompatible goals or values of different stakeholders.

3. Describe one objective that could be used to evaluate the effectiveness of mandatory sentencing policies. Pay careful attention to the four components of an objective discussed in Chapter 3.

By 1994, all 50 states had enacted one or more mandatory sentencing laws,[1] and Congress had enacted numerous mandatory sentencing laws for federal offenders. Furthermore, many state officials have recently considered proposals to enhance sentencing for adults and juveniles convicted of violent crimes, usually by mandating longer prison terms for violent offenders who have a record of serious crimes.

A second frequently mentioned mandatory sentencing enhancement is "truth-in-sentencing," the provisions for which are in the Violent Crime Control and Law Enforcement Act of 1994. States that wish to qualify for federal aid under the Act are required to amend their laws so that imprisoned offenders serve at least 85 percent of their sentences.

Rationale for Mandatory Sentencing

Mandatory sentences are based on two goals—deterrence and incapacitation. The primary purposes of modest mandatory prison terms (e.g., three years for armed robbery) are specific deterrence, which applies to already sanctioned offenders, and general deterrence, which aims to deter prospective offenders. If the law successfully increases the imprisonment rate, the effects of incapacitation also will grow because fewer offenders will be free to victimize the population at large. The intent of three-strikes (and even two-strikes) laws is to incapacitate selected violent offenders for very long terms—25 years or even life. They have no specific deterrent effect if those confined will never be released, but their general deterrent effect could, in theory, be substantial.

By passing mandatory sentencing laws, legislators convey the message that certain crimes are deemed especially grave and that people who commit them deserve—and may expect—harsh sanctions. These laws are a rapid and visible response to public outcries following heinous or well-publicized crimes. The high long-term costs of mandatory sentencing are deferred because the difficult funding choices implicit in this policy can be delayed or even avoided.

---

[1]   Tonry, M., *Sentencing Matters*, Oxford, England: Oxford University Press, 1995.

Case Study 3.2, *continued*

Impact of Mandatory Sentencing Laws

Mandatory sentencing has had significant consequences that deserve close attention, among them its impact on crime and the operations of the criminal justice system. The possible differential consequences for certain groups of people also bear examination.

Crime. Evaluations of mandatory sentencing have focused on two types of crimes—those committed with handguns and those related to drugs (the offenses most commonly subjected to mandatory minimum penalties in state and federal courts). An evaluation of the Massachusetts law that imposed mandatory jail terms for possession of an unlicensed handgun concluded that the law was an effective deterrent of gun crime,[3] at least in the short term.

However, studies of similar laws in Michigan[4] and Florida[5] found no evidence that crimes committed with firearms had been prevented. An evaluation of mandatory gun-use sentencing enhancements in six large cities (Detroit, Jacksonville, Tampa, Miami, Philadelphia, and Pittsburgh) indicated that the laws deterred homicide but not other violent crimes.[6] An assessment of New York's Rockefeller drug laws was unable to support the claim for their efficacy as a deterrent to drug crime in New York City.[7] None of the studies examined the incapacitation effects of these laws.

The Criminal Justice System. The criminal courts rely on a high rate of guilty pleas to speed case processing and thus avoid logjams. Officials can offer inducements to defendants to obtain these pleas. If only in the short term, mandatory sentencing laws may disrupt established plea-bargaining patterns by preventing a prosecutor from offering a short prison term (less than the new minimum) in exchange for a guilty plea. However, unless policymakers enact long-term mandatory sentences that apply to many related categories of crimes, prosecutors usually can shift strategies and bargain on charges rather than on sentences.

---

[2]   In mid-1996 the California Supreme Court ruled the State's three-strikes law an undue intrusion on judges' sentencing discretion. State legislative leaders immediately announced plans to introduce legislation that would reinstate the law.

[3]   Pierce, G.L., and W.J. Bowers (1981). "The Bartley-Fox Gun Law's Short-Term Impact on Crime in Boston." *Annals of the American Academy of Political and Social Science*, 455:120-132.

[4]   Loftin, C., M. Heumann, and D. McDowall (1983) "Mandatory Sentencing and Firearms Violence: Evaluating an Alternative to Gun Control," *Law and Society Review*, 17:287-318.

[5]   Loftin, C. and D. McDowall (1984). "The Deterrent Effects of the Florida Felony Firearm Law." *Journal of Criminal Law and Criminology*, 75:250-259.

[6]   McDowall, D., C. Loftin, and B. Wiersema (1992). "A Comparative Study of the Preventive Effects of Mandatory Sentencing Laws for Gun Crimes," *Journal of Criminal Law and Criminology*, 83:378-394.

[7]   Joint Committee on New York Drug Law Evaluation (1978). *The Nation's Toughest Drug Law: Evaluating the New York Experience*. A project of the Association of the Bar of the City of New York, the City of New York and the Drug Abuse Council, Inc. Washington, DC: U.S. Government Printing Office.

Case Study 3.2, *continued*

The findings of research on the impact of mandatory sentencing laws on the criminal justice system have been summarized by a prominent scholar.[8] He found that officials make earlier and more selective arrest, charging, and diversion decisions; they also tend to bargain less and to bring more cases to trial. Specifically, he found that:

- Criminal justice officials and practitioners (police, lawyers, and judges) exercise discretion to avoid application of laws they consider unduly harsh.

- Arrest rates for target crimes decline soon after mandatory sentencing laws take effect.

- Dismissal and diversion rates increase at early stages of case processing after mandatory sentencing laws take effect.

- For defendants whose cases are not dismissed, plea-bargain rates decline and trial rates increase.

- For convicted defendants, sentencing delays increase.

- Enactment of mandatory sentencing laws has little impact on the probability that offenders will be imprisoned (when the effects of declining arrests, indictments, and convictions are taken into account).

- Sentences become longer and more severe.

The research review concluded that mandatory sentencing laws:

- Do not achieve certainty and predictability because officials circumvent them if they believe the results are unduly harsh.

- Are redundant with respect to proscribing probation for serious cases because such cases generally are sentenced to imprisonment anyway.

- Are arbitrary for minor cases.

- May occasionally result in an unduly harsh punishment for a marginal offender.[9]

Racial and Ethnic Minorities. One issue that has received considerable attention in recent years is whether racial or ethnic minorities are treated unfairly in the courts' application of mandatory minimum sentences. The ques-

---

[8] Tonry, M. (1987). *Sentencing Reform Impacts*. Washington, DC: U.S. Department of Justice, National Institute of Justice.

[9] Ibid.

Case Study 3.2, *continued*

tion cannot be answered simply by comparing the proportion of minority offenders sentenced before and after introduction of, or changes in, mandatory sentencing laws. If, for example, it is objectively determined that minorities are more likely than the general population to commit offenses that carry mandatory sentences, an equitable application of the law would result in an increase in the proportion of imprisoned minorities—and probably in the lengths of their average sentences.

Consequently, the central question is whether criminal justice officials' discretionary choices in the application of mandatory sentencing laws are made in a racially neutral manner.

Results of particular studies are relevant. In one study involving cases of federal offenders sentenced for crimes subject to mandatory minimums, the researcher examined whether sentencing severity varied by amount and type of drugs involved in the current crime, weapons, offense record, role in offense, history of drug use, age, gender, or race.[10] She found sentencing differences associated with the offender's race, even after accounting for differences associated with these other characteristics. However, the magnitude of this difference was small.

The U.S. Sentencing Commission expanded this study and found significant differences in the proportion of whites (54%), Hispanics (57%), and African Americans (68%) who received mandatory minimum sentences for the most serious offense charged against them.[11] A reanalysis of the U.S. Sentencing Commission data drew different conclusions, however.[12] The reanalysis showed that when legally relevant case-processing factors were considered, a defendant's race/ethnicity was unrelated to the sentence. Also examined in the reanalysis was why more than 40 percent of the cases apparently eligible for mandatory sentences did not receive them. Reasonable explanations include evidentiary problems and instances in which defendants provided substantial assistance to prosecutors in preparing cases against others.

In an analysis of the federal sentencing guidelines, other researchers found that African Americans received longer sentences than whites, not because of differential treatment by judges but because they constituted the

---

[10] Meierhoefer, B.S. (1992). *General Effect of Mandatory Minimum Prison Terms*. Washington, DC: Federal Judicial Center; Meierhoefer, B.S. (1992). "Role of Offense and Offender Characteristics in Federal Sentencing." *Southern California Law Review*, 66:367-404; and Meierhoefer, B.S. (1992). *General Effect of Mandatory Minimum Prison Terms: A Longitudinal Study of Federal Sentences Imposed*. Washington, DC: Federal Judicial Center.

[11] U.S. Sentencing Commission (1991) *Federal Sentencing Guidelines: A Report on the Operation of the Guidelines System and Short-Term Impacts on Disparity in Sentencing, Use of Incarceration, and Prosecutorial Discretion and Plea Bargaining*. Washington, DC: U.S. Sentencing Commission.

[12] Langan, P. (1992) "Federal Prosecutor Application of Mandatory Sentencing Laws: Racially Disparate? Widely Evaded?" Washington, DC: U.S. Department of Justice, Bureau of Justice Statistics.

Case Study 3.2, *continued*

large majority of those convicted of trafficking in crack cocaine—a crime Congress had singled out for especially harsh mandatory penalties.[13] This pattern can be seen as constituting a "disparity in results" and, partly for this reason, the U.S. Sentencing Commission recommended to Congress that it eliminate the legal distinction between crack and regular cocaine for purposes of sentencing (a recommendation Congress rejected).

Future Issues

In the interviews conducted for this review of mandatory sentencing, state policymakers expressed the need to respond to the public's fear of crime and call for tougher sanctions, but also recognized the need to rein in spiraling costs of corrections. If the costs of government are cut, spending more on prisons means spending less on other public purposes. The fiscal analysis of California's three-strikes law, for example, has implications for that state's future.

In a major study of sentencing policy, Michael Tonry of the University of Minnesota suggested that states consider the following options:[15]

- Pursue presumptive rather than mandatory sentences.

  Presumptive sentences, which are developed by sentencing commissions and set forth as guidelines, can shift overall sentencing patterns in ways acceptable to policymakers. For example, they can seek to imprison more violent offenders and fewer property offenders. A sentencing commission can help maintain sentencing policy while still preserving ultimate legislative control. Presumptive sentences have generally achieved their intended goals, and research shows high rates of conformity to the sentences by judges.

  In the rare instance in which a presumptive sentence is inappropriate (i.e., either too harsh or too lenient, given the facts of the case), judges can depart from the guidelines by providing in writing reasons that can be reviewed by higher courts. If legislatures so instruct sentencing commissions, they can craft the guidelines to control future costs and, at the same time, toughen sentences for repeat violent offenders.

---

[13] McDonald, D.C., and K.E. Carlson (1993). *Sentencing in the Courts: Does Race Matter? The Transition to Sentencing Guidelines, 1986-90*. Washington, DC: U.S. Department of Justice, Bureau of Justice Statistics.

[14] Greenwood, P.W., et al. (1994). *Three Strikes and You're Out: Estimated Benefits and Costs of California's New Mandatory-Sentencing Law*. Santa Monica, CA: RAND, 1994.

[15] Tonry, *Sentencing Matters*.

Case Study 3.2, *continued*

- Include sunset provisions to require periodic reconsideration of the propriety of the laws, if mandatory sentencing laws are enacted.

- Limit the duration and scope of mandatory sentencing laws.

  Crime is, quite literally, an activity of young men. As the study of the California law emphasized, extremely long mandatory sentences (e.g., 25 years to life) are inefficient because they confine offenders for long periods (at great cost) after they would have "aged out" of crime. Sentencing could be mandated for only a few especially serious crimes. If such laws are aimed at repeat serious offenders, they could include a requirement that only particularly serious prior and current convictions trigger them.

- Conduct some form of periodic administrative review to determine if continued confinement of the offender is required, in the event mandatory sentences are imposed.

- Closely link sentencing and fiscal policy decisions to enhance the legislative process. Legislatures could ensure that they know the financial impact of proposed sentencing legislation and, where substantial long-term costs will be incurred, a funding plan might be a required provision of the enabling law. This would prevent today's legislature from avoiding the fiscal implications of its sentencing policies.

Cultivating Alternative Sanctions

Legislatures also may want to develop policy that makes more effective and systematic use of intermediate sanctions, if the twin objectives of punishment and lower correctional costs are to be achieved. Such policy might specify goals for each particular sanction, locate each category of intermediate sanctions along the continuum between standard probation and total confinement, and define target populations for each category. For example, it could specify which confined offenders will be considered for early release, which sanctions should enhance standard probation, and which offenders need treatment or services.

In addition, states may want to develop a financial structure to steer development of intermediate sanctions in intended directions. This could be a variant of current community corrections acts, for which a central state agency sets standards for local programs and administers performance-based finan-

Case Study 3.2, *continued*

cial aid to local governments. For intermediate sanctions, the state could provide greater support to jurisdictions whose program met or exceeded the performance objectives specified by the agency.

Finally, states that make greater use of intermediate sanctions may want to develop policies that govern their use in individual cases. Examples are the development of presumptive guidelines for nonconfinement as well as confinement sanctions. Such policies could be designed to ensure that overall use of nonconfinement sanctions is consistent with goals established by the legislature and broad principles that govern sentencing generally (e.g., proportionality, uniformity, and neutrality). In particular, guidelines could limit additive use of sanctions (imposing two or three nonconfinement sanctions on a particular offender) and control revocation decisions in order to minimize needless confinement for minor rule violations.

Endnotes

1   Rothman, David J. (1980). *Conscience and Convenience. The Asylum and Its Alternatives in Progressive America*. Boston: Little, Brown.

2   Von Hirsch, Andrew (1985). *Past or Future Crimes: Deservedness and Dangerousness in the Sentencing of Criminals*. New Brunswick, NJ: Rutgers University Press.

3   Auerhahn, Kathleen (2001). *Incapacitation, Dangerous Offenders, and Sentencing Reform*. Albany, NY: State University of New York Press.

4   Braithwaite, J. (1999) "Restorative Justice: Assessing Optimistic and Pessimistic Accounts." In Michael Tonry (ed.), *Crime and Justice: A Review of Research, Vol. 25*, pp. 1-127. Chicago: University of Chicago Press.

5   Packer, Herbert L. (1968). *The Limits of the Criminal Sanction*. Stanford, CA: Stanford University Press.

6   Packer, note 5, p. 154.

7   For example, see: Walker, Samuel (2001). *Sense and Nonsense About Crime and Drugs*, 5th ed. Belmont, CA: Wadsworth.

8   Andrews, Donald, Ivan Zinger, Robert D. Hoge, James Bonta, Paul Gendreau, and Francis T. Cullen (1990). "Does Correctional Treatment Work? A Clinically Relevant and Psychologically Informed Meta-Analysis." *Criminology*, 28:369-404.

9   Ibid, note 7.

10   Sherman, Lawrence W., and Richard A. Berk (1984). "The Specific Deterrent Effects of Arrest for Domestic Assault." *American Sociological Review*, 49:261-272.

11   Summarized from Finn, Peter (1998). *Texas' Project RIO (Re-Integration of Offenders)*. Washington DC: U.S. Department of Justice, Office of Justice Programs, National Institute of Justice.

12   Further information on restorative justice is available at: *http://www.realjustice.org*

13   Shichor, David (1995). *Punishment for Profit: Private Prisons/Public Concerns*. Thousand Oaks, CA: Sage.

14   Rossi, Robert J., Kevin J. Gilmartin, and Charles W. Dayton (1982). *Agencies Working Together. A Guide to Coordination and Planning*. Beverly Hills: Sage.

15   Wright, Kevin N. (1999). "The Desirability of Goal Conflict Within the Criminal Justice System." In Stojkovic, Stan, John Klofas, and David Kalinich (eds.), *The Administration and Management of Criminal Justice Organizations*, 4th ed., pp. 37-49. Prospect Heights, IL: Waveland.

16   Cohen, Michael D., James G. March, and Johan P. Olsen (1972). "A Garbage Can Model of Organizational Choice." *Administrative Science Quarterly*, 17:1-25; Hagan, John (1989). "Why Is There So Little Criminal Justice Theory? Neglected Macro- And Micro-Level Links Between Organization and Power." *Journal of Research in Crime and Delinquency*, 26:116-135; Welsh, Wayne N. (1992). "The Dynamics of Jail Reform Litigation: A Comparative Analysis of Litigation

in California Counties." *Law and Society Review*, 26:591-625; Weick, Karl (1976). "Educational Organizations as Loosely Coupled Systems." *Administrative Science Quarterly*, 21:1-19.

[17]   See Hagan, note 15, p. 119.

[18]   Eisenstein, James, and Herbert Jacob (1977). *Felony Justice: An Organizational Analysis of Criminal Courts*. Boston: Little, Brown; Feeley, Malcolm (1983). *Court Reform on Trial: Why Simple Solutions Fail*. New York: Basic Books; Forst, Martin L. (1977). "To What Extent Should the Criminal Justice System Be a 'System'?" *Crime & Delinquency*, 23:403-416; Gibbs, Jack (1986). "Punishment and Deterrence: Theory, Research, and Penal Policy." In Leon Lipson and Stanton Wheeler (eds.), *Law and the Social Sciences*. New York: Russell Sage; President's Commission on Law Enforcement and Administration of Justice (1968). *The Challenge of Crime in a Free Society*. New York: Avon Books; Reiss, Albert (1971). *The Police and the Public*. New Haven, CT: Yale University Press; Rossum, Ralph A. (1978). *The Politics of the Criminal Justice System: An Organizational Analysis*. New York: Marcel Dekker.

[19]   See Hagan, note 16.

[20]   Skolnick, Jerome (1966). *Justice Without Trial*. New York: John Wiley.

[21]   See Hagan, note 16.

[22]   Balbus, Issac (1973). *The Dialectics of Legal Repression*. New York: Russell Sage.

[23]   Office of Homeland Security (2002). *National Strategy for Homeland Security*. Washington, DC: The White House.

[24]   Excerpted from: Parent, Dale, Terence Dunworth, Douglas McDonald, and William Rhodes (1997). *Key Legislative Issues in Criminal Justice: Mandatory Sentencing* (NCJ-161839). Washington, DC: U.S. Department of Justice, Office of Justice Programs, National Institute of Justice.

CHAPTER *4*

Designing the Program or Policy

C H A P T E R   O U T L I N E

▶ *Choosing an intervention approach* involves integrating the information assembled in previous stages. How can the information collected at previous stages be used to decide what the substance of an intervention will be? How will a specific goal be accomplished?

▶ **Major activities for program design** include the following. (1) Define the target population: At whom is the intervention aimed? (2) Define target selection and intake procedures: how are targets selected and recruited for the intervention? (3) Define program components: the precise nature, amount, and sequence of activities provided must be specified. Who does what to whom, in what order, and how much? (4) Write job descriptions of staff, and define the skills and training required.

▶ **Major activities for policy design** include the following. (1) Define the target population of the policy. Which persons or groups are included, and which are not? (2) Identify the responsible authority. Who is required to carry out the policy, and what will their responsibilities be? (3) Define the provisions and procedures of the policy. Provisions specify the sanctions or services that will be delivered as well as the conditions that must be met in order for the policy to be carried out. Individuals responsible for implementing a specific set of rules must also clearly understand the specific sequence of actions to be taken (procedures) to ensure that the policy is carried out consistently.

Stage 4 involves specifying all of the program's activities or the policy's rules and procedures. Although planning for programs and policies shares many common features (e.g., analyzing the problem, setting goals and objectives), the two types of intervention are quite different in substance (design). This chapter will treat *program design* and *policy design* separately in order to keep these two intervention approaches clear.

Choosing an Intervention Approach

Choosing an intervention approach involves integrating the information assembled in previous stages. For example, your goal might be to reduce juvenile violence, but how will that goal be accomplished? What will be the substance of the intervention—creating a boot camp, enforcing a curfew, developing community recreation programs, applying tougher punishment, or something else? How do you decide? Up to this point, you have collected and analyzed data, you have an idea of the intervention options that fit the problem or need, and your goals and objectives have been established. Your *force field analysis* (see Chapter 2) has revealed critical sources of resistance and support, and your *systems analysis* (Chapter 2) has identified important characteristics of the organizational environment in which the change effort will take place. These data should constructively inform choices about which intervention approach to choose.

Another critical ingredient is the cost of the option selected.[1] At this point, our interest is in broad cost questions. For example, is capital punishment really cheaper than a life sentence? Common wisdom may say "yes"—after all, maintenance costs end when a person dies—but experience tells us that a system of capital punishment is considerably more expensive. Jury selection, complex appeals, and incarceration on a death row add tremendous costs to case processing.[2]

In selecting among approaches, past experience is an important guide: we can learn about the potential costs of an option by examining its use in other settings. In the case where the policy results in the creation of a new agency, the costs can be very high. The Juvenile Justice and Delinquency Prevention Act of 1974 was developed to improve state-level planning for combating juvenile crime and to halt the practice of confining status offenders with delinquents. One of the Act's provisions was the creation of the Office of Juvenile Justice and Delinquency Prevention within the Department of Justice. Between 1974 and 1980, Congress increased funding for this act from 25 million to 100 million.

Program and policy options are often weighed in terms of cost. One option is compared to another in terms of its expected benefits in relation to its costs, and its costs in relation to available resources. For example, in 1997, Joan Petersilia, listed the typical annual costs of different types of intermediate sanctions and treatment approaches to assist the California Department of Corrections in making its choices.[3] We have updated the figures for state prison, county jail, and parole:[4]

Figure 4.1		
OPTION	COST	
	1997	2001
State prison	$21,000	$30,929
County jail	19,700	22,611
Boot camps (121 days prison plus 244 days intensive probation)	11,700	
House arrest with electronic monitoring	3,500-8,500	
Parole	4,000	3,364
Routine probation/parole supervision	200-2,000	
Substance abuse treatment programs		
Residential	22,400	
Social model (drug-free home)	12,500	
Outpatient	2,900	
Methadone maintenance	2,500	

Some people are surprised to learn that a residential treatment program can be more costly than imprisonment or that an in-home drug treatment program can cost more than a boot camp. Similarly, many states have chosen to invest in developing community-based correctional programs to reduce dependency on costly prisons. However, these community programs, if run well, can be costly too. Are offenders in these programs expected to work or go to school? If so, will it be necessary to purchase training, assist with job searches, monitor their behavior on the job, or intervene when conflicts occur at the place of employment? Programs that include treatment are considerably more expensive than those that do not, and yet treatment improves the effectiveness of intensive probation programs.[5] These are facts that must be known in order to avoid wasteful planning or eventual program failure because of inadequate resources.

Designing a Program

In general, in designing a program we must answer the following questions as specifically as possible: who does what to whom, where, in what order, how much, and how often? How will the program be set up? How are targets selected? What activities are delivered, and how? What training and qualifications are required for staff? By the time you reach this stage of analysis, you should have information about:

- The problem or need to be addressed
- Etiology and theory
- Possible interventions
- Potential barriers to change
- Goals and objectives

Now the change agent's task is to design the "nuts and bolts" of the *new* program. If you were acting as a program "analyst," you would look at an existing program and specify in detail exactly what it does. The goals and objectives that have previously been specified must now be translated into specific tasks and activities, and the appropriate sequencing and timing of each activity must be defined. A complete example is provided in Case Study 4.1 at the end of this chapter.

Define the Target Population of the Program

Who is to be targeted, or changed? This process often involves specifying some level of need on the part of potential targets (e.g., level of drug involvement) and the characteristics of the intended target population (e.g., age, gender, geographic residence, type of offense, prior criminal record, etc.). First, we must clarify the intervention approach to be used. In Chapter 2, recall that we discussed five levels of causality. We now need to clarify exactly who or what is the target of change. Are we trying to change:

- Individuals? (e.g., via counseling, teaching problem-solving skills)
- A group or groups? (e.g., via support groups, peer groups, family counseling)
- An organization? (e.g., via police training)
- A community? (e.g., via community policing, Neighborhood Watch, community service)
- Social structural conditions? (e.g., via welfare reform, job training, employment assistance)

Once we are clear about the intervention approach, we need to specify the target population. Usually, two major steps are required: defining eligibility and specifying numbers to be served.

1. *Define Eligibility*: Who is eligible for the program? For what kind of individuals is the program intended, and which targets are best suited to the intervention approach? Eligibility is often based on age, residence, income, gender, ethnicity, or other demographic variables. It is also based on level of need: What is the appropriate population to be targeted, in terms of how significant or urgent their needs are?

2. *Specify Numbers to be Served*: Given scarce resources, how are program funds most widely spent? How many resources are available to serve how many people? How many individuals can the program accommodate over a time period of six months? One year?

Assessing Risk and Needs

One of the most common tools for defining a target population and matching individual needs with appropriate programming is a *risk/needs assessment*. *Risk* typically refers to the likelihood of a negative outcome, such as re-arrest, while *needs* pertain to the treatment-relevant issues and problems that an individual brings to the program. The risk/needs assessment tools most commonly used are empirically based; that is, they were developed from research on actual individuals from the targeted population. Among the most widely used of these tools with delinquent youths are the Youth Level of Service/Case Management Inventory (YLS/CMI), developed by Robert Hoge and Don Andrews,[6] The Massachusetts Youth Screening Instrument, Second Version (MAYSI-2), developed by Thomas Grisso and Richard Barnum,[7] and The Psychopathy Checklist—Youth Version (PCL-YV), developed by Robert Hare.[8] The YLS/CMI is a general screening tool designed to assess a youth's criminogenic needs and the risk that the youth will commit an offense in the future. The MAYSI-2 is a tool for identifying youths who may have mental health problems and require further diagnostic testing. The PCL-YV is used to identify the extent to which a youth's delinquent behavior is due to ways of thinking about antisocial acts.

Define Target Selection and Intake Procedures

Now that we know who the targets of change are, the next question is: How are targets recruited and selected for the intervention? Given that targeted individuals and potential referral sources (e.g., police, courts, schools, probation, social services, etc.) are initially unaware of the program (or perhaps hostile toward it), how will we make them aware of this program, and how will we encourage them to use it? For example, boot camp programs are often intended for first-time, nonviolent offenders. The court might identify eligible offenders; an application from the individual may be required; and an interview and screening process may be required to determine the applicant's suitability for the program.

Keep in mind that eligibility does not guarantee selection. A number of issues aside from being eligible affect selection for a program. The following five issues should be considered when defining target selection.

1. *Access*: How are targets "recruited" (i.e., how do they become aware of the program)? How are they informed of program operations and activities? Are referrals made to the program by any outside agencies? If so, by whom and for what reasons? How do referral sources learn about the program?

2. *Screening*: How are targets screened for eligibility? Is some kind of needs assessment or other assessment tool used? Are application procedures required? How do they work? How is it decided who will be admitted to the program and who will be excluded?

3. *Intake*: Is an intake form used to record basic information when an individual is referred to the program, such as name, age, source of referral, reason for referral, etc.?

4. *Individual Records*: Is information to be recorded or stored throughout an individual's participation in the program? What kinds of information are needed for agency reporting purposes? For feedback to the individual? For treatment planning?

5. *Retention*: How long are targets to be retained in the program? What procedures will encourage them to complete the program?

Define Program Components

The precise nature, amount, and sequence of activities provided by a program must be specified. *Service delivery* refers to all those parts of the program that involve the dispensing of some "services" or program operations (counseling, training, intensive supervision, etc.) to targets. Who does what to whom, where, in what order, how often, and how much? What is the sequence of activities?

A boot camp program, for example, might contain several components: rigid military style drills and physical training; academic or vocational education; life skills or problem-solving training; drug awareness education; social skills training, and so on. We need to describe how frequently each activity is provided (e.g., how many times a week?), and how much (e.g., one hour per session?). Program evaluators often refer to these measures of exposure to an intervention as *dosage*. We need to specify which staff will be responsible for providing each activity, and exactly how it will be done (e.g., how are "life skills" taught? what approach is used: text, lectures, speakers, films, role plays, individual or group counseling?). We need to describe the sequence of activities: what happens when an individual is first admitted? What order of activities is followed: upon admission? in a daily routine? on a weekly basis? How long does the program last (e.g., six weeks? six months?). How are targets "graduated" from the program?

Output refers to criteria for defining when the program has been completed (some unit of intervention provided to a specific individual). For example: 10 counseling sessions, eight weeks of boot camp, 12 problem-solving skills training sessions, and so on.

When we review applications for funding, general program descriptions, or even academic articles, we are often surprised by the vagueness of the actual activities specified by the program. For example, we are told only that a program offers "counseling for battered women." We ask: How are women referred to this program? By whom? How is eligibility determined? Who delivers counseling? How? What kind of counseling (e.g., psychotherapy? behavior modification? cognitive restructuring?) How often is counseling given? For how long? In what setting (inpatient, outpatient)? The simple information that "counseling" is provided is, by itself, insufficient to understand anything about the program's service delivery.

Write Job Descriptions of Staff, and Define the Skills and Training Required

How many and what kinds of staff are required to operate the program? What specific duties will they carry out? What kind of qualifications do they need to possess, and what further training will be necessary? How much money is needed for staff salaries and training? *Service tasks* refers to writing job descriptions of all program staff, their qualifications and training, and the major activities that are to be completed by program staff.

Designing a Policy

Policies differ from programs in that policies are rules, principles, or guidelines that govern actions, while programs are structures created to address specific needs or problems of a target population (see Chapter 1). Often programs are created to carry out large-scale policies. For example, the policy of requiring drug-abusing defendants in criminal court to participate in drug treatment has produced both new drug treatment programs and, more recently, drug courts.[9] Drug courts possess more specialized knowledge of drug addiction and are better equipped to address the unique problems of the addicted defendant.

Policies are never designed by individuals working alone. Instead, because the decisions of a great many people will be affected, policy design occurs within a legislative process. Elected legislators of government bodies typically vote on policies designed by subcommittees. In private organizations, a similar process occurs through the board of directors. In other words, the creation of rules is usually the business of a legitimate body of rule-makers.

In Chapter 1, we noted that policies vary in terms of their complexity. For example, a policy states that visitors to the offices of a program must sign a visitors' log. This is not a rule that typically requires discussion by a legislative body. Instead, these lower-level policies are handled at an administrative level. We will concern ourselves here, however, with broader polices created to address significant criminal justice problems.

The design of a policy involves specifying in detail the elements of the policy that make it possible for others to use it appropriately. In other words, if the provisions and procedures of the policy are not laid out clearly, actions may be taken that are inconsistent with the intent of the policymakers. In addition, if elements of the policy are missing, then incomplete implementation may result.

As an example, in the early 1980s, Philadelphia's Municipal Court initiated a new policy for handling drunk drivers. The idea was that small amounts of punishment combined with education and treatment would be more effective than punishment alone. Consequently, the court created new penalties that included jail sentences of only a few days, added requirements that the offender would be tested for alcohol abuse problems immediately after sentencing, and established contracts with private programs to provide alcohol abuse treatment and education. A critical piece was missing, though: No one was made responsible to see that the sentence was carried out, and no record of participation was maintained. Over time, offenders learned that if they ignored the sentence, nothing would happen. Ironically, the more times an offender was sentenced, the less likely it was that the sentence was completed.[10]

In designing a policy, the change agent typically identifies:

- The *target population*, or who will be affected by the policy,

- The *decision authority*, or who has the authority to carry out the policy,

- The *provisions* of the policy (what "services" members of the target population will receive), and the steps that must be followed (procedures).

Define the Target Population of the Policy

Policies affect people. Much like programs, they are intended to benefit or punish specific groups of people through the actions of decisionmakers. A policy that certain juveniles will be automatically tried as adults ("direct file" or "automatic exclusion") must clearly specify the characteristics of individuals and their offenses that will make them eligible for trial in criminal court. How old must they be? What offenses are included? Do they need to have a record of prior offenses? Must the prior offenses be serious? Is there any way that these juveniles can be tried in juvenile court?

For other types of policies, the question is often one of selection: whether the rule applies to everyone or whether only certain persons or groups are being targeted. Recent research has shown that serious juvenile crimes occur at specific times of day. Many cities have instituted curfews to reduce crimes that occur between 11:00 P.M. and 6:00 A.M. This type of policy applies to all persons within a specific age range. In a South Carolina study, however, researchers found that most violent crimes occur around 3:00 P.M., right after school. This information implies that more after-school programming is needed.[11]

Identify the Responsible Authority

Who is to carry out the policy, and what will the responsibilities of those persons be? Many states, for example, have implemented sentencing guidelines that limit the ranges of sentences that judges can give to offenders, depending on current and prior offense information. Judges are required to stay within the specified reasons or to provide written justification for giving a sentence that is outside the range. In this case, the judge is the responsible authority, and the judge must consult the guidelines before assigning the sentence. This assignment of responsibility to an organizational unit or to persons occupying a specific role in an organization is important to the policy's success. It assures that relevant knowledge, credibility, and lines of authority are consistent with other policies.

In some cases, a new policy results in the creation of new agencies. In the case of sentencing guidelines, many states have created commissions that monitor implementation of the guidelines, including training judges, prosecutors, defenders, and others who need to know the new rules. Importantly, these sentencing commissions monitor use of the guidelines and learn, through the application of the guidelines, how to improve them. For example, if judges routinely make exceptions to the guidelines in cases involving use of a weapon or drug addiction, then the commission needs to review the guidelines to see if changes are needed. It may be that the justifications provided by judges are consistent and convincing and that the guidelines should reflect the values and beliefs being expressed by these judges. This example shows how important it is to assign responsibility for carrying out a policy to the right persons. Not only will implementation be more effective; the policy itself has a better chance of being improved.

Specify Policy Provisions and Procedures

In order for a set of principles or rules to be implemented well, individuals responsible for carrying them out must understand what is to be done (provisions) and the steps that must be taken (procedures) so that the policy is carried out consistently. In the case of a curfew for juveniles, the rule about "who gets what and in what order" is clear. In other cases, however, the policy statement must be more detailed. It is critical that provisions and procedures be developed and stated clearly in order to ensure consistency, fairness, and control of costs associated with the policy's implementation. Typically the policy identifies:

- What is to be done: the goods, services, opportunities, or interventions that will be delivered to members of the target population (provisions)

- The steps that need to be followed and the conditions that must be met to apply the policy (procedures).

For example, state Community Corrections Acts (CCAs) are policies that specify how community correctional programs should be developed to control the growth of prison populations. The provisions of state CCAs vary on at least four dimensions:[12]

1. The degree of decentralization of authority from state to local levels (e.g., administrative control granted to city/county networks vs. state-run programs).

2. The nature of citizen participation in the design, governance, and operation of community corrections programs (e.g., citizen advisory board, role in case screening).

3. Relative emphasis on deinstitutionalization of offenders (the degree to which reductions in local or state prison populations are explicitly mandated; funding incentives or disincentives are tied to prison populations).

4. The nature and scope of individualized sanctions and services to be offered (e.g., relative emphasis on rehabilitation, reintegration, restitution, restoration, or control).

We see that provisions may overlap to some degree with decision authority and target identification. The decision authority who chooses to keep some prison-bound offenders in the community may be bound by strict criteria for target selection that include the type of crime the offender committed, their prior court history, and their family or employment situations. In another setting, the policy may specify a requirement (provision) that a certain proportion of prison-bound offenders must stay in the community. How these offenders are selected may or may not be left to the discretion of a group of decisionmakers.

When specifying the provisions of a policy, it is also important to specify the specific steps or procedures to be followed. For example, Emergency Release Acts are controversial policy options that require a local or state correctional agency to release certain prisoners in order to bring the population down to an acceptable level.[13] Obviously, such a policy is not popular with everyone. Letting prisoners out before their sentence is completed may be regarded as cheating. After all, the judge handed down a sentence that seemed fair. The fact that the prison is crowded doesn't change the appropriateness of the sentence. The fact is, however, that criminal justice agencies are not given infinite resources. They must do the best that they can with limited resources. In designing an emergency release policy, then, it is important to state clearly the sequence of actions (procedures) that must be taken when the prison population reaches a specified level:

- Prison populations are to be monitored daily.

- Projections are made about immediate crowding problems.

- Responsible persons are designated to make release decisions.

- The governor's office must be consulted in specific cases.

- Persons with specific authority must sign orders.

- Arrangements must be made for those inmates about to be released.

- Notification to other agencies (e.g., law enforcement) may be required.

These steps are especially important when the rights of individuals are affected, eligibility might be challenged, resources are limited, and public objections are likely. Clear procedures help to ensure consistency and fairness in the application of a policy.

Conclusion

Once the intervention approach is chosen, it is necessary to specify clearly and in detail the design of the program or policy. Vague descriptions are not sufficient. Not all boot camps provide the same programming, for example, nor do all mandatory sentencing policies contain the same provisions. We want to know, in detail, who does what to whom in what order, how much and how often (see the summary table below). Only when the program or policy design has been clearly defined are we ready to move to the next stage of planning or analysis.

Figure 4.2		
Critical Elements of Program and Policy Design		
	Program Design	**Policy Design**
Who (does)	Staff	Decision authority
What	"Service delivery" (program components and activities)	Provisions
To whom	Target population	Target population
In what order	"Service delivery" (program components and activities)	Procedures
How much and	"Service delivery" (program components and activities)	Provisions
How often	"Service delivery" (program components and activities)	Procedures

DISCUSSION QUESTIONS

1. (a) Briefly describe the design of a program discussed in class, or use one that you have found while doing library research for a class paper. (b) Do you have enough published material to do this analysis? If not, what information do you need, and how might you get it?

2. What factors should you consider in choosing an intervention approach? Give a brief example to illustrate your answer.

3. What is meant by the term *service tasks*? Describe the different aspects that need to be specified.

4. What is meant by the term *service delivery*? Describe the different aspects that need to be specified.

5. What is meant by the term *policy provisions*? Give an example.

6. What kinds of factors are considered in defining the target population?

7. Identify a criminal justice policy and outline its major components, including its target population, provisions, responsible authority, and procedures.

8. Describe each of the following concepts:
   - Access
   - Screening
   - Needs/risk assessment
   - Intake
   - Client records
   - Retention
   - Direct file
   - Emergency Release Acts

Case Study 4.1

Program Design: The Checkmate Program

Instructions: *Read the case study below, and then answer the question at the end of the material.*

The Checkmate Program was one of four community-based delinquency prevention programs funded by the state of Pennsylvania under its initiative to reduce minority overrepresentation in juvenile justice.[1] The following program description was excerpted from an evaluation report to the state.[2]

Target Population and Target Selection

The Checkmate Program was intended to serve Philadelphia's 25th Police District through a close cooperative relationship with Stetson Middle School. Because the Alternative School next door to Stetson received disciplinary transfers from the rest of the school system, including Stetson, youths from the Alternative School were also eligible to attend the Checkmate Program. Inclusion criteria included truancy and disruptive behavior in school. Program staff stated that the only exclusion criteria were if "youths are too much to handle."

Programs were mandated, as a condition of PCCD [Pennsylvania Commission on Crime and Delinquency] funding, to select at least half of their clients from youths having had prior contact with the justice system. While these criteria were originally interpreted to mean "at least one prior arrest," this literal interpretation proved too restrictive and not enough eligible clients at Stetson could be found. Thus, after discussions with PCCD staff, eligibility criteria were broadened. "Police contact" was no longer limited to an arrest; it could include a warning from the police or being questioned by the police. Also, if information were available to suggest that a youth was in a gang, he/she would be eligible. Following these changes in target selection, Checkmate achieved the mandated criteria.

Intake, Exit, and Follow-up Procedures

Stetson Middle School was the major source of referrals when the program began. Police made a couple of referrals; a few clients were residents of Hancock Manor (self-referrals or referrals from parents living in the building where the Checkmate Program was located); a small number came from word of mouth. A mailing was sent to all potential referral sources explaining the purpose of the program and services provided for youths.

---

[1]   Welsh, Wayne N., Philip W. Harris, and Patricia H. Jenkins (1995b) *Evaluation of Minority Overrepresentation Programs. Appendix to Report 2: Individual Program Reports.* Philadelphia: Temple University, Department of Criminal Justice.

[2]   An Internet site that stores a number of designs of programs for delinquent youths is *http://www.temple.edu/prodes.* Click on PDI to access the Program Design Inventory.

Case Study 4.1, *continued*

About two-thirds of the referrals came from schools. Program staff also had "House Meetings" (meetings with teachers at each grade level) in the first year of the program to recruit students. These efforts were so successful that by the next year the program had received a surplus of referrals, but had already admitted the maximum number of clients they could serve. As a result, House Meetings were no longer held. School referrals came mostly from the vice-principal, counselors, and teachers. Reasons for referral included truancy, cutting classes, inappropriate behavior, and causing trouble in class.

The demand for services proved quite high. Within the first three months, the Checkmate Program had already received 100 applications. Within six months, they had received about 200 applications, with room for only 50 clients at one time. Part of the reason for high demand was that Checkmate staff were very visible in schools. This was necessary, according to staff, to maintain good relations with the school and with students.

After the referral was received, there was an intake interview by a member of the staff (all staff conducted interviews). At the interview, the benefits of the program were explained. Youths were also advised of their obligations if they chose to enroll in the program. After the intake interviews, the interviewer met with the rest of the staff to discuss the applicant's suitability for the program. At the case conference, staff discussed whether there was a "good fit" between the youth's needs and the program. If the youth had no real problems, he/she was excluded from the program. Once a decision was made, each applicant was given a verbal orientation of the rules and regulations of the program.

While youths could be terminated from the program for poor attendance and/or failure to participate, the program preferred to encourage good attendance and participation by providing incentives, which included: field trips (i.e., aquarium, ball games), recreation, and after-school homework assistance. Rewards were contingent upon fulfilling obligations. For example, if a youth completed his/her homework, he/she was allowed to participate in recreation activities.

General Program Goals and Intervention Philosophy

In its original program proposal, the Checkmate Program provided the following goal statement: "The intent of the Impact Checkmate Program is to establish an accountability system for youth with school activities, supplemental education services, evening and weekend personal development and leadership training activities, and other services that will result in positive behaviors in school and in the community." A cornerstone of the program has been its emphasis on the "Four As": attendance, academics, athletics, and attitude.

Definitions of program success and failure, as provided by staff, were modest but clear. For example, staff stated that just getting youths to attend school is a major achievement. Staff also expected progress in each youth's atti-

Case Study 4.1, *continued*

tude and behavior, physical fitness, and academic performance. The most crucial factors needed for program success, according to staff, were consistent leadership and meaningful interaction with the clients.

Perceived obstacles to program success included a lot of attrition due to the transitional nature of the neighborhood and the age of the youths. Staff felt that there was too much of a "revolving door" policy regarding attendance. Efforts were made to contact youth and encourage attendance. Unfortunately, parents were sometimes a part of the problem. Program staff were limited by lack of resources in their ability to reach out to parents who resisted or did not seek assistance.

The school setting (Stetson) provided serious obstacles as well as support. For example, original target selection procedures were not successful. "Block Rostering" of students (i.e., identifying eligible students; scheduling classes to enable program clients to attend Checkmate activities) never happened. There were also problems in classroom scheduling (Checkmate originally offered its life skills classes at Stetson). Often, neither staff nor students knew in advance which classroom they were going to be in, creating delays and confusion.

Security and safety at the school was an issue. For example, random searches with metal detectors and fire alarms that were frequently set off by students caused disruption. Also, program staff reported that about six to eight serious incidents had occurred since the beginning of the school year, and there was inadequate protection for students. "Two trained counselors cannot provide effective service delivery to the school population of approximately 1,000 students." In addition, transportation from the Alternative School was stopped because of discipline problems on the bus, and this created an important gap.

At the conclusion of the first school year, Checkmate maintained its relations with the school, but began providing services to youth in a different physical setting (Hancock Manor). Checkmate staff members began visiting the schools at least three times per week to provide support for participants and recruit clients. There was a strong relationship with school staff.

Program Content (Service Delivery)

Program activities and objectives are diagrammed in Figure A. The program offered two weekend retreats (2¹/₂ days) as part of its regular programming. The first retreat was a general orientation and introduction to the program that allowed the staff to assess individual strengths and weaknesses, and encouraged youths to develop a sense of teamwork. Orientation at the beginning of the program was important for setting expectations

Case Study 4.1, *continued*

about the program. A lot of youths had no experience with sharing or team-work. Now, the orientation was provided only for new clients. Participants even-tually recognized their own commitment toward progress and learning. They worked through goal setting, participated in "trust" activities, had several sport-ing activities, and attended several presentations (i.e., life skills, group norms). Although both retreats were intensive, the second retreat was aimed at fur-thering individual and group development, including leadership skills.

The Checkmate Program emphasized truancy reduction and follow-up. Program staff telephoned the school to make sure that youths attended school, and followed up if students did not attend (phone calls, neighborhood "roundup", home visits). Over time, limited resources (i.e., too few program staff and inconsistent police assistance) resulted in less intensive truancy follow-up, although school attendance was still closely monitored.

The Checkmate Program offered regular life skills classes. These classes discussed a variety of issues, such as dealing with anger and communicating effectively. The program's staff had a very well-organized curriculum, includ-ing lesson plans and discussion questions. At first, a "Homework Club" was originally scheduled for one hour each day after school. Staff members encouraged clients to do their homework and provide assistance. It was very difficult to get students to do homework, however, and limited resources resulted in this component being offered mainly on a voluntary basis. To develop the desire to learn, the staff provided educational activities and games. Staff members found that they needed to focus on very basic skills. Dur-ing the second year of the program, the educational component was less intensive because there was no educational coordinator. On Monday, Wednes-day, and Friday lifeskills were taught, and on Tuesday and Thursday home-work/academic work was stressed. Activities included homework assistance, but also games, discussions, and other activities. Those youths that did not have homework were allowed to participate in a game (i.e., chess), read, draw, or do other activities.

The evening recreation program was provided eight to 12 hours per week and two hours on Saturday. Structured activities (i.e., basketball, games) and supervision were provided. In the first year of the program, the "Four As" were stressed: attendance, attitude, athletics, and academics. The "Four As" were not emphasized as much in the second year. Physical activ-ities were seen as a means to specific objectives: increased sense of teamwork, increased self-esteem, improved motor skills, and development of leader-ship skills. Games like chess also teach an important process, according to the Program Director: chess teaches rules, self-discipline, and thinking skills.

The Computer Learning Center, located at Hancock Manor, provided com-puter resources and training. Assistance in developing basic skills (math, science, and reading) was offered. Staff stated that they were working on new

Case Study 4.1, *continued*

plans to get more clients involved, and were setting up some software. Unfortunately, the computers were frequently in need of repair. An educational coordinator was subsequently hired, and the educational program was reorganized.

Field trips to museums and cultural and sporting events included attending a conference on multicultural disabilities, workshops on cultural awareness, and a school fair (college and career options).

In 1992-93 program staff originally stated that they provided mediation and counseling for clients, but later agreed in discussions with evaluators that this component was really only an occasional part of their job descriptions (i.e., regular interaction with youth), and not a structured service.

The Police-Community Interracial Task Force provided nonviolent conflict resolution training on a contract basis. The basic curriculum was a 30-hour package including presentations, discussions, and assignments.

A group "rap session" where youths regularly met and discussed their goals, problems, and progress was originally planned and implemented, but this was no longer being done because of problems with poor attendance and high client turnover. Five "subgroups" were planned (i.e., Rooks, Bishops, etc.). Each group was supposed to have a weekly rap session. In place of rap sessions, staff provide more one-on-one counseling.

One-to-one mentoring with adults was also intended in the original program proposal, but this component did not fully materialize due to limited resources. The program made increasing use of "student mentors" over time, however. Volunteers from local high schools and colleges assisted with program supervision and helped monitor the program's clients. The program intended to increase the number of mentors to one for each client, and began more intensive recruiting of volunteers from sources such as high schools (community service program), colleges, the United Way, St. Christopher's Church, and Temple University.

A parent support group was also intended in the original proposal, but this got off to a very slow start due to lack of interest by parents. Participation increased gradually, however, due to persistence by staff. A handful of parents (six or seven) met regularly once a month to discuss their children's progress (in the program, at school, at home) and strategies to facilitate progress, and provide support for each other. Other activities included life skills workshops, guest speakers, and parenting skills. A stress reduction clinic and a session on parents' rights were also offered.

Youths were provided with some assistance in the area of career development. George C., the project coordinator, used an assessment tool called "The Self-Directed Search (Form E). His goal was to assess needs and skills of youths and mentors, then match up pairs with similar interests and talents. George also used the "Career Directions Series" available at the Philadelphia Free Library to provide information about careers and facilitate planning with

Case Study 4.1, *continued*

youth. The objectives were to assist staff and support youth in their progress toward their goals. A monthly "mentors" meeting was held; about 12 volunteers attended regularly.

Program Goals

The primary program goals were as follows:

- Improve attendance and achievement at school
- Increase self-awareness and self-esteem
- Improve problem-solving skills
- Improve communication skills
- Increase respect for others
- Improve school performance
- Improve basic skills (i.e., reading, writing)
- Widen the range of experiences and opportunities
- Develop life skills (i.e., job skills)
- Encourage less aggressive behavior toward others
- Increase cultural sensitivity
- Learn to resolve disputes peacefully

Program Staffing

Mike M., the Program Director, carried out administrative, coordinating, and monitoring duties. The Project Coordinator, George C., planned program activities, supervised project staff, recruited and supervised volunteers, maintained program records, and completed required reports (i.e., funding). He supervised the evening recreation program, taught life skills at the Alternative School (M, W, and Th), and provided counseling. Lela B. was the Educational Coordinator and Administrator: she served as a liaison with teachers, and helped with truancy reduction, homework, and counseling. Yvette S., the Youth Vocational Counselor, taught life skills, provided liaison with parents, and assisted with truancy reduction efforts. She also provided counseling and referral services, maintained case notes and other pertinent information in youth files, and met with school personnel to review youths' academic performance. An Evening Recreation Director, McKinley W., was added in March of 1994. Katia V. was a part-time clerical assistant, and Darren C. was a part-time recreational assistant.

Case Study 4.1, *continued*

Figure A
Checkmate Program Model

Activities	Goals
Two Weekend Retreats (2½ days each)	• Assess individual needs and strengths
Life Skills Training (90 minutes weekly)	• Improve self-esteem • Improve communications skills • Increase respect for others • Learn problem-solving skills
Truancy Reduction and Follow-up (daily checks with school)	• Reduce truancy
After-School Club (3:30 P.M.- 5:00 P.M., Monday - Friday)	• Improve school behavior and performance • Provide homework assistance
Evening Recreation: Organized Sports and Games (6:00 P.M. - 9:00 P.M., Monday - Friday; and 10:00 A.M. - 2:00 P.M. Saturday)	• Develop leadership skills • Develop teamwork • Improve self-esteem
Field Trips (1 - 2 per month)	• Increase cultural awareness • Increase awareness of diversity • Practice life skills in the field
Computer Learning (optional)	• Improve basic skills in math and reading
Nonviolent Conflict Resolution (30-hr. curriculum)	• Learn to resolve disputes peacefully • Encourage less aggressive behavior toward others • Increase cultural sensitivity
Youth Mentoring	• Assist staff in evening program and support youths.
Career Development	• Provide information about careers and facilitate planning with youths.
Date: June 1994	

Case Study 4.1, *continued*

Question

1. Review the program description and chart in Case Study 4.1, and critically evaluate it. How well is the design of this program described? Is there any other information about the program design that should be included? What questions might you ask to gain more information about the program design?

Case Study 4.2

Getting Tough with Juvenile Offenders

Instructions: Read the material below, and then answer the questions at the end of the case study.

The juvenile court underwent a number of changes, largely through legislation, during the 1980s and 1990s. Both the media and some academic scholars portrayed delinquents as increasingly violent, predicting a wave of violence as the adolescent population increased in size. During the 1990s, almost every state passed new legislation making it easier to transfer juveniles to the criminal courts for trial and removing many protections, such as the confidentiality of juvenile court records. The waiver of juvenile cases to the criminal court was facilitated by removing the decision from the juvenile court and making transfer automatic under certain circumstances, thus placing the decision in the hands of prosecutors. Moreover, the language of these new laws indicated that the purpose of the juvenile justice system had shifted from one of rehabilitation to the protection of public safety and holding youths accountable for their offenses. Thus, legal and social scholars and researchers raised questions about the "rehabilitative ideal" on which the system was founded.[1]

The experience of Pennsylvania illustrates well these changes. In 1994, the State's District Attorney's Association asked the legislature to change the Juvenile Act. The recommended change was to give prosecutors the option of filing criminal charges directly in adult court when the offense was serious or violent, or if the offender was at least 16 and a chronic offender. Armed with factual evidence of increasing youth violence and arguments that the juvenile justice system was inadequate to deal with the problem, they pressed their case even harder when a new governor was elected in November of 1994.

The juvenile court judges of the state strongly opposed this proposed change. Instead, the judges proposed enhancements of the juvenile justice system that would support a comprehensive, community-focused effort to control violent juvenile delinquency. With greater resources and continued control over the decision to transfer juveniles to the adult system, the judges believed that youth violence could be reduced.

The new governor, Tom Ridge, addressed these initiatives aggressively when he came into office in January of 1995. Within a year, new legislation had been passed that change the purpose of the juvenile court from one of rehabilitation to one of balanced and restorative justice, or "balanced attention to the protection of the community, the imposition of accountability to victims for offenses committed and the development of competencies to enable

---

[1]   Harris, P.W., W.N. Welsh, and F. Butler (2000). "A Century of Juvenile Justice." In G. LaFree (ed.), *Criminal Justice 2000, Volume 1*, pp. 359-426. Washington, DC: U.S. Department of Justice, Office of Justice Programs, National Institute of Justice (NCJ-182408).

Case Study 4.2, *continued*

children to become responsible and productive members of the community." Importantly, this legislation shifted the status of beneficiary of programs from the child to the community. Other major changes also were brought into law:

- The police were now authorized to fingerprint and photograph any child alleged to have committed a misdemeanor or felony,

- Parents could now be required to participate in summary offense hearings,

- Schools and the police must now be notified of the disposition of a case,

- Juvenile records of former juvenile offenders could now be used at bail hearings, and

- Juvenile hearings were now open to the public in cases in which the juvenile was charged with a felony.

The District Attorney's Association also got what it wanted: a number of offenses were excluded from juvenile court jurisdiction, thus enabling prosecutors to try these cases in adult court. The excluded offenses, which apply only to youths age 15 and older, are: rape, involuntary sexual intercourse, aggravated assault, robbery, robbery of a motor vehicle, aggravated indecent assault, kidnapping, voluntary manslaughter, and an attempt to commit murder. If the juvenile can demonstrate that a trial in juvenile court would be better for the public, then the criminal court can choose to transfer the case back to juvenile court. In addition, juvenile court judges are now to consider primarily the "public interest" when deciding to transfer other cases. Again, it is the public, not the juvenile, that now is seen as the beneficiary of the law.

Obviously, each of the provisions listed above requires detailed procedures for judges, administrators, prosecutors, and probation staff to follow. Let's take the direct file provision, known as Act 33. This act not only specifies what offenses are excluded from juvenile court jurisdiction, but it defines in detail each offense so that fairness can be achieved. For example, aggravated assault includes an intentional attempt to cause bodily harm to a public official, an attempt to cause bodily harm with a deadly weapon, or an attempt to cause bodily harm to a teacher or student while they are engaged in school activities.

One of the most difficult implementation issues regarding this law has been translating the goals of public safety, victim restoration, and competency development into operational terms. In particular, if the development of youth competencies is a goal, what does it mean in practice? Is competency development the same thing as rehabilitation? Is it just education, vocational training, and the acquisition of life skills? As of the beginning of 2004, questions regarding how courts and programs would translate the concept of competency development into concrete objectives and program services had yet to be resolved.

Case Study 4.2, *continued*

Questions

1. Review the policy description given in Case Study 4.2 and critically evaluate it. Is the policy design (as described here) adequate? Why or why not? Is anything missing?

2. Consider what decision issues are raised by shifting the emphasis of the juvenile justice system from "the best interests of the child" to "the protection of the community," and what cost considerations should be addressed.

3. What is the target population of Pennsylvania's new Juvenile Act? What are its provisions? Who is the authority responsible for carrying it out? What procedures have been provided, and what procedures still need to be addressed?

Endnotes

[1]   We discuss cost and resource planning in further detail in Chapter 5. In Chapter 8, we examine cost-benefit and cost-effectiveness *evaluation*.

[2]   See: Baldus, David C., George G. Woodworth, and Charles A. Pulaski, Jr. (1990). *Equal Justice and the Death Penalty: A Legal and Empirical Analysis* Boston: Northeastern University Press; Bohm, Robert M. (1989). "Humanism and the Death Penalty, with Special Emphasis on the Post-Furman Experience." *Justice Quarterly*, 6:173-195; Zimring, Franklin, and Gordon Hawkins (1986). *Capital Punishment and the American Agenda*. Cambridge: Cambridge University Press.

[3]   Petersilia, Joan (1997). "Diverting Nonviolent Prisoners to Intermediate Sanctions: The Impact of California Prison Admissions and Corrections Costs." *Corrections Management*. Vol. 1, No. 1, p.10.

[4]   To get these figures, we went to the California Department of Corrections web site (*http://www.corr.ca.gov/default.asp*) and the web site of the Criminal Justice Institute (*http://www.cji-inc.com/*). The latter gave us jail figures for three California jurisdictions (Los Angeles, Riverside, and Santa Clara), which we averaged.

[5]   Petersilia, Joan, and Susan Turner (1993). "Intensive Probation and Parole." In Michael Tonry (ed.), *Crime and Justice: A Review of Research* (Vol. 17). Chicago: University of Chicago Press.

[6]   Hoge, R., and D. Andrews (1996). *The Youth Level of Service/Case Management Inventory (YLS/CMI)*. Ottawa, Ontario: Carleton University.

[7]   Grisso, T., and R. Barnum (2000). *Massachusetts Youth Screening Instrument-2: User's Manual and Technical Report*. Worcester, MA: University of Massachusetts Medical School.

[8]   Hare, R., L. McPherson, and A. Forth (1988). "Male Psychopaths and Their Criminal Careers." *Journal of Consulting and Clinical Psychology*, 56:710-714.

[9]   See: Gottfredson, D., S.S. Najaka, and B. Kearley (2003). "Effectiveness of Drug Treatment Courts: Evidence from a Randomized Trial." *Criminology and Public Policy*, 2:171-196; Goldkamp, J. (2003). "The Impact of Drug Courts." *Criminology and Public Policy*, 2:197-206; Harrell, A. (2003). "Judging Drug Courts: Balancing the Evidence." *Criminology and Public Policy*, 2:207-212.

[10] Rourke, Nancy E., and Philip W. Harris (1988). "Evaluating Your DUI System: It Can Be Sobering." *Judicature*, 27(2):14-18, 45-49.

[11] *Juvenile Justice Update* (February/March, 1996). Vol. 2, No. 1, p. 5.

[12] Harris, M. Kay (1996). "Key Differences among Community Corrections Acts in the United States: An Overview." *The Prison Journal*, 76:192-238.

[13] Welsh, Wayne N. (1993). "Changes in Arrest Policies as a Result of Court Orders against County Jails." *Justice Quarterly*, 10:89-120.

Endnotes

CHAPTER *5*

Developing an Action Plan

CHAPTER OUTLINE

▶ *Identify resources needed and make cost projections*: How much funding is needed to implement a specific intervention? Identify the kinds of resources needed, estimate costs and make projections, and develop a resource plan.

▶ *Plan to acquire or reallocate resources*: How will funding be acquired? Identify resource providers, and be prepared for making adjustments to the resource plan.

▶ *Specify dates by which implementation tasks will be accomplished*, and assign responsibilities to staff members for carrying out tasks. A *Gantt chart* is particularly useful for this purpose.

▶ *Develop mechanisms of self-regulation:* Create mechanisms to monitor staff performance and enhance communication, including procedures for orienting participants, coordinating activities, and managing resistance and conflict.

▶ *Specify a plan to build and maintain support*: Anticipate sources of resistance and develop responses.

By now, you have the program or policy design specified; now it is time to develop a *plan* to actually put it into motion. Developing an action plan is like writing the instructions that explain how to assemble a new computer system. Let's say you're about to assemble a complex system of electronic equipment by carefully following all the manufacturer's instructions. You have all the necessary components laid out in front of you; you hook up all the wires and cords according to the instructions, and you hook up the power supply. Now it is time to turn on the switch. The questions are: *Will it run? Will it run effectively and efficiently?* and *What do you do if it doesn't?* Needless to say, simply having all the components doesn't do much good unless the instructions effectively explain what is needed to get the thing going. One needs a plan for putting the system into operation and making sure that it is working properly.

Here's another analogy: Developing an action plan is like the blueprint for building a house: in addition to the *description* of the house (e.g., a four-bedroom, two-story, brick house with a deck, modern kitchen, and landscaped yard), you need a *blueprint* that specifies all the necessary materials, supplies, and tools required; what goes where; and how things are supposed to fit together. Without the blueprint, you can't even begin. We find out how good the blueprint is when we actually put it into action step-by-step. Alas, though, the blueprint didn't just fall out of the sky into our awaiting hands. Someone (the architect) put considerable thought and effort into explaining how to translate his or her vision of a house into reality. In a sense, developing an action plan is like writing a blueprint.

Interventions are similar. You have the program or policy design on paper (i.e., descriptions of target selection procedures, job descriptions and qualifications of staff, and all the program/policy components or services to be delivered), but that is not sufficient. You need to develop an action plan, a blueprint that methodically specifies the sequence of tasks that need to be completed in order to successfully launch or implement the program or policy. These include technical and interpersonal tasks (e.g., identifying and acquiring the necessary resources for the program or policy; locating office space and/or meeting space; hiring and training staff; designing client intake and reporting forms; purchasing equipment and supplies; setting dates; and assigning responsibility for the completion of specific tasks).

Naturally, as with the hypothetical computer system above, you want the thing to run properly after you've spent so much of your

> **Action Planning**
>
> Action planning entails charting the entire sequence of activities and completion dates required to implement the program or policy design. It involves specifying, in clear and concise detail, the steps required to implement the program or policy design. It is, in essence, a "blueprint" explaining how to translate a vision of the program or policy into reality.

money (and energy) on it. If you have planned carefully, you will minimize (but not eliminate) unanticipated problems that can surface when the program or policy actually begins operations.

Identify Resources Needed, and Make Cost Projections

We need to identify all the specific resources that will be necessary to implement an intervention. In real life, this is extremely important. One cannot launch any program or policy without the fiscal and personal resources needed to translate a vision into reality. One needs to start by developing a *resource plan*, which enumerates all the specific costs associated with each program or policy component, including staff salaries, benefits, and training; supplies; physical space; and so on.

Resource Plan

A resource plan is a comprehensive statement of the specific fiscal, material, and social resources required to implement an intervention. All program or policy costs are estimated, including personnel, training, equipment, supplies, facilities, travel, and so on.

A resource plan attempts to achieve the following goals:

- It matches resources to objectives: in other words, one must carefully ensure that all the resources necessary to achieve the objectives of the program or policy are in place. It forces us to impose a test of feasibility: either resources must rise to the level needed to achieve the stated objectives of the program or policy, or the objectives must be downscaled to match the level of resources available.

- It identifies the availability of current resources and resources still needed to implement the program or policy design.

- It attempts to control expenditures over a specified period of time, usually by specifying how much money is to be spent over specific periods of time, such as each quarter (a three-month period).

- It provides data for monitoring fiscal aspects of the program or policy and providing feedback to funding sources and other stakeholders (e.g., annual reports or quarterly grant reports).

We offer a few simple guidelines for developing the resource plan. We emphasize that one need not be a financial wizard, an economist, or an accountant to understand and use basic principles of resource planning. We will not be discussing professional budgeting models such as incremental models, performance-based budgeting, program budgeting, or zero-based budgeting. The interested reader can find ample discussions on these specialized techniques elsewhere.[1] Suffice it to say we believe in the principles of *program-based budgeting* (also called *functional budgeting*). We present two basic principles of resource planning. First, we identify the kinds of resources needed. Second, we estimate costs for each type of resource needed.

First, list the different categories of resources that are needed to achieve each program or policy objective. Work closely from the program or policy design (see Chapter 4). Your list should include everything that will cost anything. For example:

- Staff: how many, with what qualifications?

- Staff training: what kind, and how much will be needed?

- Supplies: e.g., paper, printing and copying, office supplies?

- Advertising: e.g., brochures, flyers, public service announcements?

- Equipment: e.g., computers, telephones, copiers?

- Rental costs for office space, meeting space, and other specialized space, if required (e.g., private interviewing rooms?)

- Telephone, electrical, and water bills?

Some types of costs can be anticipated and calculated fairly precisely (e.g., salaries, rent); others may vary a great deal (e.g., telephone, xeroxing, supplies). How do you know? Ask around; do some research on similar programs or policies. Consult directors of other programs and agencies; see if it is possible to look at proposals that other agencies have prepared. Contact potential funding sources (e.g., state or federal government) to see if they will allow you to look at selected proposals they have funded in the past (probably with confidential financial information such as individual salaries removed, but with basic categories of costs such as personnel costs intact).

Those involved with the day-to-day operations of the program or the implementation of the policy (e.g., program or agency staff, coordinators and directors) should have some input into what fiscal and social resources are needed to run the program or administer the policy. Too often, especially in applications to government agencies for funding, we see resource plans that were developed entirely by professional grant writers outside of the agency. The problem is that those grant writers have had little or no contact with the daily operations of the program or agency, and their estimates of resources needed may not correspond very closely with the experience of the staff or the clients. Again, we emphasize the value of participation: do not exclude the input of staff persons who have valuable experience to aid resource planning.

Next, we ask how much of each kind of resource is needed? It is very important to be realistic about cost estimates. If you estimate too little, the program or policy is likely to fail. If you estimate too much, the proposal may not get funded, or the agency may face accusations of waste. A good budget will not only describe all estimated costs, but will provide a clear justification for each expenditure item.

In general, we are attempting to estimate all the costs involved with processing all clients or targets through all phases of the program or policy over a specific period of time (e.g., one year). As we are trying to estimate the costs associated with each program or policy design component, we try to be as thorough as possible. In addition to paying staff salaries, how much will it cost to train staff? How much will it cost to print and duplicate the client intake forms and other record-keeping forms needed? How much will it cost to acquire the supplies needed to deliver specific services (e.g., textbooks, learning aids, computer software, etc.)? How much will it cost to pay electrical, telephone, and water bills for the rooms or offices that are to be used?

We recommend working closely from the program or policy design. Estimate the costs involved for each program or policy design component. For example, counseling is one of several program components in a state halfway house for ex-offenders. How much staff time will be needed for each client over a specific time period, and how much will that staff time cost? Case Study 5.1 provides an example of such estimation procedures.

Some will complain that in this era of scarce resources and shrinking budgets, funding agencies expect programs to do everything for nothing, that is, provide comprehensive, intensive services on a shoestring budget. How, they will ask, can you tell us to make program-based estimates when doing so may inflate our already overstretched budgets? Program directors may complain that they are already committed to providing services far beyond what their meager budgets actually pay for. But how can they provide more services than what their budgets allow for? By overworking and burning out their most motivated staff persons, by pushing untrained staff to provide specialized services (e.g., life-skills training, conflict resolution training), by constantly training and recruiting new staff to replace the ones who left, by working hard to provide the impression (a "front") that the program is really "working," and by actively covering up any negative information that might threaten the program's survival. Such a situation is untenable. A good resource plan would never allow such a fiasco.

Plan to Acquire or Reallocate Resources

The task of obtaining funds to implement the program or policy requires a combination of experience, dedication, persistence, and patience. In most cases, the change agent or another specifically appointed individual (e.g., the program director or the agency's executive director) will scour the grant announcements of government, private, and nonprofit agencies, attempting to find some match between the interests of potential funding providers and the type of services the program is designed to provide. The interests of funding providers are usually clearly spelled out in annual program announcements, grant announcements, or solicitation for proposals. In other cases, the change agent will lobby to get individuals or agencies interested in putting up funding for the program, arguing that it addresses a compelling problem or need within the mission of the funding provider. Consider the following types of funding sources.

Figure 5.1

Potential Funding Sources

- *Local, state, or federal government agencies:* Does the program or policy address a compelling need or problem that fits within the mission statement and jurisdiction of a government agency? Federal agencies are most likely to have specific grant announcements; local (city or county) agencies are most likely to fund specific programs that address their mission.

- *Governmental funds designated for special purposes*: Find out if city, state, or federal agencies have designated specific funds for certain programming areas (e.g., crime prevention, drug awareness education, violence prevention, etc.). Funding priorities or targeted programming areas change from year to year, so one must stay up-to-date with each agency's funding priorities.

- *User fees*: In some cases, nominal fees may be charged to clients, although these fees are usually far less than actual program costs. In many criminal justice programs, such "user fees" are unpopular, but we have seen more creative user fees in recent years. (For example, one probation agency charges a daily fee to all participants to help offset costs of electronic surveillance. The incentive to pay such fees resides in offenders' motivations to be supervised in the community—rather than prison—to maintain full-time employment, and be closer to their families.)

- *Private and nonprofit agencies* (e.g., the MacArthur Foundation, the United Way, the Pugh Foundation): These agencies often provide funding for programs that address their mission statements.

- *Donations from businesses*: Many large corporations and even many small community businesses have become increasingly involved in providing support for programs or policies that address community needs. In addition to "giving something back to the community" by being good citizens, many business people may qualify for valuable tax breaks by making donations of equipment, goods, services, or money.

> **Figure 5.1,** *continued*
>
> - *Volunteers*: Many programs and agencies make extensive use of volunteers to provide some services (e.g., tutoring and mentoring in after-school delinquency prevention programs). Volunteers need to be qualified and trained to provide specific services, and the program or agency must be prepared to support its volunteers.
>
> - *Fund-raising projects*: Special projects may occasionally be undertaken to raise money for the program's services.

Acquiring the necessary resources to implement a program may involve any or all of a combination of activities: writing a formal funding application to a government or nonprofit agency; lobbying local, state, or federal politicians for funding; making informal inquiries, presentations, and solicitations to various agencies; and familiarizing oneself with the entire funding terrain of potential funding sources.

Making Adjustments to the Resource Plan

Unfortunately, one may find that potential funding providers cannot fully fund the proposed budget, or one might discover later that adjustments to the budget become necessary because resources prove inadequate. In the first instance, a potential funding source may receive the application for funding, favorably review it, then ask the proposal writer to cut program or policy expenses by say, 25 to 30 percent. In the second instance, program expenditures after implementation may begin to get too high (e.g., beyond the limit of available funds), necessitating cutbacks on the program's activities and/or its objectives. It will be better to cut back early on than to find out later that we simply didn't have the necessary resources to implement our intended program design. If the program fails to achieve its stated objectives, nobody is interested in hearing the excuse that "we just didn't have enough resources;" that is tantamount to saying: "we didn't know what we were doing when we did our budget." Such excuses do not inspire confidence in funding providers.

The *change agent* and/or members of the *action system* (e.g., the program director) must be ready to make adjustments.[2] Four options for adjusting resources are possible if resources prove inadequate to implement the intended program or policy design.

Figure 5.2

Making Adjustments to the Resource Plan: Four Options

1. *Try to increase funding to cover costs*: Multiple funding sources may be required to fund the program's expenses. Maybe more than one grant will be needed. Sometimes funding providers will ask the agency applying for funds to match the provider's contribution, with the requirement that no award will be made until the applying agency comes up with matching funds.

2. *Redefine target selection and/or eligibility criteria*: This might involve restricting the eligibility of clients (e.g., to those most in need), or lowering the number of clients to be served (e.g., perhaps only 30 high-risk youths can be effectively served by an after-school delinquency prevention program, rather than the originally intended 50).

3. *Reduce or modify program objectives* (e.g., lower the outcome expected): Perhaps a 10 percent reduction in recidivism can be realistically achieved rather than a 50 percent reduction.

4. *Modify the program design*: Eliminate one or more program components, beginning with the least essential components of the program.

Example 5.1

A Gantt Chart for a Delinquency Prevention Program

Recall Example 1.4 from Chapter 1. We examined an excerpt from a funding proposal submitted by a community-based delinquency prevention program applying for state funds. Major program components included: a seven-day challenge course in which juveniles were encouraged to examine their lives and set goals; one-to-one mentoring of youths by adult "committed partners"; and weekly "follow-through" meetings of all mentors and clients. The proposal spelled out exactly who was responsible for completing numerous activities required to launch the program. Specific job titles and descriptions were provided in Example 1.4. Activities included training, travel, site costs, seven-day course costs, and follow-through costs.

Here is the time line (Gantt Chart) submitted with the proposal. While specific completion dates are not shown here, the time line clearly indicates a time period for beginning and ending each task; it indicates clearly the sequence of activities to be accomplished (and by whom) in implementing the program. Note that the "consultants" referred to are subcontractors, trainers from a well established national youth program. Note also that additional technical tasks (e.g., acquiring office space, meeting space, etc.), while not shown, could easily be specified in such a chart.

Example 5.1, *continued*

Activity	Person Responsible	1	2	3	4	5	6	7	8	9	10	11	12
1. Hire Program Coordinator.	Consultant	▌											
2. Project Coordinator training and coaching.	Consultant	▌											
3. Recruit and train volunteers (Youth Enrollment Coaches, Outreach, Facilitators).	Three trainers provided by consultant.	▌											
4. Market the program.	Project Coordinator; Outreach volunteers.			▌									
5. Youth enrollment training.	Youth Enrollment Coaches.		▌										
6. Recruit and orient youth participants.	Project Coordinator; Youth Enrollment Coaches.		▌										
7. Conduct pre-course volunteer orientation.	Three trainers provided by consultant.			▌									
8. Conduct youth violence clearance, medical exams.	Specialists, professionals provided by consultant.		▌										
9. Conduct 10-day intensive curriculum.	Facilitators, Coaches, Course Production Team, Situation Intervention Team, Security.			▌									
10. Conduct parents' orientation.	Project Coordinator.			▌									
11. Assign adult mentors and introduce to their youth partners.	Project Coordinator.			▌									
12. Conduct monthly mentor coaching sessions.	Project Coordinator.				▌	▌	▌	▌	▌	▌	▌	▌	▌
13. Conduct monthly youth and partner follow-through sessions.	Project Coordinator; two Workshop Leaders provided by consultant				▌	▌	▌	▌	▌	▌	▌	▌	▌
14. Manage weekly youth/partner communications.	Project Coordinator.				▌	▌	▌	▌	▌	▌	▌	▌	▌
15. Provide life skills counseling, educational and job training, referral and placement.	Project Coordinator; adult mentors.				▌	▌	▌	▌	▌	▌	▌	▌	▌

Time Schedule (in months)

Specify Dates by Which Implementation Tasks Will Be Accomplished

The next task, probably the most important one at this stage, is to develop a program or policy time line, sometimes called a *Gantt Chart* (see Example 5.1), which specifies three elements: (1) all the specific implementation activities that need to be accomplished, (2) assignment of responsibility for each specific task to one or more individuals, and (3) a specific date by which each task is to be completed. This process may seem tedious, but it is a far more effective alternative than merely "winging it" or "improvising" program/policy implementation. Without a specific plan that incorporates all three elements listed above, the program or policy is likely to experience difficulty (or even mortality) before it even gets off the ground. A Gantt chart is a blueprint for putting all the program or policy elements into operation: step-by-step instructions explaining how to implement the program.

Develop Mechanisms of Self-Regulation

Orienting Participants

Everyone involved in the program or policy, including staff and clients, should know what their role is. Expectations for what kind of behavior is expected should be clearly spelled out, along with specific rewards and punishments. The program or agency director or coordinator should communicate a clear message about the rationale, values, and intent of the change effort. Prior to beginning intake of clients, for example, it is particularly important to clarify job descriptions and expectations about the program or policy, and allow program or agency staff to ask questions.

Coordinating Activities

Like the conductor of an orchestra, the change agent (with assistance from the individuals and agencies comprising the action system described in Chapter 2) must coordinate the activities of several different individuals and groups. There are various people and program parts that need to be monitored and managed on a regular basis. Program managers must hire and train their staff; they must build good relations with potential referral sources (e.g., police, schools, probation); they must train staff to use required intake forms and keep client records; they must build good relations with citizens and businesses in the neighborhood; and they must provide regular reports of program progress to their funding providers. Three guidelines help ensure smooth coordination (see Figure 5.3).

Figure 5.3

Three Guidelines for Coordinating Activities

1. *Maintain consistency*: Make sure that the actual job duties of staff are consistent with their job descriptions. Develop reward systems and incentives for good performance, and communicate to staff what these rewards are. Poor program or agency managers tend to wait until something goes wrong, and then blame (or punish) their staff. Good managers find that better performance results from communicating clear expectations and rewards. Such rewards include not just money, but privileges, responsibilities, and access to resources. For example, most staff are interested in professional development, and a paid trip to a local or national conference would be a substantial, appreciated reward. Staff development activities are usually permissible budget items, if someone had the forethought to include them in a grant proposal.

2. *Maintain clear and frequent communication among staff members, and between staff and supervisors*: Various means can be used: staff meetings, memos, conferences, informal conversations, and performance evaluations. Such attempts need to be explicit, though, and must be done on a regular basis. Staff must also feel that their opinions count. The program or agency director should encourage honest opinions and reporting about difficulties as well as successes. Some of the worst programs we have seen are those in which the director communicates a "don't rock the boat" philosophy, with the result that staff are afraid to report any problems until they reach crisis proportions.

3. *Keep an eye on the time-line*: Make sure that activities required for successful progression from one step to the next are carried out on time (e.g., make sure that staff are hired and trained by the dates specified in the action plan, that all record-keeping forms are printed, and that procedures are clearly understood by staff). Imagine if 100 clients had to be turned away because a program wasn't ready to begin when it was supposed to. Perhaps a required staff position wasn't filled; the office space or meeting space wasn't ready; or the referring agency had specific reporting requirements that weren't met by the program. Such events, although relatively rare, are tragic: the program suffers damage to its credibility and reputation.

Managing Resistance and Conflict

Some resistance is inevitable with the start-up of any new program or policy. Resistance may come from any of the participants involved: clients, targets, even the program or agency's own staff (i.e., the action system). Any kind of change threatens people because it creates uncertainty. Change challenges long-standing values and views of the world; it introduces risk. If participants have had input into the planning process, resistance can be anticipated and perhaps minimized (review *force field analysis* in Chapter 2). However, any resistance that appears should be dealt with fairly and seriously.

Conflict is *not* something to be avoided at all costs. It may provide the opportunity to identify and resolve misunderstandings, and it may also point out difficulties in implementation that deserve attention. Four general guidelines for conflict resolution are helpful (see Figure 5.4).

Figure 5.4

Four Guidelines for Conflict Resolution

1. *Avoid the use of force or coercion:* Using force is not often effective, even when one has legitimate power and authority. Attempts to stifle opposition often create or increase resistance, produce unintended side effects, and lead to intentional subversion of the program's long-term goals.

2. *Try to work for a "win-win" solution, not a "win-lose" outcome:* Look for common ground, if possible. There may be options based upon a principle of exchange (i.e., each party gives up something in order to get something) that would reduce resistance at little cost.

3. *Generate alternatives and options to deal with problems* (i.e., brainstorming): Identify all possible options before evaluating them. Only after a list of options is developed should parties begin discussing costs and benefits of specific strategies or negotiating outcomes (e.g., brainstorming).

4. *Use "principled negotiations":* There are four basic rules for negotiating fairly.[3] First, separate the people from the problem (don't take it personally). Second, focus on interests, not positions: each party should identify and communicate their needs, preferences, values, or concerns. Each party should understand what elements need to be included in a reasonable solution. Third, invent options for mutual gain: generate new options that are based on shared interests or an exchange of divergent interests. Finally, insist on objective criteria: both parties should agree on what criteria will be used to evaluate possible solutions.

Specify a Plan to Build and Maintain Support

With all the different interests represented by stakeholders and participants, one can expect that some public relations work goes with managing any program or policy, especially criminal justice interventions. The program or agency director is always trying to strengthen sources of support for the program or policy: within the staff, within the community, across other agencies with which the program links, with his or her superiors, with the funding agency, and with clients. Time for support building needs to be built into one's schedule, and the person responsible for doing it needs to make sure that different stakeholders are contacted on a regular basis throughout the year.

Conclusion

The program or policy in action will never perfectly match the program or policy on paper (i.e., the program design). Developing a good "blueprint," or action plan, however, should markedly reduce subsequent problems with program or policy implementation and will help launch an effective intervention. So does looking for implementation difficulties, as we will see in the next chapter.

DISCUSSION QUESTIONS

1. Define and describe the following terms: (a) *action planning*, and (b) *resource plan*.

2. Describe the purposes (goals) of a resource plan.

3. What does it mean to "estimate the costs involved for each program component?" How does one do this?

4. What options are possible when resources prove to be inadequate?

5. What is a "time line" or *Gantt chart*? What does it attempt to do?

6. Describe three guidelines for coordinating activities.

7. Describe four guidelines for conflict resolution.

Case Study 5.1

Halfway Houses in Ohio: Costs and Benefits[1]

Instructions: *Estimates of anticipated program costs and demonstrations of potential cost-effectiveness are often critical considerations for planning. Such considerations may either help win support or present near-insurmountable roadblocks for the intervention. As Cohen points out: "Forcing analysts to quantify expected costs and benefits sheds new light on the merits of alternative programs and will undoubtedly change the focus of the debate in many criminal justice program areas. Whereas one could previously claim that "prevention is cheaper than prison" or "'three strikes and you're out' pays for itself," the benefit-cost framework allows decisionmakers to examine these claims more carefully and begin to make more rational, scientifically based judgments."[2] The following case study illustrates how the costs of halfway house programming and traditional incarceration can be effectively estimated and compared.*

All adults convicted of felonies for which the statutory minimum is at least six months enter Ohio's prison system. If eligible, convicted felons who have served a specific amount of time in prison can be placed back into the community through Parole/Post Release Control and Transitional Control. Many ex-offenders are sent to halfway houses to enhance their reentry process. *Prisoner reentry* includes all activities and programming conducted to prepare ex-convicts to return safely to the community and to live as law-abiding citizens.[3]

Given the social and fiscal costs of current sentencing policies, and the impacts on individuals, families, and communities, there is a compelling need for valid, scientifically based research to develop better knowledge on methods of successful reintegration. To advance innovations that reflect solid research, the Urban Institute began a comprehensive program of reentry policy research,[4] and Ohio was selected to participate in a 10-state reentry initiative. The following figures describe Ohio's correctional population as of 2002:[5]

- Number of institutions statewide: 33

- Total design capacity: 36,270

---

[1] Adapted from: Power, Anne (2003). *Halfway House Utilization: The Key to Reentry A Cost Savings Report*. Cincinnati: Power & Associates. Available at: *http://www.occaonline.org/ohio costsavings.pdf*

[2] Cohen, Mark A. (2000). "Measuring the Costs and Benefits of Crime and Justice." In D. Duffee (ed.), *Measurement and Analysis of Crime and Justice. Criminal Justice 2000*, vol. 4, pp. 263-315. Washington, DC: U.S. Department of Justice, Office of Justice Programs (NCJ 182411).

[3] Petersilia, J. (2003). *When Prisoners Come Home: Parole and Prisoner Reentry*. New York: Oxford University Press.

[4] For a wealth of information on reentry, see the Urban Institute web site at: *http://www.urban. org/content/PolicyCenters/Justice/Projects/PrisonerReentry/overview.htm*

[5] Ibid, note 4.

Case Study 5.1, *continued*

- Total population: 44,936
- Population as percentage of rated capacity: 124%
- 2002 admissions: 22,035
- 2002 releases: 25,773
- Average stay in prison: 3.14 years
- Average cost per inmate: $63 daily; $22,257 annually
- Number of parole/PRC violators: 3273
- Number of technical violators: 692

Halfway houses are community residential programs providing supervision and treatment services for offenders released from state prisons, referred by courts of common pleas, or sanctioned because of a violation of conditions of supervision. Halfway houses in Ohio provide services such as drug and alcohol treatment, electronic monitoring, job placement, educational programs, and specialized programs for sex offenders and mentally ill offenders.

- In fiscal year 2002, the Bureau contracted for more than 1,626 halfway house beds in 26 facilities to house felony offenders and provided subsidized funding to divert more than 7,351 offenders from prison and local jails throughout Ohio.

- At an average length of stay in a halfway house of 90 days, these 1,626 beds turn over four times in one year saving 2,373,960 prison "man days" per year (1626 x 365 x 4).

A study funded by the Ohio Department of Rehabilitation and Corrections[6] found a 63.9 percent successful termination rate for offenders in halfway houses. During fiscal year 2002, 58 percent were employed full- or part-time at the time of discharge. During the same year, offenders placed in Ohio halfway houses:

- Earned $6,637,013 in income,
- Paid $32,308 in restitution,
- Paid $73,828 in court costs,
- Paid $90,828 in child support, and
- Completed 48,546 community service hours.

---

[6]   Lowenkamp, C . (2002). *Evaluation of Ohio's Community Based Correctional Facilities and Halfway House Programs, Final Report.* University of Cincinnati, Division of Criminal Justice, Center for Criminal Justice Research.

Case Study 5.1, *continued*

The total cost for all beds in 2002 was $32,089,140, and the average per diem rate was $54.03 (approximately a 1% decrease from the 2001 rate of $54.72).

Transitional Control

The Transitional Control program is available to inmates who are determined eligible by the Ohio Parole Board. Upon the sentencing judge's approval, inmates may be placed on Transitional Control and transferred to a halfway house to complete up to the last 180 days of their prison term.

Transitional Control offenders pay subsistence fees. With an additional 3,200 offenders in 800 halfway house beds annually, there would be a large increase in subsistence fees. This increase in funds could be allocated to offset costs for funding halfway house beds. Transitional Control offenders may also be stepped down from residential placement and put on electronic monitoring in an appropriate home placement, saving further costs.

Researchers at the University of Cincinnati found significant reductions in recidivism—an average reduction of 15 percent—when offenders complete Transitional Control programs in a halfway house.[7] Transitional Control offenders had the highest successful completion rate of all offenders in the study—76 percent as compared to 64 percent overall.

In 2002, the Ohio Parole Board considered 3,899 offenders for Transitional Control. Of these, 107 were approved, 1,643 were approved pending judicial review, 1,583 were denied, and 566 were rescheduled.

In fiscal year 2002, 1,353 offenders released on Transitional Control supervision earned $2,606,651, paid $24,102 in child support, and completed 7,680 hours of community service.

Halfway house placement has thus proven successful with the Transitional Control populations, successfully lowering recidivism rates. This group could profitably be expanded as a target group for additional halfway house beds.

Cost Savings Analysis and Implications

Increasing the number of halfway house beds by 800 would provide reentry services to an additional 3,200 offenders and save more than $12 million per year.

For every 100 funded halfway house beds (utilized for reentry prerelease/transitional control or for parole violators in lieu of returning to prison), 400 offenders could be served annually, for an annual cost savings of approximately $2 million. The following figures define the data used for the cost savings analysis:[8]

---

[7] Lowenkamp, C . (2002). *Evaluation of Ohio's Community Based Correctional Facilities and Halfway House Programs, Final Report.* University of Cincinnati, Division of Criminal Justice, Center for Criminal Justice Research.

[8] Estimates assume that 800 new halfway house beds will be available without additional capital investments.

Case Study 5.1, *continued*

- State prison costs: $63.23 per day
- Halfway house costs: $55.64 per day
- Electronic monitoring/case management costs: $26.00 per day

Halfway House Costs

One hundred halfway house beds can provide 180 days of programming and supervision for 400 offenders per year at an average cost of $7,247 per offender.

- 90 days in residential halfway house programming (90 @ $55.64 per day = $5,007)

- 90 days of electronic monitoring/case management (90 @ $26.00 per day = $2,340)

  Total cost per offender = $7,347

Prison Costs

One hundred prison beds can hold 200 inmates at 180 days each per year at an average cost of $11,381 per offender.

- 180 days in prison (180 @ $63.23 per day = $11,381)

  TOTAL Cost per offender = $11,381

Costs Savings per Offender

- Total prison cost per offender = $11,381
- Total halfway house cost per offender = $7,347
- Total cost savings per offender = $4,034 (difference)

Annual Costs Savings for each 100 Halfway House Beds

One hundred halfway house beds can provide 180 days of programming and supervision for 400 offenders per year at a cost of $2,938,800.

- Total cost savings per offender = $4,034
- Total cost savings per 400 offenders = $1,613,600

Case Study 5.1, *continued*

Annual Costs Savings for 800 Halfway House Beds

One hundred halfway house beds = annual cost savings of $1,613,600

- 800 halfway house beds = annual cost savings of $12,908,800 [$1,613,600 × 8]

- Annual prison cost for 3,200 offenders (180 days) = $36,419,200 [$11,381 × 3200]

- Annual halfway house cost for 3,200 offenders = $23,510,400 [$7347 × 3200]

- Annual cost savings = $12,908,800 (difference) [$36,419,200 − $23,510,400]

Overall, estimates of substantial reductions in costs and recidivism help make a convincing argument for further adoption of halfway house programming.

Questions

Recall that the annual halfway house cost per offender is $7,347, consisting of 90 days in residential halfway house programming (90 @ $55.64 per day = $5,007), and 90 days of electronic monitoring/case management (90 @ $26.00 per day = $2,340). Assume that 100 ex-offenders are enrolled in one of these programs at one specific site.

1. Break down the resources required for the halfway house program into at least three specific cost categories. For example, how much money might be allocated for: staff supervision? counseling? program materials? security? other costs? Provide cost estimates and show your calculations.

2. Is there likely to be enough money to meet all ex-offenders' needs? Why or why not?

3. What other program components might be needed? Try to identify at least one additional resource that might strengthen this program. Describe the resource, explain why you think it is important, and provide cost projections.

Case Study 5.2

The Brady Act: Why Action Planning is Needed[1]

Instructions: *Read the material below, and then answer the questions at the end of this case study.*

The Federal Gun Control Act (GCA), 18 U.S.C. 922, prohibits transfer of a firearm to a person who:

- Is under indictment for, or has been convicted of, a crime punishable by imprisonment for more than one year

- Is a fugitive from justice

- Is an unlawful user of, or is addicted to, any controlled substance

- Has been adjudicated as a mental defective or committed to a mental institution

- Is an illegal alien or has been admitted to the United States under a nonimmigrant visa

- Was discharged from the U.S. Armed Forces under dishonorable conditions

- Has renounced U.S. Citizenship

- Is subject to a court order restraining him or her from harassing, stalking, or threatening an intimate partner or child

- Has been convicted in any court of a misdemeanor crime of domestic violence.

The GCA categories of prohibited persons are the prevailing minimum for all states. Many states have similar prohibitions and have enacted additional categories of prohibited persons, such as those who have committed alcohol-related or juvenile offenses.[2]

Following seven years of political battles and NRA opposition, the Brady Act amended the GCA and included interim provisions (18 U.S.C. 922(s)) in effect from February 29, 1994, until November 29, 1998.[3] The U.S. Depart-

---

[1]   Adapted from: Manson, D., and G. Lauver (1997). *Presale Firearm Checks* (NCJ 162787). Washington, DC: U.S. Department of Justice, Office of Justice Programs, Bureau of Justice Statistics; and Bowling, M., G. Lauver, M.J. Hickman, and D.B. Adams (2003). *Background Checks for Firearm Transfers, 2002.* (NCJ 200116). Washington, DC: U.S. Department of Justice, Office of Justice Programs, Bureau of Justice Statistics.

[2]   See: *Survey of State Procedures Related to Firearm Sales, Midyear 2002* [Online]. Available at: *http://www.ojp.usdoj.gov/bjs/abstract/ssprfs02.htm*

[3]   *Brady Handgun Violence Prevention Act* (Brady Act), PL 103-159.

Case Study 5.2, *continued*

ment of Justice, with the states, developed the National Instant Criminal Background Check System (NICS) during the 57-month interim period, as authorized by the permanent provisions of the Brady Act, 18 U.S.C. 922(t).

Interim provisions were intended to allow states a reasonable period of time to comply with the new law, which required dramatic changes in state criminal background information systems. The interim provisions of the Act required that licensed firearm dealers request a presale check on all potential handgun purchasers from the Chief Law Enforcement Officer (CLEO) in the jurisdiction where the prospective purchaser resides. The CLEO must make "a reasonable effort" to determine if the purchaser is prohibited from receiving or possessing a handgun. The federal firearms licensee must wait five business days before transferring the handgun to the buyer unless earlier approval is received from the CLEO. The "interim provisions" also permitted states to follow a variety of alternatives to the five-day waiting period, including issuing firearm permits, performing "instant checks," or conducting "point-of-sale" checks. "Brady-alternative" states prior to November 30, 1998, included California ("point-of-sale check"), Virginia ("instant check"), and Missouri (permit).

This interim system remained in effect until November 30, 1998, when an instant background check was to become mandatory for purchasers of all firearms. Under the "permanent provisions" of the Brady Act, presale inquiries were to be made through the National Instant Criminal Background Check System (NICS). The background check would determine, based on available records, if an individual was prohibited under the federal Gun Control Act or state law from receiving or possessing firearms. The act required the NICS, which is operated by the FBI, to be established no later than November 1998.

In a close 5–4 decision on June 27, 1997, the U.S. Supreme Court ruled that the federal government cannot require local police to conduct background checks on people who want to buy handguns.[4] Justice Antonin Scalia noted in his opinion that the federal government cannot force states to enact or administer a federal regulatory program (a controversy known as federalism). The five-day waiting period specified by the Act was ruled constitutional, as long as the states retained discretion whether to perform the background checks or not. They cannot be made mandatory.[5]

Under the FBI's NICS program, state criminal history records are provided through each state's central repository and the Inter-state Identification Index. The index, maintained by the FBI, points instantly to criminal records that states hold. In addition, the FBI provides records of federal offenses, fed-

---

[4] *Printz, Sheriff/Coroner, Ravalli County, Montana v. United States* 117 S.Ct 2365,138L. Ed. 2d 914 (1997).

[5] For additional information regarding Brady Act design and implementation, go the Bureau of Alcohol, Tobacco, Firearms, and Explosives web site (*http://www.atf.gov*). Choose "Search" from the menu, and enter the words "Brady Act." You will find a wealth of relevant information about the Brady Act.

Case Study 5.2, *continued*

erally maintained state data, and federal data on nonfelony disqualifications. States responding to NICS inquiries for nonfelony prohibitions provide their records directly.

To ensure availability of complete and accurate state records, the Brady Act established a grant program, the National Criminal History Improvement Program (NCHIP). This program was designed to assist states in developing or improving existing criminal history record systems and to establish interface with the NICS. As of 2002, more than $390 million had been awarded to states.[6]

The Firearm Inquiry Statistics Program (FIST) was established under the NCHIP to develop data on the impact of presale firearm checks on the identification of prohibited firearm purchasers. Data summarizing the number of inquiries, rejections, and reasons for rejections is summarized and released annually by the U.S. Bureau of Justice Statistics (see Case Study 6.2).

Controversies about the Brady Act extended beyond arguments about the desirability of tougher handgun regulation. Disagreement ensued about who was going to pay to update and automate local criminal records information systems to comply with provisions of the Brady Act. This is a major reason why the NCHIP program described above was created. NCHIP was an excellent example of "action planning." Without this enabling legislation and funding, problems in gaining state compliance with the new Act could have been insurmountable. Similarly, the FIST program was needed to monitor implementation of the Act over time.

On November 27, 1998, ATF issued an FAQ (frequently asked questions) sheet addressing 68 specific questions about who was responsible for doing exactly what under the new provisions of the Act.[7] Twenty examples are provided below.

1. **Q. What is "permanent Brady"?**
   A. The term "permanent Brady" refers to the permanent provisions of the Brady law, found in section 922(t) of the Gun Control Act.

2. **Q. Does permanent Brady require a 5-day waiting period before a firearm can be transferred?**
   A. No. Instead of waiting 5 days for a background check through a local law enforcement officer, licensees will initiate a background check through the National Instant Criminal Background Check System (NICS). For the most part, these background checks will be immediate. In some circumstances, however, licensees will have to wait up to three business days before getting a response from NICS.

---

[5]   Bowling, M., G. Lauver, M.J. Hickman, and D.B. Adams (2003). *Background Checks for Firearm Transfers, 2002.* (NCJ 200116). Washington, DC: U.S. Department of Justice, Office of Justice Programs, Bureau of Justice Statistics.

[6]   The full text of 68 questions and answers can be found at: *http://www.atf.gov/firearms/brady law/q_abrady.htm*

Case Study 5.2, *continued*

3. **Q. Who must comply with the requirements of permanent Brady?**
   A. Federally licensed firearms importers, manufacturers, and dealers must comply with permanent Brady prior to the transfer of any firearm to a nonlicensed individual.

4. **Q. When do the provisions of permanent Brady take effect?**
   A. Permanent Brady goes into effect on November 30, 1998. Accordingly, any transfer occurring on or after November 30, 1998, is subject to the requirements of permanent Brady.

5. **Q. Is NICS operated by ATF?**
   A. No. NICS is operated by the Federal Bureau of Investigation (FBI).

6. **Q. Do all NICS checks go through the FBI's NICS Operations Center?**
   A. No. In many States, licensees will initiate NICS checks through the State Point of Contact (POC). In some cases, the State POC is also the agency that does background checks for firearms transactions under State law.

7. **Q. If the State is acting as a POC, does that mean that all NICS checks go through the POC rather than the FBI?**
   A. That depends on the State. In some States, the POC will conduct background checks for all firearms transactions. In other States, licensees must contact the POC for handgun transactions and the FBI for long gun transactions. In some States, NICS checks for pawn redemptions will be handled by the FBI.

8. **Q. How does a licensee know whether to contact the FBI or a State POC in order to initiate a NICS check?**
   A. Prior to November 30, 1998, ATF sent an open letter to licensees in each State, providing the licensees with instructions as to how to initiate a NICS check in their State.

9. **Q. Is there a charge for NICS checks?**
   A. The FBI will not charge a fee for conducting NICS checks. However, States who act as POCs may charge a fee consistent with State law.

10. **Q. Must licensees enroll with the FBI to get access to NICS?**
    A. Licensees must be enrolled with the FBI before they can initiate NICS checks through the FBI's NICS Operations Center. Licensees who have not received an enrollment package from the FBI should call the FBI NICS Operations Center at 1-877-444-6427 and ask that an enrollment package be sent to them. Licensees in States where a State agency is acting as a POC should contact the State for enrollment information.

Case Study 5.2, *continued*

11. **Q. Does permanent Brady apply to the transfer of long guns as well as handguns?**
    A. Yes.

12. **Q. Does permanent Brady apply to the transfer of antique firearms?**
    A. No. Licensees need not comply with permanent Brady when transferring a weapon that meets the Gun Control Act's definition of an "antique firearm."

13. **Q. Does permanent Brady apply to the transfer of firearms between two licensees?**
    A. No. Permanent Brady only applies when a licensed importer, manufacturer, or dealer is transferring a firearm to a nonlicensee.

14. **Q. Must licensed collectors comply with the Brady law prior to transferring a curio or relic firearm?**
    A. No. Transfers of curio or relic firearms made by licensed collectors are not subject to the requirements of the Brady law.

15. **Q. Is the transfer of a firearm by a licensed dealer to a licensed collector subject to the Brady law?**
    A. The Brady law does not apply to the transfer of a curio or relic firearm to a licensed collector. However, a licensed collector who acquires a firearm other than a curio or relic firearm from a licensee would be treated like any other nonlicensee, and the transfer would be subject to Brady requirements.

16. **Q. Must a licensed importer, manufacturer or dealer comply with the Brady law when selling firearms from his or her own personal collection?**
    A. No, provided the licensee has maintained the firearm as part of his or her personal collection for at least one year.

17. **Q. Do the provisions of permanent Brady apply to a licensee's loan or rental of a firearm to a nonlicensee?**
    A. If the firearm is loaned or rented for use on the licensee's premises, the transaction is not subject to the Brady law. However, if the firearm is loaned or rented for use off the premises, the licensee must comply with permanent Brady.

18. **Q. Must licensees conduct NICS checks for sales of firearms to nonlicensees at gun shows?**
    A. Yes. A licensee may not transfer a firearm to a nonlicensee at a gun show without first complying with the requirements of permanent Brady.

Case Study 5.2, *continued*

19. **Q. Is the redemption of a pawned firearm subject to permanent Brady?**
A. Yes. Unlike interim Brady, permanent Brady does not contain an exemption for the return of a firearm to the individual from whom it was received. Accordingly, the redemption of a pawned firearm is considered a transfer subject to permanent Brady.

20. **Q. What should a licensed pawnbroker do with a firearm he or she has in pawn when the NICS check results in a "denied" transaction?**
A. The licensee cannot transfer the firearm to the transferee without violating the law and placing the transferee in violation of the law. Licensees with additional questions should contact their local ATF office.

Questions

1. Look at three specific questions and answers about the Brady Act prepared by ATF. (a) Discuss how the "Q & A" format illustrates concepts discussed in this chapter (e.g., see "Developing Mechanisms of Self-Regulation and Managing Resistance and Conflict"). (b) Analyze how adequately the answers provided by ATF address the three questions. Is anything still unclear? Should further difficulties in implementing the Act be anticipated? Why or why not?

2. Read one of the dissenting opinions of the four Supreme Court Justices who opposed the majority decision in *Printz v. the United States*. Dissenting and concurring opinions are available at: *http://supct.law.cornell. edu/supct/html/95-1478.ZS.html*. (a) Identify the judge who wrote the opinion, and summarize his or her arguments in your own words. (b) Do you agree or disagree with those arguments? Why or why not? Provide evidence to support your position.

Endnotes

[1]   For a summary, see: Kettner, Peter M., Robert K. Moroney, and Lawrence L. Martin (1999). *Designing and Managing Programs: An Effectiveness-Based Approach*, 2nd ed. Thousand Oaks, CA: Sage.

[2]   See Chapter 2 for discussion of relevant stakeholders.

[3]   Fisher, R., and W. Ury (1981) *Getting to Yes: Negotiating Agreement Without Giving In*. Boston: Houghton Mifflin.

CHAPTER *6*

Developing a Plan for Monitoring Program/Policy Implementation

CHAPTER OUTLINE

▶ *"Monitoring"* refers to the collection of information to determine to what degree the program or policy design (see Chapter 4) is being carried out as planned. Is the intended target population being reached? Are program/policy activities or provisions actually being carried out as planned? Are appropriate staff or responsible authorities selected and trained, and are they carrying out their assigned duties?

▶ *Design monitoring instruments to collect data* (e.g., observations, surveys, interviews). Data is collected to find out what is actually being delivered to clients or targets. The purpose is to identify gaps between the "program/policy on paper" (design) and the "program/policy in action."

▶ *Designate responsibility for data collection, storage, and analysis*: Ensure that there is no ambiguity about what information is to be collected, who is responsible for collecting it, or how it is to be collected, stored, and analyzed.

▶ *Develop information system capacities.* Information systems may consist of written forms and records that are filed, or fully computerized data entry and storage systems.

▶ *Develop mechanisms to provide feedback to staff, clients, and stakeholders.* Depending on the results of monitoring analyses, it may be necessary to make adjustments either to what is being done ("the program or policy in action") or to the intended design ("the program or policy on paper").

At a designated point in time, as specified in the action plan, it will be time to begin program or policy operations by following the sequence of steps specified in the action plan. At this point, before continuing the planning process, we need to develop a strategy to observe the program or policy in action. History has taught us well that good intentions alone are insufficient: we cannot assume that everything planned will actually be done. The example below illustrates the all-too-frequent gap between intentions and actions.

Example 6.1

Is "Weed and Seed" Bearing Fruit?

Initiated in 1991, Operation Weed and Seed now includes 200 sites nationwide. Operation Weed and Seed is a federally funded strategy to mobilize and coordinate anti-drug resources in high-crime communities. Four key components are included:[1]

1. **Weeding:** Concentrated and enhanced law enforcement efforts to identify, arrest, and prosecute violent offenders, drug traffickers, and other criminals operating in the target areas.

2. **Seeding:** Human services, including after-school, weekend, and summer youth activities; adult literacy classes; parental counseling; and neighborhood revitalization efforts to prevent and deter further crime.

3. **Enhanced Coordination:** Coordinated analysis of local problems and developing strategies to address them. The federal oversight responsibility for each participating site rests with the U.S. Attorney's Office for the corresponding district.

4. **Community Policing:** Proactive police/community engagement and problem solving in which police officers are assigned to specified geographic locations. This effort is seen as the bridge between weeding and seeding. By gaining the trust and support of the community, police engage residents and businesses as problem-solving partners in the law enforcement effort (e.g., Neighborhood Watch, citizen marches and rallies, and graffiti removal).

A national evaluation of eight cities examined program implementation and effects on crime and public safety.[2] Each site had high rates of violent crime related to drug trafficking and drug use. The study included a review of funding applications and other program documents; interviews with key program administrators, senior law enforcement staff, managers of seeding activities, service providers, and community leaders; analyses of automated, incident-level records of crimes and arrests; group interviews with participants in seeding programs; and two surveys of residents in target areas.

Example 6.1, *continued*

Developing appropriate seeding strategies in specific communities proved to be more difficult than anticipated. Seeding efforts (e.g., youth prevention and recreation programs, family support services, community economic development) required participation and commitment from many diverse organizations with many different goals. Community participants discovered that much more time was needed for planning, relationship building, and gaining consensus and commitment. Weeding, in contrast, had a relatively clear mission and was carried out within the more established structures of law enforcement and criminal justice.

Within the target areas of each site, evaluators compared Part 1 crime trends for the year prior to implementation of Weed and Seed and the second year after Weed and Seed began. Five target areas had double-digit percentage decreases: (Stowe Village in Hartford, 46%; Crawford-Roberts in Pittsburgh, 24%; North Manatee, 18%; the Shreveport target area, 11%; and the Central District in Seattle, 10%). One target area (West Las Vegas) had a single-digit decrease (6%), and three target areas experienced increases in Part 1 crime (South Manatee, 2%; Meadows Village in Las Vegas, 9%; and Salt Lake City, 14%).

Because a controlled experimental study was not possible, researchers could not state definitively the extent to which Weed and Seed or other factors contributed to observed changes in crime. Available evidence, however, suggested that Weed and Seed had little effect on crime rates. Crime rates in the surrounding (nontarget) areas mirrored increases or decreases in the target areas. For example, Hartford and Pittsburgh achieved the largest Part 1 crime decreases in their target areas, but they also experienced the largest Part 1 crime decreases in nontarget areas (i.e., areas where there was no intervention).

Changes in drug arrest rates appeared to be associated with changes in the overall Part 1 crime rates. Among six target areas for which arrest data were available, the four areas reporting decreases in Part 1 crime from the year prior to Weed and Seed through the second year of implementation (Hartford, Pittsburgh, North Manatee, and Shreveport) all experienced initial high rates of drug arrests, suggesting an initial period of intense weeding activities followed by declining drug arrest rates. Assuming that levels of law enforcement remained somewhat constant, this trend may reflect some success in reducing drug activity.

Participant interviews and community surveys were also conducted. According to the residents interviewed, the seeding programs provided services that otherwise would not have been available in the target areas. Most of those interviewed indicated that participation in the seeding programs was a positive experience that helped them feel more secure emotionally, physically, or both. Benefits perceived by participants included providing additional structure and discipline in the lives of target area youths, and opportunities and assistance for adults to work toward personal and professional growth.

Community surveys, however, suggested inconsistent effects. Residents in only two areas (Manatee and Pittsburgh) perceived substantial improvements in police effectiveness and decreases in crime severity. Residents in Akron

---

Example 6.1, *continued*

and Seattle perceived slight reductions in drug-related crime; Hartford residents perceived some reduction in violent and gang-related crime. Residents in three areas (Las Vegas, Salt Lake City, and Shreveport) perceived little improvement in general public safety or the severity of specific types of crime.

In sum, the implementation and effectiveness of weeding and seeding activities varied considerably across the eight sites. Pre-existing community features (e.g., community cohesion) likely played a key role in enhancing or weakening Weed and Seed efforts. Important factors included the strength of the existing social and institutional infrastructure (e.g., an established network of community-based organizations and community leaders), the severity of crime problems, geographical advantages favoring economic development, and transience of the population. Finding the appropriate mix and sequence of "weeding" and "seeding" activities for specific communities remains a compelling challenge.

Before we continue, it is useful to distinguish implementation from monitoring.

Previously, in the design stage (see Chapter 4), we talked about *identifying* "who does what to whom in what order, how much, and how often?" Now at the monitoring stage, we are concerned with finding out whether the intended design has been properly implemented. How do we measure whether implementation succeeded? Monitoring, as we will see shortly, requires ongoing data collection throughout the life of the program or policy.

Implementation

Implementation is the initiation, management, and administration of the action plan (see Chapter 5). Once the program or policy actually begins, we want to minimize discrepancies between what was planned (i.e., the program or policy design) and what was actually done (i.e., the "program *or* policy in action").

Monitoring

Monitoring is an attempt to determine whether program or policy implementation is proceeding as planned. It is a process that attempts to identify any gaps between the program or policy on paper (design) and the program or policy in action (implementation).

At the monitoring stage, then, we attempt to find out if the program or policy was implemented properly. Sometimes called "process evaluation," *monitoring* refers to the collection of information to determine to what degree the design or blueprint (the program or policy "on paper") is being carried out as planned. Data (e.g., observations, surveys, interviews) are collected to find out what is actually being delivered to clients (the program or policy in action). Adjustments will then need to be made to revise either the design of the intervention (e.g., either service delivery or policy provisions) or to make what is currently being done conform to the intended design.

Outline the Major Questions for Monitoring

Monitoring relates directly back to the design stage (see Chapter 4). How do we measure whether the critical elements of program or policy design have been implemented properly? We can specify all the key questions for monitoring in terms of their corresponding program or policy design features.

Figure 6.1

Target Population

- What are the characteristics of the actual persons targeted by the program or policy? Are appropriate targets selected?

- Is the program or policy meeting its specified criteria in terms of client eligibility (e.g., age, sex, income, region, etc.) and numbers to be served?

- Are proper target recruiting, referral, screening, and intake procedures followed? How are target selection decisions made?

Figure 6.2

Program Components or Policy Provisions

- *Who did what to whom in what order, how much, and how often?* We need to identify some unit of measuring what was done. In a drug treatment program, for example, one way of measuring services delivered to clients is to record the total hours of counseling that are actually delivered to clients. We could also measure the number of clients admitted, attendance at regular program sessions (e.g., group meetings), and the number of clients who successfully completed a program. For three-strikes laws, in addition to describing the rules for charging and processing suspects, we could count the number of people charged and convicted.

- *Were there variations in how program services or policy provisions were delivered?* In a program, for example, did one client receive different amounts or types of services than another (e.g., frequency or quality of treatment)? Was there more than one site or location where a program or policy was carried out, and if so, were services administered consistently across different sites? Within a state, for example, were courts in some cities or counties more active than others in charging under three-strikes provisions?

Figure 6.3

Program Staff or Individuals Designated to Implement the Policy

- *For a program*: Are proper staff selected and trained? Do they fit the specified job descriptions? Do staff understand their duties and perform them as expected? Do different program staff provide services in a different manner?

- *For a policy*: Have the individuals responsible for carrying out a policy been clearly identified? Do they understand the policy and their specific responsibilities? Are proper procedures for implementing a specific policy being consistently followed by the designated authorities? Do different policy authorities implement the same rule differently?

We can illustrate the correspondence between program or policy design and monitoring by referring to the chart in Figure 6.4, and we can easily see what kinds of questions we need to ask. In Column 1, we summarize all the key design features in terms of targets, staff, or responsible authority, and program components or policy provisions. We should have all this information available from our previous assessment of program or policy design (see Chapter 4). Then, as Column 2 indicates, we need some method of collecting data (to be discussed shortly) to find out whether intended design features were properly implemented. In Column 3, we report the results of monitoring: How was the program or policy actually implemented? Finally, in Column 4, we summarize any gaps detected between program or policy design and implementation (compare Column 1 with Column 3). Information collected from monitoring analysis is vital for modifying the program or policy to correct any implementation gaps detected.

Design Instruments to Collect Monitoring Data

There are four major data collection techniques for monitoring:[3] (1) observational data, (2) service records (documents), (3) service provider data (staff), and (4) participant data (targets). Wherever possible, it is best to use more than one technique, and, depending on the time and resources available, as many as possible. Each has its advantages and limitations.

Figure 6.4

Monitoring Analysis

	1. **What was intended?** (i.e., the program or policy on paper, the design of the program or policy).	2. **How was monitoring done?** (i.e., which of the four data collection methods were used?)	3. **What were the results of monitoring?** (i.e., how was the program or policy actually implemented?)	3. **What gaps were found** between the program or policy on paper (design) and the program or policy in action (implementation)?
Targets (e.g., eligibility, numbers to be served, access, screening, intake).				
Program Staff or Individuals Responsible for Implementing the Program or Policy (e.g., selection, training, duties).				
Program Components or Policy Provisions (e.g., specific goods, services, opportunities, or interventions to be delivered).				

Observational Data

Observational data may provide a rich and detailed source of information about program activities and policy provisions. By observational data, we mean that evaluators and/or trained observers actually participate in or observe the program or policy in operation. For example, in the classic Minneapolis Domestic Violence Experiment,[4] trained observers rode along in police cars to observe how police handled domestic violence calls and to determine whether they followed agreed-upon procedures for administering one of three interventions (arrest, mediation, or separation). Good observational data is rarely obtained simply by "hanging out" at the program or policy site. Observers must be trained in how to make observations and how to record their observations. We need some systematic method for making and recording observations. Three main observational techniques are possible: (1) the narrative method, (2) the data guide method, and (3) the structured rating scheme.[5]

Narrative Method

When using the *narrative method*, an observer records events in detail, in the order in which they occur. This is very much like a diary. It is the least structured of the three observational methods, but it may provide rich detail on implementation. The observer describes what services were provided, how the clients reacted, how the staff acted, and so on.

Data Guide

In the *data guide method*, the evaluator or change agent gives observers specific questions that they are required to answer from their observations. This technique is more structured than the narrative method but less structured than the structured rating scheme. For example, observers may go out with police to observe DUI stops. Observers are given a list of questions that they attempt to answer for each stop:

- How did police officers select the vehicle for a DUI check?
- How many people were in the car?
- What kind of car was it (model, year)?
- Describe the driver (age, sex, race).

- Was the suspect: respectful? cooperative?

- Was the officer respectful? Did the officer explain the purpose of the stop?

- What police action was taken? (e.g., sobriety test, Breathalyzer, warning, other, none?)

- Did anything unusual or significant happen during this stop?

Structured Rating Scheme

The structured rating scheme is the most structured of the three observational methods. We can ask observers to rate some kind of behavior on a standardized scale or checklist. Using the same example as above, where observers go out on police DUI stops, the observer may be given a checklist that he or she completes for every police stop. The checklist may contain items such as those in Figure 6.5.

Figure 6.5

Observer Checklist for DUI Stops

Name of observer: _____

Date and time of DUI stop: _____

Type of vehicle: _____

Observer Instructions: Rate the behavior of the suspect and the police officer on the five-point scales provided below. Circle the number that best fits your perception of what happened.

1. The suspect was:
         1   2   3   4   5
         polite   abusive

2. The police officer was:
         1   2   3   4   5
         polite   abusive

3. The police instructions were:
         1   2   3   4   5
         clear   vague

4. Action taken (check one):

   _____ Field sobriety test

   _____ Breathalyzer

   _____ Warning

   _____ No action taken

   _____ Other (Please specify: _____)

In general, the major advantage of observational methods lies in the first-hand description of program activities that observers can provide. The major problem with these techniques is that the presence of observers may actually alter the behavior of program personnel or participants. Might police officers, for example, be more guarded in their speech and actions when they know a civilian observer is watching them? A less frequent, but not unusual, problem is that observers may not report or record information consistently or accurately. The less structured the observational scheme is (e.g., the narrative method), the greater the concerns with observer reliability and subjectivity.

Service Record Data

Service record data refers to written, typed, or computerized records that are kept by staff. Many programs require staff to collect certain information on program clients, service delivery, and staff duties. One simple example is program attendance data: staff may be required to record whether clients are absent or present for scheduled meetings, or they may be required to record the total number of hours each client participates in the program. As a graduate student, the first author once worked at a federal forensic prison in Canada. This facility provided psychological assessments for the courts and treatment services for convicted offenders. Because the facility was an accredited hospital, as well as a prison, medical records had to be kept. Staff (e.g., psychiatric nurses, psychologists, psychiatrists, and research staff) were required to make an entry in a medical records binder each time they visited a prisoner, describing the purpose of the visit, the length of the visit, what happened, the client's state of mind, and whether any action was taken with that client. In general, for many programs, we could ask program staff to make regular entries in a logbook describing what they did with each client, how much time they spent on different activities, and so on. These records, depending upon their complexity and reliability, may provide a good source of monitoring information.

Service record data have at least two advantages: such data is (1) inexpensive, and (2) easily obtainable. However, service record data also present two common disadvantages: (1) program records may not contain sufficient information needed to monitor clients and the services provided adequately; and (2) staff may not record this information consistently, accurately, or completely. There may be sizable gaps in the information that is actually recorded. There are three possible solutions to these problems: (1) seek participation by staff in developing monitoring instruments, (2) train staff in how to use these instruments, and (3) conduct regular quality-control checks to make sure that records are being kept properly. There are three key guidelines for using service record data:

1. It is better to gather a few items of data consistently and reliably than to gather a lot of data poorly.

2. Recording forms should be structured as checklists whenever possible to simplify usage by program staff.

3. Service records should be checked immediately after completion for consistency and accuracy. Checks should be conducted on a regular basis, and corrective feedback should be given to staff as needed.

Service Provider Data

Service provider data refers to information that the evaluator or change agent obtains from program or agency staff members directly. As opposed to service records, for example, we could ask staff about the specific activities and services being provided. We could ask them whether client participation was high or low, how much time was spent on different activities, how clients responded, and so on. We could use relatively informal or more structured interviews to obtain staff perceptions, or we could use questionnaires or surveys. The major advantage of this technique is that program or agency staff have regular involvement in the intervention, and they can often provide detailed, first-hand experience and knowledge. The major problem is potential subjectivity: program staff or policy authorities may answer questions so as to make themselves or the program/policy look good. Staff may also dislike the extra time or work required by this method (e.g., more paperwork), so the researcher or change agent must make sure that the information provided by staff is not incomplete or inaccurate.

Participant Data

Participant data refers to information that the evaluator or change agent obtains from clients or targets directly. Too often, client perceptions of interventions are ignored. It is important to get clients' perceptions not only of what services were actually delivered, but often their degree of satisfaction with program services or policy provisions. In asking about services provided by a DARE (Drug Awareness Resistance Education) program, for example, we might ask participants whether the information they received was understood and whether the information was utilized (e.g., were students less likely to use drugs as a result of participating in the program?). Evidence has suggested that information provided by DARE programs may be well understood but rarely utilized.[6]

As was the case with measuring staff perceptions of program services, we can assess client perceptions by using questionnaires and/or interviews. The advantages of obtaining client perceptions are that clients have abundant first-hand experience with program or policy services, and they are the only ones who can provide the perspective of the intended targets of change. Disadvantages to be considered are possible subjectivity (clients or targets may want to make the intervention look either "good" or "bad" depending on their personal experience and possible mistrust of unfamiliar evaluators or "outsiders." It takes some skill to get valid responses from participants, but these problems are by no means insurmountable.

Designate Responsibility to Collect, Store, and Analyze Data

We emphasize that monitoring requires collecting information. What this usually means more work for program or agency staff, on top of their service delivery duties. Such information is indispensable, however, and no program or agency can survive or grow without it. For example, all programs need to record some basic information for accountability purposes. Examples might include the number of contacts made with clients in an intensive supervision probation program, the number of hours of participation in an after-school delinquency prevention program, or weekly attendance at group counseling sessions in a substance abuse program.

In the authors' work with nonprofit groups and criminal justice agencies, we have often found that funding agencies or program supervisors do not always clearly communicate or emphasize the information reporting requirements for programs, and we have found that staff who have been assigned the responsibility for collecting monitoring data often lack the training, skills, and time needed to fulfill such tasks. These are not excuses. The program manager or director bears full responsibility to make sure that certain information is recorded consistently and accurately. Expect that stakeholders will want regular reports on the numbers and characteristics of clients served, their level of need, their progress and participation in the program, and, eventually, their outcomes.

Someone must take responsibility to ensure that the job gets done. If the program manager assigns responsibility to staff to undertake these tasks, he or she is also responsible to make sure that it gets done. If there is any ambiguity at all about what information is to be collected, who is responsible for collecting it, or how it is to be collected, recorded, and stored, the program manager must alleviate any such ambiguities before the program or policy begins operations. If such gaps are detected afterwards, they must be filled. The risk of not taking such "mundane" considerations seriously is the potential death of the program or policy when those funding it or authorizing it lose faith in it.

Develop Information System Capacities

A good information system can serve several purposes. First and foremost, a good information system can demonstrate accountability to funding agents, the community, and other stakeholders who may provide either critical support or resistance. A good information system is also useful for planning: it allows program managers or policy authorities to see how well plans are going and what problems emerge, and then make decisions about adjustments. A useful information system allows for continuous monitoring over time: it is sensitive to both intended and unintended changes in program or policy design.

Information Systems

Information systems are ongoing methods of collecting data about clients, staff, and program or policy activities. They may consist of written forms and records that are filed, or fully computerized data entry and storage systems.

Several guidelines should facilitate the development of a useful information system. First, it is vital to gain staff acceptance. Extra paperwork is unwelcome unless you can show that it provides meaningful and useful information. For example, staff may be more receptive to doing the work if they find out that they receive useful feedback about client performance, program services, and their own performance. Cost is another consideration. Even printing new forms can be expensive for a small, nonprofit agency. Certainly purchasing new computers or setting up a coordinated computer network can be very expensive. The bigger the agency and the greater the number of clients, however, the greater the likelihood that more sophisticated information storage systems are needed. Greater needs are also implied by detailed and regular client assessment and re-assessment procedures (e.g., risk and needs classifications of ex-offenders), and sophisticated, multiple services provided to a diverse clientele. We should also consider compatibility. What information is already being collected? Can current information systems be modified somewhat, rather than designing a brand new information system? Safeguarding of information is important. In a delinquency prevention program, for example, staff need to protect the identity of the juvenile. To assess a juvenile's needs adequately, however, the program must gather sensitive information about the juvenile's previous criminal record and his or her current school performance. Strict procedures must be developed for handling, using, and storing such information (see Case Study 7.1). In general, training of staff is essential if good information is to be collected. One should never simply hand someone a package of forms and say that instructions are enclosed. Make sure that staff members understand what is being asked of them. Consider these guidelines as you read Case Study 6.3.

Develop Mechanisms to Provide Feedback to Stakeholders

Finally, make plans for how monitoring information is to be used. The change agent should identify the appropriate stakeholders (e.g., program clients, staff, other agencies, legislators, funding agencies, community representatives), and schedule individual and/or group meetings to communicate results. Some reporting, particularly to funding agencies, will come in the form of program reports or research reports. Wherever gaps are detected, corrective action should be discussed and implemented. The bottom line is that any effective organization—private, public, or nonprofit—requires monitoring information on a regular basis to figure out how well it is doing. Can you imagine an effective business that examines its sales only once a year? A stock market that reports transactions only once a month? A television network that examines ratings only at the end of the season? Ignoring monitoring is not good business. Extreme cases of inattention are likely to be fatal to the program or policy.

Conclusion

Monitoring is a process that attempts to identify any gaps between the program or policy on paper (design) and the program or policy in action (implementation). We can specify all the key questions for monitoring in terms of corresponding program or policy design features: what was intended in terms of targets, staff, and program/policy services? Second, how do we collect data to determine the degree to which these design features are actually being implemented? Third, what gaps exist (if any) between the program or policy on paper, and the program or policy in action? Where gaps are found, adjustments must be made: either the design (the program or policy on paper) must change, or the way the program or policy is being implemented (the program or policy in action) must change.

We emphasize that the purpose of monitoring is not simply to ensure compliance with the original program or policy design. There is always some drift between the original design and actual implementation of any program or policy. Over time, as conditions in the environment change, and as unanticipated difficulties emerge, modifications to the original design are inevitably made. Leadership changes, staff persons come and go, and services are altered. Sometimes these changes are necessary and for the better. What we are seeking, after all, is better programs and policies, not blind obedience to a piece of paper. If monitoring is timely and consistent, we can observe these changes in program or policy design can be observed and explicit, intentional decisions can be made about whether to adopt certain changes.

Consider this example. A residential drug treatment program's funding from the county is in jeopardy because it is serving too few clients with serious drug abuse problems. Monitoring data has indicated that the staff persons responsible for client intake have been turning away seriously addicted clients because they are too disruptive. Different options are possible. First, less stringent client eligibility criteria might be adopted to maintain funding levels. Alternatively, the program may seek funding from a different sponsor that will be more sympathetic to their existing client selection and treatment procedures. In the first case, changes in client selection (e.g., more clients with more serious drug abuse problems) will also necessitate changes in program design (e.g., type of counseling and total hours of counseling needed for seriously addicted clients). In the second case, changes in program funding may affect the program's entire mission and goals. We emphasize: Any deviations from the original program or policy design should be consciously intended, explicit, and visible. Monitoring facilitates deliberate decisions about program or policy design and helps prevent unintended or invisible "drift."

Monitoring provides essential, continuous information that can be used to satisfy accountability requirements, improve program services or policy implementation on a regular basis, and move toward desired outcomes. As we will see in the next chapter, thorough monitoring should precede and accompany any valid evaluation of a program or policy. Though the two are linked, monitoring more closely emphasizes process; evaluation emphasizes outcome.

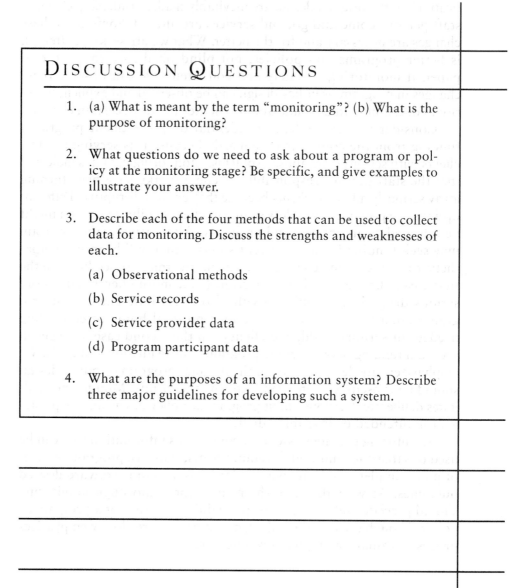

DISCUSSION QUESTIONS

1. (a) What is meant by the term "monitoring"? (b) What is the purpose of monitoring?

2. What questions do we need to ask about a program or policy at the monitoring stage? Be specific, and give examples to illustrate your answer.

3. Describe each of the four methods that can be used to collect data for monitoring. Discuss the strengths and weaknesses of each.

    (a) Observational methods

    (b) Service records

    (c) Service provider data

    (d) Program participant data

4. What are the purposes of an information system? Describe three major guidelines for developing such a system.

Exercise 6.1

Read the SEARCH report, *Drug Court Monitoring, Evaluation, and Management Information Systems*,[7] or read a different one assigned by your instructor. Complete a monitoring analysis by using the Monitoring Analysis Chart as a guide (see Figure 6.1).

Case Study 6.1

Program Monitoring: The Correctional Program Assessment Inventory (CPAI)

Professors Don Andrews and Paul Gendreau have inquired extensively into the characteristics of effective correctional treatment programs and how those characteristics can effectively be shaped to improve treatment outcomes. This approach is based upon empirical evidence that rehabilitation *is* sometimes effective, at least with certain offenders under certain circumstances. Following a review of relevant outcome literature, and using a technique called meta-analysis, they examined the average "effect size" produced by different programs with different characteristics. They wanted to know what the characteristics of "effective" programs are (i.e., programs that have produced larger than average decreases in reoffending)? Their argument is simple but convincing: there are identifiable characteristics of effective programs that can be assessed and adjusted so as to improve the achievement of program outcomes (e.g., reduction of recidivism). According to Andrews et al., effective programs evidence the principles of risk, need, and responsivity.[1]

1. *Risk:* Effective programs clearly differentiate between low-risk and high-risk clients. The largest effects on recidivism are likely to be achieved by targeting high-risk rather than low-risk offenders. High-risk cases should receive high levels of intervention and services; low-risk cases should receive minimal intervention.

2. *Needs:* Criminogenic needs are dynamic (i.e., changing) risk factors that are predictive of recidivism (e.g., antisocial cognitions and emotional states, association with antisocial peers, substance abuse, weak self-control, and problem solving skills). Programs that effectively target and reduce such individual needs accomplish larger decreases in reoffending.

3. *Responsivity:* Programs that *appropriately* target the specific needs and learning styles of their clients are more effective. For example, clients who are interpersonally and cognitively immature require more structured services, but more mature clients benefit from more flexible approaches. Andrews et al. argue that the

---

[1]   Andrews, Donald, Ivan Zinger, Robert D. Hoge, James Bonta, Paul Gendreau, and Francis T. Cullen (1990). "Does Correctional Treatment Work? A Clinically Relevant and Psychologically Informed Meta-Analysis." *Criminology* 28:369-404; see also: Cullen, Francis, and Paul Gendreau (2000). "Assessing Correctional Rehabilitation: Policy, Practice and Prospects." In J. Horney (ed.), *Criminal Justice 2000, Volume 3*, pp. 109-175. Washington, DC: U.S. Department of Justice, Office of Justice Programs, National Institute of Justice (NCJ-182410). Available at: *http://www.ojp.usdoj.gov/nij/criminal_justice2000/vol3_2000.html* (retrieved March 12, 2004).

Case Study 6.1, *continued*

most effective styles of treatment have been cognitive-behavioral and social learning strategies that focus on skill development in a variety of areas. Conversely, programs that incorrectly target the criminogenic needs of their clients may actually increase rather than decrease re-offending.

The Correctional Program Assessment Inventory (CPAI) was designed to assess, in a fairly structured and objective manner, the degree to which a program has been adequately designed and implemented. It is sensitive to the three principles of risk, need, and responsivity derived from empirical research. The instrument is still being developed and studied, but it has demonstrated its usefulness in a wide variety of correctional settings so far.[2] The CPAI assesses a specific program by tabulating the presence, number, and variety of the best-validated elements of effective correctional programs. There are six primary sections of the CPAI:

1. *Program implementation*: This section assesses the qualifications and involvement of the program director, the extent to which the treatment literature was considered in the program design, and whether the program is consistent with existing values in the community, meets a local need, and is perceived to be cost-effective.

2. *Client pre-service assessment*: This section examines the program's offender selection and assessment processes to ascertain the extent to which clients are appropriate for the services provided. It also addresses the methods for assessing risk, need, and responsivity factors.

3. *Characteristics of the program*: This section examines whether the program is targeting criminogenic attitudes and behaviors, the specific treatment modalities employed, the use of rewards and punishments, and the methods used to prepare the offender for release from the program.

4. *Characteristics and practices of the staff*: This section identifies the qualifications, experience, stability, training, and involvement of the program staff.

---

[2] Andrews, D. A. (1995) *Assessing Program Elements for Risk Reduction: The Correctional Program Assessment Inventory (CPAI)*. Paper presented at the "Research to Results" conference, sponsored by IARCA, Ottawa, Canada, October 11-14, 1995; Gendreau, P., and D.A. Andrews (1994). *Correctional Program Assessment Inventory*, 4th ed. St. John, New Brunswick: University of New Brunswick.

Case Study 6.1, *continued*

5. *Evaluation*: This section centers on the types of feedback, assessment, and evaluations used to monitor how well the program is functioning.

6. *Miscellaneous*: This final section of the CPAI includes miscellaneous items pertaining to levels of funding and community support for the program.

Each section of the CPAI consists of six to 26 items for a total of 77 items designed to operationalize the principles of effective intervention. The number of items in each section represents the weight given to that particular section relative to the other sections of the instrument. Each item is scored as "1" or "0." To receive a "1" programs must demonstrate that they meet the specified criteria (e.g., the director is involved in some aspect of direct service delivery to clients; client risk of recidivism is assessed through a standardized, quantifiable measure).

Based on the number of points earned, each section is scored as either "very satisfactory" (70% to 100%); "satisfactory" (60% to 69%); "satisfactory, but needs improvement" (50% to 59%); or "unsatisfactory" (less than 50%). The scores from all six areas are totaled and the same scale is used for the overall assessment score. Some items may be considered "not applicable," in which case they are not included in the scoring. Data for the CPAI are gathered through structured interviews with program staff at each of the sites. Other sources of information include the examination of program documentation, the review of representative case files, and some observation of program activities. As you read the example below, think of the basic elements of program design and monitoring discussed in Chapters 4 and 6, and note how the CPAI assesses critical features of program design.

Example: The MonDay Community Correctional Institution. The MonDay Community Correctional Institution (MonDay), located in Dayton, Ohio, is a state-funded, community-based facility for both male and female felony offenders. Offenders are sentenced to MonDay in lieu of prison for a period not to exceed six months. In October 1997, MonDay was awarded a federal grant for the purpose of implementing a Residential Substance Abuse Treatment Program (RSAT). Thirty beds (20 male and 10 female) were designated as RSAT beds for offenders identified as needing long-term residential treatment. In conjunction with the RSAT grant, MonDay developed a Therapeutic Community (TC) that was fully implemented by January 1, 1998. The University of Cincinnati conducted a process evaluation that included a CPAI assessment.[3]

---

[3] Betsy Fulton, E. Latessa, and J. Pealer (2001). *MonDay Community Correctional Institution: RSAT Process Evaluation, Final Report.* [Online] Available at: *http://www.ncjrs.org/pdffiles1/ nij/grants/188871.pdf* (retrieved September 6, 2004).

Case Study 6.1, *continued*

The average overall CPAI score for 150 programs across the United States was 54.4; MonDay's RSAT program scored a commendable 74.2 percent (Figure 6.6). The following areas were identified as program strengths:

- Both the Program Director and the Clinical Director have extensive experience working with offender populations and the requisite educational background. Both have been intricately involved in all aspects of program development. The program development process was extremely thorough and included a comprehensive literature review, a formal pilot period, and a needs assessment that identified many offenders in need of long-tern residential treatment.

- A comprehensive screening and assessment process that includes the Level of Service Inventory LSI-R, the ASUS, and a social history interview facilitates the identification of appropriate clients for the RSAT program. Combined, these instruments provide MonDay with a quantifiable measure of client risk and need and a detailed assessment of the offender's substance abuse history.

- The treatment and services offered by MonDay's RSAT program are designed to target criminogenic needs.

- The program is theoretically based: the TC model is rooted in a social learning approach that provides opportunities for modeling and behavioral rehearsal techniques that engender self-efficacy; and the specific treatment groups provided within the TC (e.g., chemical dependency education, relapse prevention, criminal thinking errors, anger management, problem-solving) incorporate a cognitive behavioral approach that aims to challenge antisocial attitudes and develop self-control procedures.

- Close offender monitoring and detailed treatment manuals contribute to the consistency in services and help maintain program integrity.

- Treatment is individualized for the RSAT participants with the duration, intensity, and nature of treatment varying according to the level of client risk and need.

- The RSAT staff are well qualified with appropriate educational backgrounds and licensures. Turnover is low, and staff are involved in program development and modifications.

- MonDay has several mechanisms in place to monitor how well the program is functioning. First, ongoing quality assurance mechanisms include file reviews, group observation, and client satis-

Case Study 6.1, *continued*

faction surveys. Second, client progress in treatment is monitored during treatment team meetings and through a reassessment of client risk using the LSI-R. Third, MonDay is participating in an outcome evaluation of RSAT that incorporates a quasi-experimental design.

The following areas were identified as needing improvement:

- The clinical director is not systematically involved in the delivery of direct services to offenders (e.g., conducting groups, assessing offenders, individual counseling). This is recommended as a means of staying abreast of the challenges faced by staff and clients and the skill level and resources necessary for the effective delivery of services.

- Information regarding responsivity factors, or personal characteristics that may interfere with treatment, were not available to treatment staff for consideration in treatment planning. Assessing and disseminating this type of information facilitates improved treatment matching (e.g., between client and program; between client and staff).

- The MonDay program utilized both rewards and punishments in response to client behavior. These rewards and punishments, however, could be used more systematically to ensure achievement of the recommended ratio of at least four rewards to one punishment and to promote consistency and immediacy in the administration of punishment.

- MonDay has developed specific program completion criteria to guide successful terminations that are based on the acquisition and demonstration of prosocial attitudes, skills, and behaviors. The 180-day maximum stay mandated by the state, however, negates the ability of the program to keep clients who could benefit from a longer stay.

- MonDay does not systematically involve family members or significant others in the offender's treatment.

- Because of the number of different county probation departments responsible for post-release supervision, there is inconsistency in the extent to which aftercare and/or booster sessions are provided to MonDay clients.

Case Study 6.1, *continued*

- Staff training is accomplished primarily through a 40-hour on-the-job orientation. It is recommended that program staff receive three to six months of formal training in theory and practice of interventions employed by the program.

- Although the clinical staff receives group supervision, it is recommended that individualized clinical supervision be provided on a routine basis for the purpose of discussing problem cases and enhancing clinical skills.

CPAI Results of MonDay Correctional Institution Compared to National Average Scores

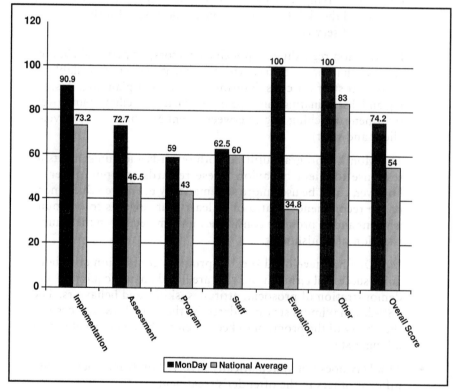

A CPAI assessment provides valuable data for programs to articulate what they are about: for example, who is served, with what intent, in what ways, and with what intermediate and long-term changes expected. Similar to the

Case Study 6.1, *continued*

process of "evaluability assessment,"[4] examination and clarification of program goals and structure can provide valuable learning opportunities for program staff and directors, and can inform useful and necessary program adjustments prior to undertaking formal outcome evaluation (see Chapter 7).

What Andrews, Gendreau, and their colleagues prescribe for correctional programs may be applicable to a wider variety of interventions: drug treatment programs, delinquency prevention programs, counseling programs for domestic violence offenders, and so on. Their approach is based on sound principles of program development, and it utilizes a scientific approach that reduces the subjectivity of judgments about adequate program functioning.

Question

1. Describe how the CPAI assesses basic dimensions of program design and monitoring. Using Figure 6.1 ("Monitoring Analysis") as a guide, briefly describe one example for each of the cells in Column 1 ("what was intended": clients, staff, and program services) and Column 4 ("gaps": clients, staff, and program services).

---

[4] See: Rutman, Leonard (1984). *Planning Useful Evaluations: Evaluability Assessment.* Beverly Hills: Sage; Wholey, J.S. (1994). "Assessing the Feasibility and Likely Usefulness of Evaluation." In J.S. Wholey, H.P. Hatry, and K.E. Newcomer (eds.) (1994), *Handbook of Practical Evaluation* (pp. 15-39). San Francisco: Jossey-Bass.

Case Study 6.2

Monitoring Presale Firearm Checks Under the Brady Act[1]

Instructions: *Read the case study below, and then answer the questions that follow. You will find it helpful to review concepts in Chapter 4 (especially "Designing the Policy") and Chapter 5 (especially Case Study 5.2).*

Recall that the Firearm Inquiry Statistics program (FIST) was established to provide monitoring data on presale firearm checks, as specified by the Brady Act (Case Study 5.2). This type of data collection is essential to planned change. We want to determine the degree to which a policy is actually used and enacted as planned (i.e., the policy as specified "on paper" by the provisions of the Brady Act). We are also interested in the degree to which there are any gaps between what was planned and what was actually done (i.e., the policy "in action").

Highlights of the 2002 Report[2]

- From the inception of the Brady Act on March 1, 1994, to December 31, 2002, nearly 46 million applications for firearm transfers were subject to background checks. About 976,000 applications (2.1%) were rejected.

- Total applications for firearm transfers or permits nationwide decreased 2 percent, from 7,958,000 in 2001 to 7,806,000 in 2002.

- State and local agencies conducted background checks on about half of the applications for firearms transfers or permits in 2002, while the FBI was responsible for the remainder.

- In 2002, 136,000 (1.7%) of approximately 7,806,000 applications for firearm transfers or permits were rejected by the FBI or state and local agencies. This national rejection rate in 2002 declined from 2001 (1.9%).

- The rejection rate for applications checked by the FBI (1.4%) was lower than the rate for checks by state and local agencies (2.1%). Rejection rates for individual state points of contact (POC's) ranged from more than 4 percent to less than 1 percent.

---

[1] Adapted from: Bowling, M., G. Lauver, M.J. Hickman, and D.B. Adams (2003). *Background Checks for Firearm Transfers, 2002* (NCJ 200116). U.S. Department of Justice, Office of Justice Programs, Bureau of Justice Statistics. Available at: *http://www.ojp.usdoj.gov/bjs/pub/pdf/bcft02.pdf*

[2] This report is one in a series. More recent editions may be available. To view a list of all in the series go to *http://www.ojp.usdoj.gov/bjs/pubalp2.htm#bcft*

Case Study 6.2, *continued*

- In 2002, the majority of rejections for state and local agencies (52%) were due to applicants' felony convictions or indictments; about 14 percent were rejected for a domestic violence misdemeanor conviction or restraining order. Other reasons for rejection—including state or local law prohibitions, fugitives, mental illness or disability, drug addiction, juveniles, dishonorable military discharge, and illegal aliens—accounted for the remaining 34 percent.

- Checking agencies reported an estimated 2,000 arrests of persons with outstanding warrants or who submitted false information on an application.

The Brady Handgun Violence Prevention Act (Brady Act) mandates criminal history background checks on persons applying to purchase firearms from federally licensed firearm dealers, Federal Firearm Licensees (FFLs). The permanent provisions of the Brady Act became effective on November 30, 1998. The act established the National Instant Criminal Background Check System (NICS) and required a background check by the Federal Bureau of Investigation (FBI) or a state point of contact (POC) on persons applying to receive firearms from a FFL.

The Bureau of Justice Statistics (BJS) began the Firearm Inquiry Statistics (FIST) program in 1995 to collect information on background checks conducted by state and local agencies. The state and local data—when combined with FBI NICS data—provide national estimates of the total numbers of applications and rejections resulting from the Brady Act and similar state laws. In 2002, FIST collected information from 19 statewide POCs and approximately 700 state and local agencies that conduct their own checks under federal and state laws. The FBI also compiled data on the inquiries or transactions handled by the NICS operations center.[3] Nearly all applications included in the 2002 FIST survey were subject to a NICS check, as well as checks to fulfill any additional state requirements.

Fewer applications were filed in 2002 than in 2001, decreasing from 7,958,000 to 7,806,000, or 2 percent (Table A). Rejections fell from 151,000 in 2001 to 136,000 in 2002, a decrease of 10 percent. In addition to the nearly 4.2 million applications for firearm transfers processed by the FBI in 2002, state and local checking agencies processed 3.6 million applications (see Table B).

---

[3] The number of background checks handled by state POCs as reported in the *National Instant Criminal Background Check System (NICS) 2002 Operations Report*, published in May 2003, may be higher than the estimates reported here because multiple inquiries or transactions for the same application (which may be done at the discretion of the agency) are a normal part of FBI operations. FIST only counts the first of multiple inquiries.

Case Study 6.2, *continued*

When a background check produces evidence of factors that disqualify an applicant from owning a firearm, the application is rejected. In 2002, the FBI rejected 60,739 firearm transfer applications, a 1.4 percent rejection rate, while state and local agencies rejected 75,000, a rate of 2.1 percent. Together, approximately 136,000 firearm transfer applications were rejected in 2002, a rate of 1.7 percent. This overall rate of rejection continued a four-year decline.

Table A
Number of Applications and Estimates of Rejections for Firearm Transfer, 1994-2002

	Number of applications		Rejection Rate
	Received	Rejected	
Total	45,717,000	976,000	2.1%
Interim period	12,740,000	312,000	2.5%
1994[a]	2,483,000	62,000	2.5%
1995	2,706,000	41,000	1.5%
1996	2,593,000	70,000	2.7%
1997	2,574,000	69,000	2.7%
1998[b]	2,384,000	70,000	2.9%
Permanent Brady	32,977,000	664,000	2.0%
1998[c]	893,000	20,000	2.2%
1999	8,621,000	204,000	2.4%
2000	7,699,000	153,000	2.0 %
2001	7,958,000	151,000	1.9%
2002	7,806,000	136,000	1.7%

Note: Counts are rounded. Statistics for national totals from 1999 to 2002 combine FIST estimates of the number of checks and rejections done by state and local agencies and the FBI number of actual transactions and rejections reported by the NICS operations reports. Data through November 29, 1998, are primarily for handguns. For information about FIST estimates before 1999 see *Presale Handgun Checks, the Brady Interim Period, 1994-98* (NCJ 175034). Available at: *http://www.ojp.usdoj.gov/bjs/pub/pdf/phc98.pdf*

[a] March 1 - December 31, 1994.
[b] January 1 - November 29.
[c] November 30 - December 31, 1998. Counts are from the National Instant Criminal Background Check System (NICS) Operations Report (November 30, 1998 - December 31, 1999) and may include multiple transactions for the same application.

Approval Systems

State systems for approval of a prospective firearm purchaser can be classified as "instant approval," "purchase permit," "exempt carry permit," or "other approval" systems.

Instant approval systems. Instant approval (instant check) systems require a seller to transmit the applicant's information to a checking agency by tele-

Case Study 6.2, *continued*

phone or computer. The checking agency is required to respond to the seller at once or as soon as possible (generally within three days). State agencies conducted more than 2.1 million instant checks in 2002. About 48,000 (2.2%) of the applications were rejected (Table B). The FIST survey also included all state permits required to purchase firearms and certain "exempt carry permits" that can be used to make purchases without a background check at the actual time of purchase (federal law does not mandate a permit to purchase firearms).

Table B
FIST Estimates, by Type of Agency and Approval System
and Total FBI Checks, 2002

Type of checks conducted	Applications	Rejections	Rate of rejection
State agencies			
Total	3,004,901	63,939	2.13%
Instant checks	2,153,358	47,613	2.21%
Purchase permits	297,992	6,683	2.24%
Carry permits	176,204	5,332	3.03%
Other approvals	377,347	4,311	1.14%
Local agencies			
Total	672,211	11,295	1.68%
Purchase permits	440,909	7,641	1.73%
Carry permits	181,960	3,211	1.76%
Other approvals	49,342	443	0.90%
Unadjusted state and local total	3,677,112	75,234	2.12%
Adjustment (see note)	(120,213)	—	—
State and local total (FIST)	3,556,899	75,234	2.12%
FBI total	4,248,893	60,739	1.43%
National total (FIST and FBI)	7,806,000	136,000	1.74%

Note: Agencies that conduct checks for exempt carry permits in Alaska, Arkansas, Mississippi, North Dakota, South Carolina, Texas, and Wyoming request that the FBI conduct the background check, but the state agency makes the decision to reject. Thus, the total number of applications in these states is included in the FBI checks, but the number of rejections is included in the state and local checks.

Purchase permit systems. State purchase permit systems require firearm purchasers to obtain, after a background check, a government-issued document (such as a permit, license, identification card, or other document) that must be presented to a seller in order to receive a firearm. Most agencies issuing purchase permits operate under statutes that allow between seven and 30 days to complete a background check. There were 739,000 applications

Case Study 6.2, *continued*

filed for state and local purchase permits in 2002, while 14,000, or about 2 percent, were rejected.

Exempt carry permit systems. An exempt carry permit is not required for purchase but can be used to exempt the holder from a background check at the point of sale. A permit is exempt if it is issued after a check that includes the NICS and meets other requirements of the Brady Act under an ATF ruling. Agencies issuing exempt carry permits access the NICS Index themselves or request a check by sending information to the FBI. In 2002, state agencies received an estimated 176,000 exempt carry permit applications, of which 5,300 (3%) were rejected. Besides the state agencies, local agencies received an additional 182,000 applications for exempt carry permits, an increase of more than 7 percent from 2001. Local agencies rejected about 3,200 applications for exempt carry permits for a rejection rate of 1.7 percent. Nine states reported statewide data on exempt carry permits for 2002.

Other types of approval systems. Other approval systems require a seller to transmit the applicant's information to a checking agency by mail, telephone, or computer. The checking agency is not required to respond immediately but must respond before the end of a state statutory time limit, generally within seven to 10 days. Other types of approval systems processed 427,000 applications in 2002; about 1 percent of them were rejected.

Rejection rates varied for different types of statewide approval systems, with exempt carry permits having the highest rate (3.0%), followed by purchase permits (2.2%), instant checks (2.2%), and other approvals (1.1%).

Analysis of Rejection Rates

Although state points of contact received the majority of applications made to state and local checking agencies, local agencies accepted a significant number. Moreover, rejection rates among state and local checking agencies varied by type and age of approval system.

Statewide Reporting. In 2002 the FIST survey obtained statewide data from 20 NICS points of contact (including Hawaii) and Delaware. The 16 states that provided complete statewide data processed checks for 2.1 million applications in 2002, rejecting 45,000 (see Table C).

Generally, the higher rejection rates occurred in states that implemented an instant approval system on or after the effective date of the Brady Act. These states included Colorado (3.8%), Tennessee (3.3%), and Georgia (2.9%). In each of these states, the rejection rate has been decreasing since the instant check system began operation. Approval systems established before passage of the Brady Act generally had lower rejection rates. In addition to Connecticut, Illinois, and New Jersey, these systems include California (1.1%), Virginia (1.3%), and Wisconsin (1.6%).

Case Study 6.2, *continued*

Table C
Number of Firearm Purchase Applications Received and Rejected
by State Agencies, 2001-2002

	2002			2001			Percent change, 2001-2002	
	Number of applications	Rejections	Rejection rate	Number of applications	Rejections	Rejection rate	Number of Applications	Rejections
All statewide agencies	2,148,773	44,715	2.1%	2,199,890	52,053	2.4%	-2.3%	-14.1%
California	352,425	3,833	1.1	354,202	3,607	1.0	-0.4	6.3
Colorado	138,779	5,315	3.8	145,403	6,705	4.6	-4.6	-20.7
Connecticut[a]	55,216	137	0.2	51,339	170	0.3	7.6	-19.4
Delaware[b]	9,464	407	4.3	9,615	535	5.6	-1.6	-23.9
Florida	266,249	6,331	2.4	275,755	6,873	2.5	-3.4	-7.9
Georgia	189,906	5,456	2.9	209,202	8,545	4.1	-9.2	-36.1
Hawaii[c]	6,990	103	1.5	6,829	134	2.0	2.4	-23.1
Illinois	376,587	7,002	1.9	380,586	5,866	1.5	-1.1	19.4
Purchase permits	225,067	5,695	2.5	222,610	4,616	2.1	1.1	23.4
Instant checks	151,520	1,307	0.9	157,976	1,250	0.8	-4.1	4.6
Nevada	45,593	1,089	2.3%	48,309	1,340	2.8%	-5.6%	-22.6%
New Hampshire[d]	12,752	149	1.2	13,870	165	1.2	-8.1	-9.7
New Jersey	88,038	1,065	1.2	74,060	927	1.3	18.9	17.5
Purchase permits	48,716	993	2.0	38,019	806	2.1	28.1	23.2
Instant checks	39,322	96	0.2	36,041	121	0.3	9.1	-20.7
Oregon	118,023	2,699	2.3	124,754	3,175	2.5	-5.4	-15.8
Tennessee	205,204	6,746	3.3	216,066	9,114	4.2	-5.0	-26.0
Utah[e]	66,100	1,550	2.3	65,696	1,830	2.8	0.6	-15.3
Virginia	187,959	2,363	1.3	192,653	2,612	1.4	-2.4	-9.5
Wisconsin[d]	29,488	474	1.6	31,551	455	1.4	-6.5	4.2

Note: Each of the 16 listed states reported complete statewide data for applications and rejections in 2002. Pennsylvania reported 378,728 instant checks for 2002, but the number rejected is unavailable.

[a] Connecticut, Illinois, and New Jersey conduct checks on permits or identification cards and again at the time of firearm transfer.
[b] Delaware is not a POC for the NICS; dealers must contact the FBI for handgun, rifle, and shotgun checks required by the Brady Act.
[d] Counts in this table include handguns only for these states.
[e] Applications for carry permits are listed separately elsewhere.

Local Reporting. Local agencies mainly conduct checks for purchase and exempt carry permits. In 2002, local agencies received 672,000 applications, of which 11,000 (1.7%) were rejected. Rejection rates varied among local agencies by size of the population served, by the jurisdiction, and by the type of permit. For purchase permits, rejection rates were highest in jurisdictions with populations more than 100,000 and lowest in those with populations under 10,000. Overall, rejection rates in 2002 were higher for purchase permits than for exempt carry permits.

Availability of Records. During 2002, all states maintained databases that recorded felony convictions. Many maintained data on other disqualifying fac-

Case Study 6.2, *continued*

tors such as fugitive status, court restraining orders, mental illness, and domestic violence misdemeanor convictions. States differed in the degree of automation used in record searching and whether records were in a central database or in databases maintained by county courts or other local agencies.

In 2001, states held approximately 63.6 million criminal records on individuals, about 90 percent of which were automated. About 75 percent of automated records were accessible for conducting presale firearm and other background checks. From 1995 to 2001, the number of criminal records accessible for background checks increased 60 percent, about twice the rate of growth in the number of automated records over the same time period.[4]

Checking agencies often encounter delays if they attempt to access records in other jurisdictions. The most frequent delays occur when researching the final disposition of a criminal charge indicated in another jurisdiction's arrest or indictment record. If the final disposition cannot be found during the time allowed for a background check, the agency must decide, based on federal or state law, whether the application will be approved, denied, or delayed pending further research.

The Brady Act allows a transfer to proceed if a disqualifying record is not found within the three-day limit for a NICS check. Some states have laws and regulations that allow their agencies to deny or delay a transfer if an incomplete record is being researched when the time limit expires.

Reasons for Rejection

About 52 percent of rejections for firearm transfer among state and local checking agencies (39,000 applications in 2002) occurred because the applicant had a felony conviction or was under felony indictment (Table D). The second most common reason for rejection was a domestic violence misdemeanor conviction or restraining order (about 14% of rejections or approximately 11,000 applications). A portion of all rejections reported by state and local agencies fall under the categories of state and local law prohibitions (11% of rejections) and mental illness (1.4%).

The FBI reported that 42 percent of their rejections were for felony-related reasons (about 26,000 of the total rejections in 2002). A domestic violence misdemeanor conviction or restraining order was the next most common reason for rejection (nearly 18% or about 11,000 rejections). Drug addiction, fugitive status, and mental illness accounted for smaller proportions of rejections.

---

[4]   See *Improving Criminal History Records for Background Checks*, available at: *http://www.ojp. usdoj.gov/bjs/abstract/ichrbc.htm*

Case Study 6.2, *continued*

Table D
Reasons for Rejection of Firearm Transfer Applications, 1998-2002

	FBI	State and local agencies				
Reason for rejection	**2002**	**2002**	**2001**	**2000**	**1999**	**1998**
Total	100%	100%	100%	100%	100%	100%
Felony indictment/conviction	42.5	51.8	57.7	57.6	72.5	63.3
Domestic violence						
Misdemeanor conviction	12.5	10.4	10.6	8.9	9.0	9.9
Restraining order	5.3	3.5	3.7	3.3	2.1	3.4
State law prohibition	—	9.9	7.0	4.7	3.5	6.6
Fugitive	3.9	8.0	5.8	4.3	5.0	6.1
Mental illness or disability	0.4	1.4	1.2	1.0	0.5	0.7
Drug addiction	6.6	1.3	1.0	0.7	1.0	0.9
Local law prohibition	—	0.9	0.5	0.2	0.2	0.3
Other*	28.7	12.8	12.5	19.4	6.2	8.8

—Not available or not applicable.

*Includes illegal aliens, juveniles, persons dishonorably discharged from the Armed Services, persons who have renounced their U. S. citizenship, and other unspecified persons.

Mental Health and Domestic Violence Records

During 2002-03, REJIS conducted a survey of mental health and domestic violence records accessed during background checks. One goal of the survey was to identify impediments and improvements to the availability and accessibility of these records. Forty-nine state contacts returned the survey. Nearly all states reported at least one impediment to sending records to the FBI or to checking agency access to records. Common impediments included:

- Privacy laws.

- Incomplete automation.

- Incomplete records.

- Inability to distinguish domestic violence misdemeanors from other misdemeanors.

Despite these impediments, more than one-half of the states reported at least one initiative underway to improve access to mental health records, domestic violence misdemeanor convictions, and/or restraining order records.

Case Study 6.2, *continued*

Overall, the survey results indicated that:

- Domestic violence restraining orders are the most readily available of the record types identified above.

- Accessing and sending mental health data pose the greatest challenge.

- Several impediments hinder access to domestic violence misdemeanor convictions, but the impediments are not widespread among states.

The number of rejections by state and local agencies for reasons other than felony convictions increased 294 percent from the first year of the Brady Act to 2002, compared to a 119 percent increase in total rejections and a 48 percent increase in rejections for felony convictions (Table E). This represents an increase from 29 percent of all rejections in 1994 to 52 percent in 2002. Several factors likely contributed to these increases, including greater accessibility to records of disqualifying factors other than felonies.

For example, states have used funds from the National Criminal History Improvement Program (NCHIP) to initiate the flagging of criminal history records evidencing convictions for domestic violence or the issuance of a protection order. Forty-two states submit data to the NCIC Protection Order File, which became operational in May 1997 and includes more than 750,000 records of protection orders.

Table E
Trends in Applications, Rejections, and Reasons for Rejection Since the Beginning of the Brady Act, Among All Agencies Conducting Such Checks, 1994-2002

	2002	2001	2000	1999	1998	1997	1996	1995	1994	Percent Change, 1994-2002
Inquiries	7,806,000	7,958,000	7,699,000	8,621,000	3,277,000	2,574,000	2,593,000	2,706,000	2,483,000	214.4%
Rejections	136,000	151,000	153,000	204,000	90,000	69,000	70,000	41,000	62,000	119.4
Felons rejected	65,000	87,000	88,000	147,000	57,000	43,000	47,000	30,000	44,000	47.7
All other	71,000	64,000	65,000	57,000	33,000	26,000	23,000	11,000	18,000	294.4
Percent felony	48%	58%	58%	72%	63%	62%	68%	72%	71%	
Felons per 1,000 inquiries	8.3	10.9	11.4	17.0	17.3	16.0	18.1	10.9	17.7	-53.1

Note: Counts are rounded. See notes on Table A.

Case Study 6.2, *continued*

Questions

When we are doing monitoring, we want to find out the degree to which the policy design was actually carried out as planned. Review the section in Chapter 4 titled "Designing a Policy." Recall that at this stage the change agent typically identifies: (1) the target population, or who will be affected by the policy; (2) the provisions of the policy, or what members of the target population will receive; (3) the decision authority, or who has the authority to carry out the policy; and (4) the procedures that must be followed by the decision authority.

1. Briefly describe the four policy components of the Brady Act (i.e., "policy design").

2. Now, using the Monitoring Analysis in Figure 6.1 as a guide, describe the degree to which these four design components have been carried out, and describe any gaps that you find. For example: Is the Brady Act doing what it is designed to do, and are state and local officials doing what they are supposed to be doing? What specific data reported in Case Study 6.2 helps to answer these questions?

Case Study 6.3

Why Drug Courts Need Good Information Systems[1]

Drug courts are a growing phenomenon. As of June 2001, more than 697 drug courts were operating in the United States, and 427 more were in the planning phases. Drug courts represent a unique, information-intensive approach to managing drug-related cases. Drug courts were developed to reduce substance abuse and recidivism through techniques such as treatment, judicial supervision, and graduated sanctions.

Typically, each drug court team—judge, drug treatment providers, court coordinator, prosecutor, defense attorney, and other integral players such as probation and pretrial services—carefully monitors and continually reports on the nonviolent defendant's journey to a drug-free life. For example, almost all drug courts require participants to obtain a General Educational Development (GED) diploma, to keep a job, and to pay current financial obligations, including drug court fees and child support (where applicable).

As team members track participants' compliance with program requirements, the "total progress picture" must be available quickly and accurately so drug court team members can manage the participants effectively. The drug court team must be able to analyze and summarize these progress pictures to provide the data that drug courts need to monitor their day-to-day operations, evaluate their processes and impact, and demonstrate the costs and benefits of their programs to their communities.

Unfortunately, most programs began and continue without the benefit of rigorous evaluation plans or automated management information systems (MISs). In recognition of this gap, the Drug Courts Program Office (DCPO) established initiatives to quantify the courts' needs for information technology and evaluation training and technical assistance, and to develop training and technical assistance solutions to address drug court priority needs.

More than 75 percent of the drug courts in the United States participated in a national survey designed to help those dealing with large drug caseloads assess their needs for enhanced information-gathering tools. The survey queried the entire population of known drug courts in the United States. Survey responses were received from 257 of the 340 (76%) drug courts that were operational at the time of the survey. The major findings were summarized in 10 key points:

---

[1] Adapted from: SEARCH, The National Consortium for Justice Information and Statistics. (2003). *Drug Court Monitoring, Evaluation, and Management Information Systems: National Scope Needs Assessment* (NCJ 195077). Washington, DC: U.S. Department of Justice, Office of Justice Programs, Bureau of Justice Assistance. Available at: *http://www.ncjrs.org/pdf files1/bja/195077.pdf*

Case Study 6.3, *continued*

1. Although there was widespread access to personal computers, vital data were not generally entered into automated systems, and there was not widespread, appropriately shared access to data among drug court team members. Less than one-quarter of courts surveyed use automation to help judges interact with their case-load of defendants.

2. A strong relationship existed between automation and the time it took for the judge to get failed drug test results. The critical factor was the importance that the drug court places on the value of information.

3. An overwhelming majority of the drug courts surveyed expressed their willingness to use every technical assistance option offered to acquire the proper automation, maintain the technology, and obtain the education needed to generate regular productivity reports.

4. A lack of funding was the top reason drug courts did not acquire the additional automation needed and the training and technical assistance to improve the administration of drug court justice.

5. In addition to funding barriers, drug courts also listed difficulty with linking to other systems as a prime barrier to automation.

6. The largest drug courts—those with 200 or more participants— were highly automated with good MIS support. The majority of courts (the smaller ones), however, lacked such resources.

7. Drug courts clearly specified that they needed technical assistance with all aspects of automation—including help with initial steps, such as developing needs assessments and technology plans and preparing funding proposals for stakeholders.

8. Surveyed drug courts expressed a desire for additional education and training to deal specifically with evaluation and management information systems. Targeted workshops and videotaped training sessions dedicated to monitoring, evaluation, and MIS development rated highly among surveyed courts.

9. Difficulty with data entry and sharing were not a result of drug court indifference to the need to provide regular evaluation information. Indeed, fewer than one-half of the drug courts surveyed rated their current systems as "good" or "very good" at providing information for evaluations.

Case Study 6.3, *continued*

10. Less than 15 percent of all surveyed courts reported that they had completed the necessary automation required to produce reports needed for overall program evaluation.

The results of the survey clearly showed that the automated support being provided to the drug courts by existing computer systems is inadequate. Without technology, it is difficult for drug courts to link the information about their results with the goals of the court. It is also difficult to produce the reports and evaluations needed to persuade stakeholders to allot more funding for technology.

Questions

1. Describe the information needs of different stakeholders for drug courts. How well do current information systems satisfy those needs?

2. What improvements might be needed? Review the guidelines for developing useful information systems discussed in Chapter 6, and discuss how they apply to this case study:

   • Staff acceptance

   • Cost

   • Compatibility

   • Safeguarding of information

   • Staff training

   • Staff understanding

Endnotes

¹   Dunworth, T., and G. Mills (1999). *National Evaluation of Weed and Seed* (NCJ-175685). Washington, DC: U.S. Department of Justice, National Institute of Justice.

²   Dunworth, T., G. Mills, G. Cordner, and J. Greene, (1999). *National Evaluation of Weed and Seed: Cross-Site Analysis* (NCJ-176358). Washington, DC: U.S. Department of Justice, National Institute of Justice.

³   For further information, see: Rossi, P.H., M.W Lipsey, and H.E. Freeman (2003). *Evaluation: A Systematic Approach*, 7th ed. Thousand Oaks, CA: Sage.

⁴   Sherman, Lawrence W., and Richard A. Berk (1984). "The Specific Deterrent Effects of Arrest for Domestic Assault." *American Sociological Review*, 49:261-272.

⁵   Ibid, note 3.

⁶   Ringwalt, C.L., J.M. Greene, S.T. Ennett, R. Iachan, R.R. Clayton, and C.G. Leukefeld (1994). *Past and Future Directions of the D.A.R.E. Program: An Evaluation Review*. Draft Final Report, September 1994. Washington, DC: U.S. Department of Justice, Office of Justice Programs, National Institute of Justice. Available at: *http://www.ncjrs.org/txtfiles/darerev.txt*; for a review, see: Gottfredson, D.C. (1998). "School-Based Crime Prevention (Ch. 5)." In L.W. Sherman, D.C. Gottfredson, D. MacKenzie, J. Eck, P. Reuter, and S. Bushwa (eds.), *What Works, What Doesn't, What's Promising: A Report to the United States Congress*. Prepared for the National Institute of Justice [Online]. Available at: *http://www.ncjrs.org/docfiles/wholedoc.doc* (retrieved March 12, 2004).

⁷   SEARCH, The National Consortium for Justice Information and Statistics. (2003). *Drug Court Monitoring, Evaluation, and Management Information Systems: National Scope Needs Assessment* (NCJ 195077). Washington, DC: U.S. Department of Justice, Office of Justice Programs, Bureau of Justice Assistance. Available at: *http://www.ncjrs.org/pdffiles1/bja/195077.pdf*

CHAPTER 7

Developing a Plan for Evaluating Outcomes

CHAPTER OUTLINE

▶ *Evaluations can measure impact, performance, or efficiency.* More specifically, is the program or policy achieving its objectives, how do outcomes change over time, and is it worth the investment of resources devoted to its implementation?

▶ *Impact evaluation*: This most common type of evaluation attempts to establish causality between intervention (program or policy) and outcome (a specific change in the problem).

▶ *Meta-analysis:* This is a method for combining the results of many individual program evaluations to determine if different intervention approaches or methods work better than others.

▶ *Two prerequisites for evaluation must be met*: (1) objectives must be clearly defined and measurable, and (2) the intervention must be sufficiently well designed and well implemented.

▶ *Develop outcome measures based on objectives*. Good outcome measures should be *valid* and *reliable*.

▶ *Specify the research design to be used*. Examples include: the simple pre-post design; the pre-post design with a control group; the pre-post design with multiple pre-tests; the longitudinal design with treatment and control groups; and the cohort design.

▶ *Identify potential confounding factors* (factors other than the intervention that may have biased observed outcomes). Common confounding factors include biased selection, biased attrition, and history.

▶ *The two major techniques for minimizing confounding effects are random assignment and nonequivalent comparison groups*. Each involves creating some kind of comparison or control group.

▶ *Identify users and uses of evaluation results*: Who is the intended audience, and how can results be effectively and efficiently communicated? How will the results be used?

▶ *Reassess the entire program or policy plan:* Review the entire planning process from start to finish, looking for any *inconsistencies, contradictions,* or *inadequacies*.

Now the time has come to measure the impact of the intervention: Has the program or policy achieved its intended effect(s)? How can we tell? The goal at this stage is to develop a research design for measuring program or policy outcome (a specific, intended change in the problem, defined by objectives). Did the program or policy achieve its intended objectives? Why or why not?

In spite of how obvious the need for evaluation may seem, many programs and policies have never been evaluated. Cost is often given as a reason for not conducting evaluations, but we must also recognize that evaluation can be threatening to stakeholders because their public image, political power, and/or agency budget may be linked to the success or failure of a specific program or policy. Sometimes not evaluating is an effective means of avoiding accountability.

Increasingly, however, funding agencies are demanding accountability for outcomes. Grants made to public and private agencies by federal agencies such as the National Institute of Justice typically require an evaluation component, and often an independent researcher must do the evaluation. In the fields of health and mental health, managed care agencies carefully measure outcomes and costs in order to ensure that the money they manage is being used effectively. This kind of thinking is making its way into the criminal justice system.

All stages of planning, including the formulation of an evaluation plan, should precede the actual start-up of the program or policy. Evaluation should never be an afterthought. In most cases, the research design depends very critically on the design stage, at which crucial decisions are made about target recruitment or selection. Evaluation is a critical component of the planning stage, not an activity that should be done "after the facts are in."

Types of Evaluation

Before you define what kind of evaluation data to collect, it is important to know about different approaches to evaluation. Before designing the evaluation, we need to be clear about the kinds of evaluative questions we are going to ask. Evaluations of programs and policies typically take one of three major approaches: (1) impact evaluation, (2) performance evaluation, or (3) efficiency evaluation.

Note that we do not intend (or pretend) in this chapter to cover evaluation methods in all their complexity.[1] We do hope that readers become familiar with some basic concepts necessary to understand evaluation. We will not attempt to teach students or practitioners how to design their own measures in this book. That is a task for a good course in research methods.

Impact Evaluation

The most common type of evaluation, and the type we focus on mainly in this chapter, is an *impact evaluation*. To assess impact, we want to compare *actual* outcomes to *desired* outcomes (objectives). In order to do this, we need valid measures of the desired outcomes and information about the status of clients on these measures prior to their exposure to the intervention. For example, the fact that a high proportion of clients of a delinquency prevention program end the program with high self-esteem is meaningless if they started the program with high self-esteem. It is not sufficient to know simply that a change occurred: we need to determine whether the program or policy in question caused the observed change. We need to know that this change wouldn't have happened without the intervention. To know this, we will also need information on similar types of persons who were not exposed to the intervention. If the same change occurred in this second group, then we are unable to attribute the change to the intervention.

Performance Evaluation: Outcome-based Information Systems

One weakness of many impact evaluations is that their results are limited to a specific point in time. Programs, in particular, are constantly changing in terms of their staff, clients, services, and goals. Staff turnover, intervention fads, changes in the political environment, and changes in the characteristics of incoming clients can all produce changes in program outcomes. The results of even the best-designed impact evaluation gradually become obsolete. *Performance evaluation* offers an alternative: Why not collect and analyze outcome information on all clients on a permanent basis? This way, stakeholders could learn from the outcome data, make adjustments, and see the consequences of their responses over time. The growth of computerized information systems within criminal justice is making this approach increasingly viable and useful.

This incremental learning process incorporates much of what we talked about in the last chapter with regard to monitoring, but the focus is on improving outcomes rather than assessing the adequacy of implementation. Moreover, this interactive approach to evaluation incorporates the concept of "action research" that was introduced by Kurt Lewin (see Chapter 2). In terms of design, an outcome-based information system is a *multiple cohort design* (see the section called "Specify the Research Design" in this chapter) in which the outcomes for each cohort (a specific group of clients) can be compared as a trend over time.

Let's add one more step to this idea: Such a system of learning is even stronger when outcome information is monitored in an entire system of programs. For example, a city or state could monitor specific outcome data on all programs that serve a specific population of clients, such as drug offenders or juvenile delinquents. With this information, comparisons of programs over time generate more information about why certain outcomes are being produced. The control group is not made up of clients who receive no services but of very similar clients (a matched control group) who receive different services.

Computerized information systems are increasingly common in the criminal justice field. Although the focus of such systems is typically on management needs—for example, personnel, finance, and case control—client-specific outcome information can easily be added to enhance the capacity of the organization to assess a program or policy's success. One example of such a system is *ProDES*, Philadelphia's Program Development and Evaluation System (See Case Study 7.1).

Efficiency Evaluation

Finally, we may want to know how efficient a given program or policy is. In *efficiency evaluation*, two types of analyses are useful: *cost-benefit analysis* and *cost-effectiveness analyses*. In cost-benefit analysis, we ask if the amount of change that is being produced (the benefit) is worth the cost (usually in monetary terms). Cost-effectiveness analyses, in contrast, express outcomes in substantive terms so as to compare programs and policies that produce similar outcomes.

For example, let's look at a three-month school-based curriculum for teaching problem-solving skills to eighth graders determined to be at high risk for delinquency. If desired changes are taking place, then various measures of benefit can be established (e.g., a unit increase in problem-solving skills as measured by a standardized test; the number of children who avoid any subsequent arrest up to age 18). The costs, some of which may be less obvious than others, must now be accurately measured. For example, how much money did it cost to buy course materials (notebooks, videos, etc.) and train classroom teachers to administer the curriculum? Was there a cost in terms of what students *did not* get (e.g., a reduction in mathematics or science training to make way for the problem-solving skills curriculum)? We may then compare the difference between total dollars saved by preventing each arrest (e.g., costs of arresting, processing, charging, and supervising each adjudicated delinquent) and dollars expended on operating the problem-solving skills curriculum. In other words, we calculate ratios of costs to benefits. If there is no benefit, the cost is irrelevant. However, a moderate gain at a low cost may often signal a more worthwhile program than a slightly higher gain at a much more substantial cost. A cost-effec-tiveness analysis of the same program might estimate the total dollars spent to convert each delinquent into a nondelinquent, and then com-pare this approach with others that attempt to produce similar out-comes (e.g., secure detention).

We also can compare actual costs against projected costs: an "effi-cient" program might be one that came in on budget or under budget, but produced a tangible benefit. In many cases, the costs of achieving the same level of benefit can be compared across different programs, policies or even settings. Efficiency analyses, therefore, can provide valu-able information to assist stakeholders and policymakers in making choices from among competing programs, policies, and projects.

Exactly how specific costs and benefits should be defined, however, is a matter of some controversy, and procedures for conducting effi-ciency analyses tend to be quite complex. For all three types of eval-uation, we expect our readers to be aware of why, how, and where such analyses are used, but their actual conduct requires sophisticated training and expertise. This is particularly true of efficiency analyses.[2]

Meta-Analysis

Although an impact evaluation can tell us about the success or fail-ure of a particular program, we can't be sure what components of the program are causing the observed outcomes. Most programs provide several discrete activities, such as group counseling, recreation, behav-ioral contracting, and education. How can we be sure which of these activities or which combination of activities is causing success? Of course, programs are more than activities: there are other clients attending the program, the staff, the facility, and the management of the organization providing the program. All of these program char-acteristics can affect a client's experience in a program, and conse-quently affect program outcomes.

In order to discover whether certain treatment approaches work, researchers such as Mark Lipsey[3] and Paul Gendreau[4] have made use of a statistical method that allows us to examine alternative causes of program outcomes. Often selecting only those evaluations that are well designed (meaning that the study used an experimental or suitable quasi-experimental design) meta-analysis involves calculating the size of the difference between those who received the intervention and those who did not in each study, called an "effect size," and then combin-ing these effect sizes across different studies into one measure of the impact of the treatment approach.[5]

To date, meta-analyses have found that behavioral and cognitive-behavioral methods are more effective for delinquent youths than various types of client-centered, nondirective therapies.[6] For adult correctional treatment, cognitive-behavioral and behavioral approaches work better than other treatments. Intensive prison drug treatment appears to be effective, especially when combined with community aftercare. Education, vocational training, and prison labor programs have modest effects. Effects of sex offender treatment are uncertain. It is important to remain aware that findings of meta-analyses are often limited by methodological weaknesses of the studies analyzed (e.g., selection bias), a lack of detailed information about the subjects and the treatment, and/or questionable implementation or program fidelity.[7]

Two Prerequisites for Evaluation

Before actually evaluating a program or policy, two main criteria (prerequisites) must be satisfied. If either prerequisite is not met, any attempt at evaluation is likely to be unsuccessful, and the results will be unconvincing. Indeed, an entire methodology called "evaluability assessment"[8] has been developed to address these critical concerns.

Figure 7.1

Two Prerequisites for Evaluation

1. Program or policy objectives must have been clearly specified, and those objectives must be measurable (see Chapter 3).

2. The intervention should have been sufficiently well designed (see Chapter 4) and sufficiently well-implemented so that there is no question that its critical elements (activities) have been delivered to clients as planned. Remember, this is why you do monitoring: to find out whether the "program or policy in action" matches the "program or policy on paper" (see Chapter 6).

Evaluability Assessment

Under circumstances in which we intend to evaluate an existing intervention, it is often advisable to first examine the program or policy to determine what aspects of the intervention can be measured. It may be that a program has clearly articulated goals but has not completed the task of creating measurable objectives. If one program goal is to see an improvement in offenders' perceptions of their opportunities for the future, how will the program know if these perceptions have changed? It may also be the case that different program staff members have different opinions regarding the program's goals. To the extent that these differences exist, the evaluation may be targeting the wrong objectives.

An evaluability assessment is a method for uncovering actual program components and isolating those elements that can be measured.[9] This evaluable model of the program is the program that is tested in the evaluation. Any program elements that cannot be measured are put aside. The assessment typically involves reading written documents that describe the program, interviewing administrators and line staff members, reading case files, and even interviewing program clients. Each of these sources of information is queried as to program goals and objectives, program activities, impact models, program resources, planning mechanisms, and areas in which change is needed. The result of the evaluability study is a single program model that is then reviewed by program administrators and staff for accuracy. The model often forces program personnel to confront their differences and for the first time achieve consensus regarding important facets of their program.

Develop Outcome Measures

To develop outcome measures, refer back to objectives. How will we adequately measure these objectives? Remember that an adequate objective contains four components (see Chapter 3): time frame, target population, a key result, and a criterion for measurement. We are trying to determine whether a specific intervention (program or policy) produces an intended change in the problem. Recall from Chapter 3 that an impact model specifies such a prediction or hypothesis.

Establishing the impact of a program amounts to establishing causality. In other words, we want to determine whether the intervention produces a specific effect, an intended change in the problem. To do so, we need adequate measures and an adequate research design.

The *validity* of a measure refers to the degree to which any measure or procedure succeeds in doing (measuring) what it purports to do. Most experts refer to this type of validity as *construct validity*. In other words, how can you tell whether the measure actually assesses the construct or concept that it is supposed to assess?

For example, we might be using a measure of self-esteem, such as the Rosenberg Self-Esteem Scale,[10] or we might be using a measure of self-reported drug use, such as the National Household Survey on Drug Abuse.[11] The question is: How accurate is each measure? Is it a good indicator of the construct you are trying to measure? These questions are often investigated through research that attempts to demonstrate that the measure relates to some known indicator of the same concept. We might measure a student's self-esteem and then correlate self-ratings with ratings from that student's friends and family members. We want to see if there is a relationship between our measure and some other indicator of the same concept. Alternatively, we might validate self-reported drug use with actual drug-testing technology to determine if self-reports are under- or over-inflated. Wherever possible, one should try to use existing measures for which previous research has indicated reasonable evidence of validity.

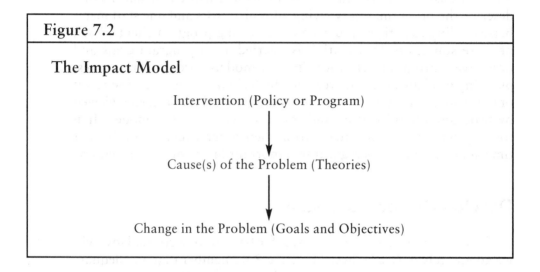

Figure 7.2

The Impact Model

Intervention (Policy or Program)

Cause(s) of the Problem (Theories)

Change in the Problem (Goals and Objectives)

The *reliability* of a measure refers to its consistency. For example, what is the probability of obtaining the same results upon repeated use of the same measuring instrument (i.e., test-retest reliability)? We want to be sure that the measure is somewhat consistent over time and that results do not vary dramatically from one time to the next. For example, self-esteem is seen as a relatively stable personality trait. Any reliable measure should not yield wildly disparate results about a person's self-esteem from one week to the next. Attempts to establish reliability of a self-report measure such as self-esteem usually examine, through research, the internal consistency of the items in a measure (i.e., do items correlate with one another) or relationships between scores obtained from two or more separate administrations of the same test.

Identify Potential Confounding Factors

As noted above, establishing the impact of a program amounts to an attempt to establish causality. Did the intervention produce an observed change in the problem? Before we look at a few basic research designs, we need to discuss *confounding factors* (sometimes called confounds). These refer to any factors, other than your program, that may account for observed changes on the outcome measure (e.g., an increase or decrease in the problem). Confounding factors bias the measurement of program outcomes. In research design textbooks, these confounding factors are often labeled threats to the internal validity of the experiment.

Biased selection is one common confound of which to be careful. In many criminal justice interventions, especially offender treatment and post-release programs, researchers view reducing recidivism as a primary objective. However, upon close inspection of many interventions, we often find that many of the clients who were selected to receive the treatment were not high-risk to begin with. If youths in a delinquency prevention program had no observable risk factors to begin with (such as previous arrests, truancy, academic failure, or family problems), it is not surprising if they show a low rate of recidivism upon graduation from the program. Does this mean that the intervention worked? Or does it mean that client selection was so biased that we have no way of knowing whether the program actually works?

When we refer to confounding factors, we are saying that something else (other than the intervention itself) may have caused the observed change in the problem, or something may have disrupted ("confounded") the way we measured a change in the problem. Confounding factors introduce bias into our measurement of outcomes. One should try to anticipate potential confounds and design the evaluation to minimize them. The evaluation of every intervention should address potential confounds. Here are three of the most typical confounds:

1. *Biased selection*: Systematic bias in client selection procedures results in the treatment group not including adequate numbers of clients with demonstrated needs or problems. Sometimes called "creaming," this problem occurs when a program deliberately or unknowingly selects those clients most likely to show a favorable outcome, rather than those clients most in need of the intervention. For example, many private drug treatment programs claim phenomenal rates of success, but we often find that they have limited their client selection to those with the least severe problems. In other words, clients most in need were not selected. Suspicions should be further aroused if no control group was used to compare program outcomes.

2. *Biased attrition*: Bias is introduced into the outcome measure because subjects dropped out of one comparison group at higher rates than subjects in other comparison groups. For example, it is a common difficulty in drug treatment programs that those with the most severe problems drop out before the end of program. The observed result is that those who remained in the treatment program had lower rates of relapse than similar subjects in a control group. The result is biased, however, because the treatment program lost those subjects who were most likely to show the highest rates of relapse.

3. *History:* Some unanticipated event, occurring between the beginning and the end of the intervention, introduces bias into the measurement of program objectives. For example, if a major change in a state's criminal laws occurred during the course of a mandatory arrest experiment, the new law, rather than the intervention, might explain the observed result of increased arrests for domestic abuse.

Two Major Techniques for Minimizing Confounding Effects

There are two major techniques for minimizing confounding effects: (1) *random assignment*, and (2) *nonequivalent comparison groups*. Each involves creating a comparison group: a different group of clients that is equivalent to the treatment group on any factors that might influence the outcome measure, such as recidivism, but does not receive the intervention.

Random Assignment

Random assignment means that researchers randomly assign eligible clients to separate treatment and control groups. This is not the same as random selection, which would make absolutely no sense. Students often have a hard time keeping these two concepts separate. As a sampling strategy, one might randomly select subjects to participate in a survey or opinion poll. The purpose would be to obtain a representative, random sample of the population. In contrast, nobody would ever randomly select clients for an intervention: they would instead determine who is eligible for the program and who needs the program. Once the eligible pool of clients is determined, they would then randomly assign subjects to the treatment and control groups. Clients in any intervention are not randomly selected; they are deliberately selected on the basis of need and eligibility. Once selected, though, they can be randomly assigned to treatment or control groups.

What random assignment does, in theory, is equalize two different groups on unknown differences (e.g., intelligence, previous criminal history, etc.) that might bias the outcome results. With a large enough sample, the chances of equally distributing characteristics of subjects across the treatment and control groups is very good. This is the best method for dealing with confounds, when possible. For ethical and practical reasons, however, random assignment is not always possible. In many social interventions, those most in need of the intervention must be selected, and randomization would be unfair or even unethical (see the example at the end of this chapter).

Example 7.1

Potential Confounds in the Minneapolis Domestic Violence Experiment

The Minneapolis Domestic Violence Experiment[12] has been criticized for potential confounding factors. Some suggest that one cannot adequately determine from this experiment whether a mandatory arrest policy works better than mediation or separation. One measure used was a follow-up interview with victims to ask about victimization following the police intervention. Victims were interviewed immediately after the intervention, then every two weeks for 24 weeks. Researchers reported a decrease in the problem, as measured by fewer victim reports of repeat abuse. Of couples that received the mandatory arrest intervention, only 19 percent of victims reported further abuse in the follow-up study, compared to recidivism rates of 33 percent and 37 percent, respectively, in the separation and mediation interventions.

Here is the difficulty: What if women were scared to report further incidents of abuse because they had been threatened or beaten by their spouse following the previous police intervention (arrest, mediation, or separation)? Sherman and Berk reported that a substantial number of victims in their sample dropped out of the study. Initial interviews with victims were completed in only 62 percent of all cases. Others could not be found or refused to be interviewed. Biweekly interviews were completed for only 49 percent of subjects in the original sample. The study may have lost many of those who were victims of repeat abuse following the experiment.

Maybe some of these victims who refused to be interviewed were afraid to talk to the interviewers for fear of retaliation by their spouse. Perhaps some of these women had already experienced retaliation from spouses who had been temporarily detained under mandatory arrest provisions but were subsequently released a day or two later.

Sherman and Berk reported that of those victims they actually contacted, there was no "differential" attrition (i.e., the victim dropout rate for the experiment was about the same for each of the three interventions).[13] However, we have no way of knowing how many of those not contacted actually experienced further abuse. Critics expressed doubts about the experimental results because of this potential confound.[14] Moreover, attempts to replicate the results of the Minneapolis experiment in other jurisdictions have not been very successful.[15]

In summary, it is not entirely clear that the intervention (mandatory arrest) was responsible for the observed results (a decrease in reported incidents of abuse). We cannot entirely rule out the possibility that the results were biased due to the attrition (dropping out) of more than one-half of the original subjects. We are suspicious that those victims who refused to be interviewed in the follow-up study might have been more likely to experience further victimization than those who agreed to be interviewed. The observed reduction in repeated incidents of abuse may be due to the fact that victims who dropped out of the experiment were afraid to report further incidents of abuse to police or interviewers.

Nonequivalent Comparison Groups

Often we cannot randomly assign subjects to treatment and control groups, but we can attempt to construct treatment and comparison groups made up of clients with similar characteristics. It is especially important that the two groups are similar in terms of their level of need and the characteristics that might influence the outcome of interest (e.g., recidivism). We must decide with care exactly which factors might be important to control for. We usually look to previous research to determine important variables. We might then attempt to create matched control groups so that average client characteristics are distributed relatively equally across the two groups (aggregate matching), or so that every client in the treatment group is matched one-to-one with a similar nonclient in the control group (individual matching). Aggregate matching is much easier than individual matching, unless one is dealing with an extremely large pool of eligible clients. Individual matching is more precise, but we lose a very large number of potential cases as we try to match individuals rather than groups on a large number of variables. For example, we may be measuring recidivism as a program outcome. It would be important to match our treatment and control groups on variables known to influence recidivism, such as previous criminal behavior, age of offender, employment and job skills, and so on.

Specify the Research Design

In this section, we attempt to acquaint readers with a few of the most basic research designs used to evaluate program impacts. In general, such designs specify when and how measures will be collected to assess program impact. Each involves comparisons of certain groups of subjects, and measurement on specific variables, over particular time periods, to evaluate outcome. We will diagram and describe several of the most commonly used research designs.

You might want to think of an example as you go through the diagrams and descriptions of different research designs. Imagine, for example, a six-week prevention program designed for adolescents at high risk of abusing drugs. The program attempts to raise youths' self-esteem. The program's rationale is that increasing self-esteem is a means of increasing one's ability to make independent decisions without being unduly influenced by one's peers. A self-report self-esteem measure such as the Rosenberg Self-Esteem Scale is used.[16]

Figure 7.3

Legend For Diagrams of Research Designs

In each of the diagrams below:
"X" represents the intervention or "treatment"
"O" represents the observation or measure
"PRE" refers to a pre-intervention observation
"POST" refers to a post-treatment observation

Figure 7.4

The Simple Pre-Post Design

O_1 X O_2

PRE   TREATMENT   POST

$\longrightarrow$

PASSAGE OF TIME

The simple pretest-posttest is an easy-to-use design, but it is not a good one. Because there is no comparison or control group, we cannot adequately determine whether the program or some other unmeasured influence (confounding factor) produced the observed change from O_1 to O_2. How do we know, for example, whether self-esteem would have increased (or decreased) even without the intervention? How do we know whether clients were high or low on this measure to begin with? How do these clients compare to a similar group who did not receive the intervention?

Figure 7.5

The Pretest-Posttest Design with Control Group

O_1 X $O_{2\ (treatment\ group)}$

O_1 $O_{2\ (control\ group)}$

PRE   TREATMENT   POST

$\longrightarrow$

PASSAGE OF TIME

The pretest-posttest with control group is a much better design than the simple pre-post design. A control group provides us some means of comparing initial measures with later measures. If the two groups are relatively equivalent on variables likely to influence the outcome measure, we can compare the outcomes observed for the two groups to evaluate program impact.

The Pretest-Posttest Design with Multiple Pretests

The pretest-posttest design with multiple pretests is a slight improvement over the pretest-posttest design with a control group. It gives us a better assessment of the condition of clients and nonclients before treatment. This design allows us to obtain a baseline of behavior or attitudes for each group before the intervention begins. A baseline is always preferable to a one-shot (cross-sectional) assessment of pre-intervention characteristics. This is valuable because it gives us a much better indication of how stable or unstable the specific behavior of interest is, and whether treatment or comparison groups differ in their baselines prior to treatment.

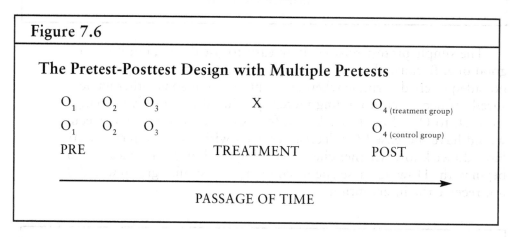

Figure 7.6

The Pretest-Posttest Design with Multiple Pretests

O_1 O_2 O_3 X $O_{4 \text{ (treatment group)}}$

O_1 O_2 O_3 $O_{4 \text{ (control group)}}$

PRE   TREATMENT   POST

PASSAGE OF TIME

The Longitudinal Design with Treatment and Control Groups

The longitudinal design with treatment and control groups is the most favorable design, but it tends to be expensive, takes a long time, and is difficult to conduct. It is the most favorable because it gives us a baseline for both the treatment and control groups, both before and after the intervention begins.

Figure 7.7

The Longitudinal Design with Treatment and Control Groups

O_1 O_2 O_3 X O_4 O_5 O_6 O_{7} (treatment group)

O_1 O_2 O_3 O_4 O_5 O_6 O_{7} (control group)

PRE   TREATMENT   POST

PASSAGE OF TIME

The Cohort Design

When it is difficult to actually assign clients to treatment and control groups, the evaluator may decide to follow different cohorts: similar groups of people who go through the same system or experience, but at different times. One cohort gets the intervention program, the other cohort (the control group) does not. This design is often used for school studies. For example, if you have identified the ninth grade in one school as a group particularly vulnerable to experimentation with drugs, but still "reachable," the following steps might be taken to set up a cohort design:

1. Measure self-reported drug use of the ninth-grade class in 1996-97.

2. At the beginning of the next school year (1997-98), you start a drug awareness education program.

3. At the end of the school year (1997-98), you measure the level of drug use in this second cohort.

4. You determine whether drug use is lower in the second group (the 1997-98 cohort) than the first cohort (1996-97), the one that did not receive the program. This design assumes that all other conditions in the school (e.g., funding, security measures) have remained relatively constant from one year to the next.

Figure 7.8

The Cohort Design

O_1 X O_{2} (1997-98 Cohort)

O_1 O_{2} (1996-97 Cohort)

PRE   TREATMENT   POST

PASSAGE OF TIME

Identify Users and Uses of Evaluation Results

Who will be interested in the results of this evaluation, and how will they use the information? If any evaluation is to be useful, it should serve the information needs of the program or policy and its stakeholders (see Chapter 2). Any intervention has multiple stakeholders such as the funding agency, citizens, politicians, criminal justice officials, volunteers, targets, and so on. The time spent previously (at Stage 1) identifying stakeholders should not be wasted. Evaluation is a critical means of demonstrating accountability—and hopefully, effectiveness—to stakeholders.

The change agent should develop plans and assign responsibility for packaging and communicating evaluation results to different users. It is particularly important to find means of communication that different audiences can understand. Even at academic conferences, for instance, many eyes in the audience glaze over when a presenter puts up overheads cluttered with complicated statistical results. If the results are to be useful, and used, one must create means of communication that intended audiences could understand and react to. Stakeholders must be able to participate in a dialogue with the report writer or presenter.

Reassess the Entire Program Plan

At this point, we review the entire planning process, from Stage 1 (problem analysis) through Stage 7 (evaluation). Remember that (ideally) we are doing all this planning before the program is actually implemented. Far too many program people, researchers, and funding agencies still fail to see that critical decisions that have been made at earlier stages affect later stages.

For example, if an evaluator has had no input into decisions regarding client selection processes, he or she often finds that it is impossible to construct an adequate comparison group. This is particularly true in cases in which the selection process is biased in favor of low-risk clients, or there are multiple referral sources, or selection criteria are simply too vague to define any specific target population.

This is just one example of the type of problem that can occur if one fails to examine how all the different planning pieces fit together. Once the plan is complete, it is time to go back and review the entire planning process from start to finish. No doubt, there will be inconsistencies, contradictions, or inadequacies. The whole puzzle rarely fits together perfectly on the first try. Taking this step of review and reassessment, however, is much less burdensome if done before the program starts than if done later, when program operations demand constant attention, and stakeholders expect results, not excuses. Review and reassessment of the entire program planning process is a step that must be taken with deliberation and care. Answering the questions that follow Case Study 7.2 will provide a good test of how well you understood some of the major concepts presented in this chapter.

DISCUSSION QUESTIONS

1. What is meant by the term *evaluation*?

2. What are the main differences between performance and impact evaluations?

3. How can an automated information system increase the availability of evaluation data?

4. Define and describe an example of efficiency analysis.

5. What are the two prerequisites for evaluation? Explain.

6. Define: (a) reliability, and (b) validity.

7. (a) Define confounding factors. (b) Describe the three most common types of confounding factors.

8. Refer back to Example 7.1 (the Minneapolis Domestic Violence Experiment). How were confounding factors illustrated by this example?

9. How does one minimize possible confounding effects in an evaluation? Make sure you discuss the two major techniques.

10. Describe each of the following research designs: (a) simple pretest-posttest, (b) pretest-posttest with a control group, (c) pretest-posttest with multiple pretests, (d) longitudinal design with treatment and control groups, and (e) cohort design.

EXERCISE 7.1

Your instructor may ask you to analyze a published evaluation study. One good example is the Kansas City Gun Experiment summarized briefly in Chapter 1.[17] Retrieve and read the article and answer the following questions: (a) What were the program's intended outcome objectives? (Hint: remember the distinction between process versus outcome objectives; see Chapter 3). (b) To what degree, if any, did the program achieve its intended outcome objectives? Give specific examples and evidence from the article to support your answer.

Case Study 7.1

ProDES—An Information System for Developing and Evaluating Services to Delinquent Youths

Philip W. Harris and Peter R. Jones[1]

Instructions: *Read the case study below, then answer the questions that follow.*

ProDES (the Program Development and Evaluation System) is an outcome-based information system that tracks every Philadelphia delinquent for the duration of his or her involvement with the juvenile justice system. Its primary focus is development of the entire system of programs that serve delinquent youths. That is, it provides programs and the system as a whole with a continuous flow of intermediate (changes during the program) and ultimate (recidivism and community adjustment) outcome information. The information is then used for program development, matching youths to programs, and assessments of the program resources available to system-level decision-makers, such as judges and probation officers.

ProDES was also designed to study key policy questions. Questions such as whether more resources are needed for female delinquents or sex offenders have already been investigated with these data. Trend information produced by ProDES (such as the growing number of delinquent youths with drug and alcohol abuse problems and the dramatic increase in the number of Hispanic youths entering the system) lead to the need for new policies. Moreover, because information is collected continuously, ProDES can measure the impact of policy and program changes on specific outcomes. ProDES is the product of a unique effort in Philadelphia to enhance existing juvenile correctional programs and simultaneously develop new programs and approaches that are more effective in meeting the goals of the system. ProDES has three goals:

1. To facilitate the development of intervention programs for delinquent youths by providing those programs with continuous outcome information that is relevant to the ways in which program personnel think about change,

2. To facilitate planning of the entire array of delinquency services provided by the Department of Juvenile Justice Services through the provision of program-level outcome information that identifies program strengths and weaknesses as well as strengths and weaknesses in the entire array of services available, and

---

[1] Philip W. Harris and Peter R. Jones are professors of Criminal Justice at Temple University in Philadelphia. ProDES is operated by the Crime and Justice Research Center at Temple University. Reprinted with permission of authors.

Case Study 7.1, *continued*

3. To facilitate the rational matching by probation officers and judges of adjudicated youths to programs that can meet their needs and the needs of the community.

Most students of corrections are familiar with the term "recidivism." Among the definitions of recidivism are re-offending, new arrests, new charges, new adjudications, and new commitments. The usefulness of these measures for program development, however, is extremely limited. Thus, while recidivism data are important for some purposes, we recognized from the beginning the need for outcome measures that would speak directly to the purposes of those persons directly serving delinquent youths. Harris and Jones found, too, that these service providers needed more than descriptions of their clients. They needed multiple measures that demonstrated change over time.

The first phase of the developing ProDES involved visits to 15 agencies selected to represent the broad range of programs. Within each program, evaluability assessments were conducted that sought to articulate the goals and objectives of the various programs, their measures of success or failure, and the range of information they routinely collected and utilized. These assessments demonstrated that no common base of information existed across all community programs. However, commonalties did exist in terms of information that agencies thought to be important to the evaluation of their own programs and to the system as a whole. Agreement was also found in terms of the ideal structure of an information system—one that went beyond simply describing program clients at one point in time (usually at intake) and included multiple measures to demonstrate change over time.

The second phase of the research involved the testing of outcome measures and the development and implementation of an information system that monitors case-level outcomes and provides data previously identified as central to the mission of individual programs, the Department of Human Services, and Family Court. With this in mind, a system of data collection, analysis, and feedback was designed that would use case-level data collected at four points in time: (1) record data are collected immediately by ProDES staff following disposition in juvenile court, (2) program intake data are collected by program staff shortly after a youth was admitted into the program, (3) discharge data are collected by program staff shortly before release from a program, and (4) follow-up data, including recidivism measures and interviews with the youths and caregivers whose cases are being analyzed, are collected by ProDES staff six months following departure from the program.

The content of the ProDES database includes the entire court record of the youth:

- Current offense and related decisions,
- Prior offenses and related decisions,
- Sociodemographic variables,

Case Study 7.1, *continued*

- Family and educational information, and
- Psychological assessments.

Shortly after the youth arrives at the program, staff of the program collect the intake information:

- A risk assessment,
- A needs assessment,
- Family structure and attitudes toward family,
- Self-esteem,
- Values,
- School bonding (7 dimensions),
- Family bonding (5 dimensions),
- Drug and alcohol use, and
- Employment experience.

At discharge, all of the intake information is repeated in order to determine if changes on these key outcome dimensions have taken place during the course of the program. In addition, information is collected on the interventions used, in-program behavior, program completion, and reason for discharge.

Six months after a youth leaves the program, a follow-up is conducted. The follow-up includes a record check to see if there have been new juvenile or adult charges filed, and telephone interviews are conducted with the youth and a parent concerning community adjustment and satisfaction with the program.

ProDES became fully operational in January of 1994. Over time the number of programs feeding data into the system and receiving case-level and aggregate reports grew from 64 to 90. Data are fed back to programs, family court, probation staff, and the Department of Human Services on a continual basis. Additionally, multivariate analyses of data are conducted to focus attention on policy issues of importance to the field, and system-wide trends are reported regularly. Most importantly, each ProDES program receives an annual report of its outcome information.

In designing ProDES, Harris and Jones gave recognition to potential confounding factors. One such factor is the risk of future recidivism that already existed before the program started. That is, one youth might begin the program with a high risk of future offending (usually based on past behavior such as previous arrests), while another presents a low risk. If the high-risk youth recidivates and the low-risk youth does not, how would we know that the program was making a difference? ProDES, using an empirically developed scale, predicts risk of recidivism for each youth, and controls for risk statistically when examining program outcomes.

Case Study 7.1, *continued*

A second confounding factor is that the attitudes, values, perceptions, and complexity of a youth's view of the world can affect a youth's reaction to the program. It is well recognized that not all youths respond to a particular program in the same way. Maturity, personality characteristics, and cultural background can affect whether or not a youth relates to program staff, feels comfortable in the program's environment, finds the program content stimulating, enjoys the experiences, or learns from the program's interventions. ProDES contains a typology of delinquent youths, based on self-reported standardized scales. By analyzing the responses of more than 2,500 youths on 14 scales, ranging from a measure of values to several scales that measure family bonding and school bonding, Harris and Jones identified five types of youths. Program outcomes are assessed for each type, with the expectation that patterns of outcomes will vary by type.

The decision of what program to attach to a specific youth involves matching. It is at this point that program designs (objectives, activities/services, staff, and resources) are examined in terms of how well they fit the characteristics and needs of the youth. To do this, Harris and Jones created the Program Design Inventory (PDI), a database of program designs for all of the programs available to the court. Using a search screen, the user can identify youth characteristics, type of youth (see above paragraph), and desirable program characteristics (e.g., location, level of security, coed or not), and the PDI will identify programs fitting that set of requirements. The PDI also provides comparisons of programs in terms of key program characteristics and in terms of outcomes for youths similar to the one in question.

ProDES was designed from the beginning as an information system that would support performance evaluation research. As such, it can serve as an adjunct to a management information system, but it is not a substitute for a good management information system. It collects more than 800 items of information on every case, and is, therefore, a tremendous resource for developing systems of programs and for examining complex policy questions.

Questions

1. Discuss the usefulness of ProDES, using concepts from Chapter 7. How is ProDES useful for evaluating programs? How about policies?

2. How did Harris and Jones account for confounding factors that might bias observed outcomes?

3. Do you see any problem with a six-month follow-up? Explain.

Case Study 7.2

Evaluating Outcomes of Community-Based
Delinquency Prevention[1]

Instructions: Read the case study below, then answer the question that follows.

The Problem, Program Design, and Goals

To assess concerns of minority overrepresentation in the Pennsylvania juvenile justice system, and to respond to changes in federal guidelines for states participating in the Juvenile Justice and Delinquency Prevention (JJDP) Formula Grant Program, the Minority Confinement Subcommittee of the Pennsylvania Commission on Crime and Delinquency (PCCD) Juvenile Advisory Committee concluded that some action could be taken to slow the entry or re-entry of minorities into the juvenile justice system. They recommended the development and support of community-based intervention activities. Five programs were funded in Dauphin County (Harrisburg) beginning in 1991-92; those programs concluded their third and final year of PCCD funding early in 1994. It was expected that programs would obtain their own funding after two and a one-half years of initial funding from PCCD.

All programs stressed the value of supervised activities to keep youths out of trouble. All provided "life skills training," which often included training in problem-solving skills, conflict resolution, and cultural diversity and awareness training. Most provided homework or tutoring assistance, structured recreation and/or field trips, some form of career development or vocational training, and community service. All programs, as requirements of their PCCD funding, had two mandated goals: (1) to reduce future involvement with the juvenile justice system, and (2) to improve school behavior and performance.

Research Design

The authors were contracted as evaluators quite some time after the programs began operations, and agencies were already utilizing diverse referral sources. Because neither randomization nor matched constructed control groups were possible, our choices for forming comparison groups were limited. We had no control over client selection and referrals, and referrals came from different sources (e.g., self and family, probation, school, and police). Requirements of informed consent also limited research design options. To gain access to inspect agency records (e.g., police, probation, school) for individual program clients, we were required to obtain a release form signed by the client and a parent. As a result, a strict "control" group

---

[1] Adapted from: Welsh, Wayne N., Patricia H. Jenkins, and Philip W. Harris (1997) *Reducing Minority Over-Representation in Juvenile Justice: Results of Community-Based Intervention in Pennsylvania, 1992-95.* Philadelphia: Temple University, Department of Criminal Justice. See also Welsh, W.N., P.H. Jenkins, and P.W. Harris (1999). "Reducing Minority Over-Representation in Juvenile Justice: Results of Community-Based Delinquency Prevention in Harrisburg." *Journal of Research in Crime and Delinquency*, 36:87-110.

Case Study 7.2, *continued*

was not possible (i.e., one that was identical to the intervention group in all respects except that no treatment was delivered). It was not possible to obtain police and school records for nonclients unless they had already granted consent but never subsequently participated in any of the programs.

Comparison groups were constructed on the basis of frequency of client participation in the programs. Numerous studies have suggested that the intensity of treatment (e.g., frequency of contacts; number of contact hours) is one of the most crucial variables influencing the success of intervention, including drug and alcohol treatment and delinquency prevention.[2] We would expect that if a program works at all, a critical variable affecting client outcome is treatment intensity or degree of exposure to the program. We were aided by the fact that many of the clients referred to the programs signed a release of information form but never attended the programs.

To determine the adequacy of these constructed comparison groups for each cohort, we examined the possibility of biased selection (i.e., did the groups differ on critical pre-selection variables that might affect the outcomes of interest?). While our data allow us to examine group differences on numerous risk factors, the most crucial factors to examine are those most likely to affect the dependent variables. Recidivism, for example, is known to be related to previous delinquent activity and age (older juveniles are at greater risk of arrest and rearrest). Sources of referral could potentially bias comparison groups (e.g., probation referrals may be more likely to have been arrested than other referrals). For analyses of school outcomes, it is advisable to examine possible pre-selection differences that could influence educational outcomes (suspensions, truancy, and core GPA). We also examined demographic factors that could have influenced selection (e.g., ethnicity, family structure, parental employment).

We report results for two separate client groups in Harrisburg: those who attended programs during the 1992-93 school year, and those who attended programs during the 1993-94 school year.

The 1992-93 sample consisted of 187 clients. Our first comparison group (the "control" group) was made up of 80 clients (43%) who never participated in any program. The second comparison group was made up of 45 clients (24%) who participated occasionally but accumulated less than 30 total program hours over the 1992-93 school year. Our third comparison group was made up of 62 clients (33%) who accumulated greater than 30 program hours during the 1992-93 school year. The three groups did not differ significantly in terms of prior arrests, gender, family structure, parental employment, previous truancy, or prior suspensions. However, the comparison groups did differ in terms of age (high attenders were slightly younger), referral source (probation referrals had poorer attendance; self or family

---

[2]   Palmer, Ted (1992). *The Re-Emergence of Correctional Intervention.* Newbury Park, CA: Sage.

Case Study 7.2, *continued*

referrals had higher rates of attendance), ethnicity (75% of the total sample were African American, but Latino children were slightly overrepresented in the low and high attendance groups), whether the student was promoted the previous school year, and academic performance the previous year (nonattenders had slightly lower grades and were less likely to have been promoted). Because randomized assignment of subjects to comparison groups was not possible, we cannot rule out the possibility that comparison groups differed on other, unmeasured pre-intervention variables related to the dependent variables of interest. For analyses of recidivism and educational outcomes, we can be assured that factors of most concern (prior arrests, suspensions, and truancy) do not contaminate the results. All pre-selection factors that statistically differentiated the comparison groups (e.g., age, referral source, ethnicity, previous school promotions, and grades) were examined in statistical analyses as control variables.

In the 1993-94 sample, 97 clients were examined. Our first comparison group (the "control" group) was made up of 32 students (33%) who never participated in the programs. The second comparison group was made up of 31 clients (32%) who participated occasionally but accumulated less than 50 total program hours over the 1993-94 school year. Our third comparison group was made up of 34 clients (34%) who accumulated greater than 50 program hours during the 1993-94 school year. To determine the adequacy of these constructed comparison groups, we examined the possibility of biased selection (i.e., did the groups differ on critical pre-selection variables that might affect the outcomes of interest?). Upon intake, the three comparison groups did not differ significantly in terms of prior arrests, age, gender, ethnicity, family structure, parental employment, academic retention (1992-93 school year), prior suspensions (1992-93 school year), or core GPA (1992-93 school year). The comparison groups did differ in terms of referral source (probation and police referrals had poorer attendance; self or family referrals had higher rates of attendance; referrals from human services had the highest rates of attendance) and truancy the previous school year (nonattenders and low attenders had higher rates of truancy than high attenders). Once again, because randomized assignment of subjects to comparison groups was not possible, we cannot rule out the possibility that comparison groups differed on other, unmeasured pre-selection variables related to the dependent variables of interest. For analyses of recidivism and educational outcomes, then, critical factors (prior arrests, age, previous suspensions, previous grades) do not contaminate the results. All pre-selection factors that differentiated the comparison groups (i.e., referral source, truancy) were examined in statistical analyses as control variables.

Case Study 7.2, *continued*

Results

Recidivism. Results for the 1992-93 Harrisburg sample suggest that programs had success in reducing recidivism for high-risk clients. The rate of recidivism over a three-year period for the high-attendance group (25.8%) was impressive, especially considering that nearly one-half of these clients had previous arrests prior to their referral. In contrast, the control group had a recidivism rate of 53 percent for the same period.

Recidivism results for the 1993-94 Harrisburg sample were less positive. The rate of recidivism over a two-year period for the high-attendance group (23.5%) was satisfactory, but nearly the same proportion (about one-fourth) of these clients had previous arrests prior to their referral. A prior arrest, then, rather than programmatic intervention, was the strongest influence of recidivism. Compared to the previous year (1992-93), programs in 1993-94 targeted clients who were much younger and much less likely to have previous arrests.

Academic Performance. Impacts on academic performance were somewhat disappointing, although missing data resulted in smaller samples than desirable for multivariate tests. For both the 1992-93 and 1993-94 samples, Harrisburg programs had no significant effects on academic performance. For the 1993-94 sample, academic performance either remained stable or declined slightly for all comparison groups over a two-year period, and statistical analyses suggested that programs had no significant effect on grades. The absence of any directional improvement in grades over time suggests that programs have made little progress in impacting upon their clients' educational performance.

Dropout Rates. For the 1992-93 sample, Harrisburg programs had no significant effects on dropout rates. Only previously poor academic performance significantly explained dropout rates. Although the 1993-94 sample was young and the follow-up period brief, results did not reveal any statistically significant program effect on dropout rates. However, results for the 1993-94 sample were in a positive direction (the high program attendance group had a dropout rate of 4.3 percent compared to 26.9 percent for the control group).

Truancy. For the 1992-93 sample, Harrisburg programs had no significant effects on truancy. All comparison groups showed a large increase in truancy from 1991-92 to 1993-94. Although the sample was young and the follow-up period brief, results for the 1993-94 sample were similarly disappointing. However, while no statistically significant programmatic effect on truancy was found, results were in a positive direction (i.e., there was a slight but statistically nonsignificant decrease in truancy from 1993-94 to 1994-95). The only significant predictor of post-intervention truancy for the 1993-94 sample was previous (pre-intervention) truancy.

Implications

Although the results were somewhat disappointing, it is important to recognize that results do not reflect the total success or failure of the programs.

Case Study 7.2, *continued*

For example, findings about recidivism were compromised by the fact that there were so few youths with prior arrests in the 1993-94 sample. Academic performance, dropout rates, and truancy did not improve significantly, but it may be unrealistic to expect dramatic changes in youths who participated in the programs only sporadically. Further, programs may influence educational outcomes only to a small degree compared to the more pervasive effects exerted by schools and families.

Results may be influenced by various factors, some of which we can account for in our data (e.g., gaps in the delivery of program services, inconsistent patterns of youth participation in programs, insufficient program resources, inadequate measures of client skills and attitudes), and some that lie outside the parameters of our evaluation (e.g., poverty, family trauma, and inadequate funding for public schools). It may also be the case that some programs, if evaluated individually rather than as a combined sample, would produce more positive results. Because the number of clients in each program was so small, and there was so much missing data, we could not effectively evaluate outcomes for individual programs.

Another problem is presented by the need for adequate measures of additional objectives that programs attempt to achieve (e.g., improved self-esteem, problem-solving skills, and interpersonal behavior). We vigorously attempted to measure such outcomes using self-report measures and staff ratings of client behavior in the 1994-95 cohort, but program staff did not have the time or resources to complete the assessment process at required three-month intervals. Thus, there may be areas of program impact that we were unable to adequately measure.

Concern was raised by the diverse nature of referral sources during the 1993-94 school year. Rather than selecting clients on the basis of their suitability for each program, intakes during the 1993-94 school year were marked by a high diversity of client characteristics and needs, perhaps indicating a desperate attempt by the coalition to get referrals from anywhere possible. Program funding, therefore, may not yet have stabilized to the degree necessary for programs to concentrate more intensively on defining their intended target population and strengthening their service delivery to meet specified client needs.

Question

1. Explain how Case Study 7.2 illustrates concepts discussed in Chapter 7, providing evidence to support your answer: (a) reliability and validity; (b) nonequivalent comparison groups; (c) confounding factors; and (d) reassessing the entire program or policy plan.

Case Study 7.3

Evaluation of Prison-Based Therapeutic Community Drug Treatment Programs in Pennsylvania[1]

Instructions: Read the case study below, then answer the question that follows.

This project built upon a collaborative research partnership between Temple University and the Pennsylvania Department of Corrections (PA-DOC) that began in 1999. A steering committee consisting of senior executive, research, and treatment personnel from the Pennsylvania Department of Corrections and Center for Public Policy researchers was formed to guide research activity and facilitate the department's overall research agenda. This group continues to meet regularly to provide oversight of the research process and consider the larger organizational and policy issues that the research raises. Steering committee members participated in the oversight of this entire project. Findings were regularly presented and discussed at steering committee meetings, and members provided numerous helpful comments on an earlier version of this report.

An in-prison Therapeutic Community is an intensive, long-term, highly structured, residential treatment modality for hard-core drug users convicted of a criminal offense. TC emphasizes the necessity of the inmate taking responsibility for his or her behavior before, during, and after treatment. Several evaluations of in-prison TCs have produced promising results. However, studies have been criticized for small sample sizes, faulty research designs (e.g., selection and attrition biases), and inadequate attention to interactions between inmate characteristics, treatment process, and treatment outcomes. No studies have examined prison-based TCs across multiple sites or attempted to include programmatic and contextual variations in analyses of outcome. Numerous questions remain about the potential impacts of unmeasured variations in inmate characteristics, treatment programs, and multiple outcome measures.

In this study, we examined in-treatment measures and multiple post-release outcomes for 2,809 inmates who participated in TC drug treatment programs (n = 749) or comparison groups (n = 2,060) at five state prisons. Matched comparison groups made up of TC-eligible inmates participating in less intensive forms of treatment (e.g., short-term drug education and outpatient treatment groups) at the same five institutions were constructed based upon known predictors such as drug dependency, need for treatment, and criminal history. Process and outcome measures incorporated a range of institutional, intermediate (e.g., attitudinal and behavioral change, participation in treatment), and post-release measures (e.g., drug relapse, rearrest

---

[1]   Welsh, Wayne (2003). *Evaluation of Prison-Based Therapeutic Community Drug Treatment Programs in Pennsylvania: Executive Summary*. Philadelphia: Department of Criminal Justice, Temple University. Available at: *http://www.pccd.state.pa.us/pccd/site/lib/pccd/stats/completedprojectdocs/tc_eval_-_finalreport.pdf*

Case Study 7.3, *continued*

and reincarceration, employment, levels of parole supervision). At the time of this report, 462 TC inmates and 1,152 comparison inmates had been released from prison, with follow-up periods extending up to 26 months (mean = 13 months). The two groups did not differ significantly on amount of time at risk since their release from prison. We continue to track releases and recidivism for the entire sample. Below we summarize our major findings, recommendations, and conclusions. Details of analyses and further discussion are provided in the full final report for this project.

Major Findings

- Offenders in TC received 15 times the treatment "dose" that the comparison group received.

- We found positive effects of TC treatment upon reincarceration and rearrest rates but not drug relapse rates (Table A).

- Post-release employment strongly and significantly reduced the likelihood of drug relapse, rearrest, and reincarceration (Table B).

Table A
Effects of TC vs. Comparison Group on Three Measures of Recidivism

	Comparison Group	TC Group
Reincarceration Rate	41%	30%*
Rearrest Rate	33%	24%*
Drug Relapse Rate	39%	35%

*$p < .05$
Note. Statistics shown are based on logistic regression results where all control variables including a categorical variable indicating membership in the TC vs. the comparison group were entered into analyses. Results shown thus reflect outcomes controlling for the effects of all other variables (see Results section in full report for further detail).

Table B
Effects of Post-Release Employment on Three Measures of Recidivism

	Full-Time	Part-Time	Unemployed and Able to Work	Unemployed and Unable to Work
Reincarceration Rate	17%	26%	24%	65%*
Rearrest rate	21%	34%	27%	41%*
Drug Relapse rate	30%	39%	38%	44%*

* $p < .05$
Note. Statistics shown are based on logistic regression results where all control variables including a categorical variable indicating membership in the TC vs. the comparison group were entered into analyses. Results shown thus reflect outcomes controlling for the effects of all other variables (see Results section in full report for further detail).

Case Study 7.3, *continued*

- Treatment outcomes were generally invariant across institutions, with one important exception. Significantly higher rates of drug relapse were observed for inmates treated at Cresson (44%) and Houtzdale (43%), compared to Waymart (24%), Huntingdon (32%), and Graterford (35%).

- TC inmates evidenced numerous, positive improvements in psychosocial functioning and involvement in treatment over the first six months of treatment, as indicated by subscales of the TCU Resident Evaluation of Self and Treatment (REST) form and the TCU Counselor Rating of Client (CRC) form. TC inmates showed significant decreases in depression and risk-taking behavior, and significant increases in self-esteem, therapeutic engagement, personal progress, trust in group, opinions of program staff, and perceptions of counselor competence. The strongest area of consistency across the five TC programs was in the high ratings that inmates gave of counselor rapport and counselor competence.

- Each unit, while implementing the basic TC philosophy, also exhibited some programmatic variations. For example, two of the five TC units were rather large (100+ inmates). Large units make it difficult to properly implement the TC philosophy, which depends heavily upon positive peer interactions. Second, while the overall termination rate for TC (26%) was reasonable, one program (Waymart) was very low (5%) and another (Graterford) was very high (71%).

- Eighteen REST scales and eight CRC scales measuring various dimensions of inmate psychosocial functioning and responses to treatment were entered into logistic regression analyses as predictors of the three measures of recidivism (controlling for all other variables). Significant predictors of reincarceration included anxiety, hostility, therapeutic engagement, counselor rapport, ratings of program structure, and rapport with other inmates. No additional predictors of rearrest were statistically significant. Significant predictors of drug relapse included self-efficacy, risk taking, and self-confrontation.

- The validity of our findings were bolstered by the fact that we that we were able to account precisely for total treatment exposure for all inmates in our sample, and we examined the effects of treatment exposure as a control variable. Previous studies have failed to do so.

Case Study 7.3, *continued*

Limitations

- The major limitation was the brevity of the follow-up periods and associated sample sizes available for multivariate analyses so far. As more inmates are released, and as average time at risk increases, we will revisit the analyses and conclusions formulated in this report.

- Our ability to examine post-release outcomes was limited by the unavailability of automated data regarding participation in after-care treatment. Aftercare may interact with employment and other observed predictors to influence outcomes. Further research should examine ways to better integrate prison-based drug treatment with post-release needs and resources.

- It was difficult to determine the degree to which employment was a cause or an effect. To do so, it would be useful to obtain more detailed information on parolees' type of post-release employment, employee performance, income, etc. To disentangle potential causes, research should also determine how other factors (e.g., intelligence, cognitive abilities, education, in-prison and pre-prison work history, job training) might interact with drug treatment to influence post-release outcomes (employment, drug relapse, reincarceration, and rearrest).

- However, none of the control variables examined in this study (e.g., assessed level of need for drug treatment, prior and current offense severity, age) substantially weakened the observed relationship between employment and reduced recidivism, leading us to conclude that the effect of post-release employment is quite robust.

Question

1. Explain how Case Study 7.3 illustrates concepts discussed in Chapter 7, providing evidence to support your answer: (a) nonequivalent comparison groups; (b) confounding factors.

Endnotes

[1] For more thorough discussions of evaluation concepts and methods, we recommend the following works: Berk, Richard A., and Peter H. Rossi (1998). *Thinking About Program Evaluation*, 2nd ed. Newbury Park, CA: Sage; Patton, Michael Quinn (1996). *Utilization-Focused Evaluation: The New Century Text*. Thousand Oaks, CA: Sage; Rossi, Peter H., Mark W. Lipsey, and Howard E. Freeman (2003). *Evaluation: A Systematic Approach*, 7th ed. Thousand Oaks, CA: Sage; Wholey, Joseph S., Harry P. Hatry, and Kathryn E. Newcomer (eds.) (1994). *Handbook of Practical Evaluation*. San Francisco: Jossey-Bass.

[2] See for example: Thompson, M. (1980). *Benefit-Cost Analysis for Program Evaluation*. Beverly Hills: Sage; and Stokey, E., and R. Zeckhauser (1978). *A Primer for Policy Analyses*. New York: Norton.

[3] Lipsey, M.W., and D.B. Wilson (1993). "The Efficacy of Psychological, Educational and Behavioral Treatment: Confirmation from Meta-Analysis." *American Psychologist*, 48:1181-1209.

[4] Gendreau, Paul, and T. Little (1996). "A Meta-Analysis of the Predictors of Adult Offender Recidivism: What Works!" *Criminology*, 34:575-608.

[5] For a detailed description of meta-analysis, see Lipsey, M.W., and D.B. Wilson (2001). *Practical Meta-Analysis*. Thousand Oaks, CA: Sage.

[6] Lipsey, M.W., and D.B. Wilson (1993) "The Efficacy of Psychological, Educational and Behavioral Treatment: Confirmation from Meta-Analysis." *American Psychologist*, 48:1181-1209.

[7] Gaes, G.G., T.J. Flanagan, L.L. Motiuk, and L. Stewart (1999) "Adult Correctional Treatment." In M. Tonry and J. Petersilia (eds.), *Prisons. Crime and Justice, A Review of Research*, Vol. 26, pp. 361-426; Welsh, W.N., and G. Zajac (2004). "A Census of Prison-Based Drug Treatment Programs: Implications for Programming, Policy and Evaluation." *Crime & Delinquency*, 50:108-133.

[8] Rossi, Peter H., Mark W. Lipsey, and Howard E. Freeman (2003). *Evaluation: A Systematic Approach*, 7th ed. Thousand Oaks, CA: Sage; Rutman, Leonard (1984). *Planning Useful Evaluations: Evaluability Assessment*. Beverly Hills: Sage; Wholey, Joseph S., Harry P. Hatry, and Kathryn E. Newcomer (eds.) (1994). *Handbook of Practical Evaluation*. San Francisco: Jossey-Bass.

[9] Wholey, J.S. (1994). "Assessing the Feasibility and Likely Usefulness of Evaluation." In J.S. Wholey, H.P. Hatry, and K.E. Newcomer (eds.), *Handbook of Practical Program Evaluation* (pp. 15-39). San Francisco: Jossey-Bass.

[10] Rosenberg, Morris (1965). *Society and the Adolescent Self-Image*. Princeton, NJ: Princeton University Press.

[11] Available at: *http://www.samhsa.gov/oas/nhsda.htm*

[12] Sherman, Lawrence W., and Richard A. Berk (1984). "The Specific Deterrent Effects of Arrest for Domestic Assault." *American Sociological Review*, 49:261-272.

[13] Ibid, note 12.

[14]   Lempert, Richard (1989). "Humility is a Virtue: On the Publicization of Policy-Relevant Research." *Law and Society Review*, 23:145-161.

[15]   Sherman, Lawrence W. (1992). *Policing Domestic Violence: Experiments and Dilemmas*. New York: Free Press.

[16]   Ibid, note 10.

[17]   Sherman, L.W., J.W. Shaw, and D.P Rogan, (1995). *The Kansas City Gun Experiment* (NCJ-150855). Washington, DC: U.S. Department of Justice, Office of Justice Programs, National Institute of Justice. Available at: *http://www.ncjrs.org/pdffiles/kang.pdf* (retrieved March 17, 2004).

CHAPTER *8*

Initiating the Program or Policy Plan

CHAPTER OUTLINE

▶ *Planning for failure.* Exaggerated goals can hasten implementation failure.

▶ *Planning for success.* Ongoing reassessment, learning, and revision are crucial elements of successful interventions. Four tasks increase chances of success: (1) communication with stakeholders, (2) building internal capacities for leading and learning, (3) studying information about program or policy performance, and (4) increasing the fit between needs and characteristics of the environment and capacities of the program or policy.

▶ *Learning and adapting.* Interventions, their organizations, and surrounding environments change over time, and successful interventions must adapt to change by consciously tailoring the program or policy.

▶ *A caution about program and policy survival.* Interventions sometimes survive long after they are known to be ineffective. Survival is often dependent on how well the intervention serves the personal goals of key stakeholders.

▶ *The tasks of implementation.* Plans from Stages 3 – 6 are finally implemented: Initiating the Design (implementing Stage 3 plans); Initiating the Action Plan (implementing Stage 4 plans); Monitoring Program/Policy Implementation (implementing Stage 5 plans); and Evaluating and Providing Feedback to Users and Stakeholders (implementing Stage 6 plans).

At this point, the program or policy is ready to be launched. Ideally, all six stages of planning should be completed prior to the initial start date for the intervention. We recognize, however, that time constraints imposed on the planning process may result in less-than-optimal program designs and action plans. Nonetheless, at this stage, for the first time, the program or policy takes on life. While planning and reviewing is a continuous process, we now begin doing what we have planned.

We rarely have any control over the environments within which policies and programs are implemented: they have lives of their own, driven by visions and goals that may be independent of our new innovation. They may even be wholly driven by political and financial arrangements that often appear irrational and chaotic. Because any program or policy operates in a dynamic organizational or system environment, we need to pay attention to changes that occur in areas such as political climate, fiscal health of funding sources, key policymakers, and policies related to the intervention. Sometimes these changes will occur independently of our intervention, but in other cases our interventions will cause reactions that require adaptation. As we discussed in Chapter 2 in relation to force field analysis, some of the forces that sustain a problem or issue over time are more potent than others. As these potent forces shift in strength, it becomes critical for programs and policies to change. As an example, consider the economic issues surrounding the export of jobs to other countries.

Example 8.1

Exporting Jobs and the Global Economy

While the development of a global economy and a growth in businesses that span national boundaries is inevitable, there is growing concern in the United States that outsourcing production to countries that can provide cheaper labor will harm the American economy. Because fewer jobs are being created here at home, and because health care and energy costs are rising, worries are growing about how workers who have lost their jobs can be trained and supported to move on to jobs that are likely to be available. As companies in other countries develop and compete with American companies, companies in the United States will have to find ways to cut costs, or will need to constantly innovate in order to stay ahead of innovation elsewhere. However, the answer is often to seek cheaper labor overseas. At the same time that we need resources to train workers who have lost jobs, the current Presidential administration [Bush] is cutting back on support for community colleges, a likely source of this training.

We repeat our warning from Chapter 1: *Planned change improves the likelihood of successful intervention, but it cannot guarantee it.* Good planning increases the odds of success by explicitly considering important factors that might lead to failure or success.

Example 8.2

Criminal Justice Planning and the Lesson of Jurassic Park

Our preference for rational planning is a value that guides our writing and research. We are not so naïve, however, to believe that careful planning always produces successful outcomes. Even the most carefully crafted plans can have no effect, make problems worse, or create unintended effects. There are other times when energy and resources are wasted because planning processes are terminated prematurely. In general, subtle facets of the criminal justice system (see Chapter 2) can frustrate good planning. In real life, systems do not always behave the way we want them to.

In *Jurassic Park*,[1] Ian Malcolm, a mathematician (played in the 1993 film by Jeff Goldblum[2]), warns of the larger, more powerful natural rhythms of nature that can undermine what appear to be great scientific advancements. "My point is that life on earth can take care of itself," he raves. "In the thinking of a human being, a hundred years is a long time. . . . But to the earth, a hundred years is nothing. A million years is nothing. This planet lives and breathes on a much vaster scale. We can't imagine its slow and powerful rhythms, and we haven't got the humility to try. We have been residents here for the blink of an eye. If we are gone tomorrow, the earth will not miss us."

Eugene Doleschal[3] sounded a similar warning, this one directed at criminal justice reform efforts. He argued that forces that continually shape the justice system should be allowed to interact naturally. When reforms are implemented, the results are often the opposite of those intended. For example, many efforts intended to reduce prison populations through the creation of community-based program have failed to do so. Instead, community programs have often extended supervision and control of less serious offenders. Other examples include policy changes intended to reduce discretion that only moved discretion to other, less visible, decision points in the system. He likened these reforms to a program conducted in Alaska and Canada to protect herds of caribou from their natural predator, the wolf. By shooting the wolves, environmentalists hoped to increase the caribou population. Instead, old and sick caribou that previously were killed and eaten by the wolves faced death by starvation and disease.

Rather than give up on planning, we can learn from these experiences. In many cases, failures become the means for discovering the nature and strengths of forces we are trying to change. Sometimes we may decide that our knowledge and resources are inadequate to the task, but in other cases we become better equipped to try again.

Planning for Failure

Failure of any program or policy is related to two broad types of difficulties: (1) insurmountable obstacles within the implementing agency or its environment, and (2) breakdowns or omissions in the planning process.

First, it is possible for a program or policy to fail even when its designers have planned thoroughly and carefully. It may be the case that certain obstacles are too big or powerful to overcome—or that inadequate resources are available to do so. As discussed in Chapter 2, such obstacles may be *physical* (e.g., the physical design of a courthouse precludes more efficient case processing), *social* (e.g., existing barriers related to class, gender, or race are unchanged by the program or policy), *economic* (lack of sufficient funding), *educational* (e.g., special training or education is required to implement an intervention), legal (e.g., criminal justice agencies are legally obligated to do certain things and prohibited from doing other things), *political* (e.g., motivations of partisan stakeholders can block a specific change), or *technological* (e.g., problems with managing the information system required to implement a new policy). A criminal justice systems analysis and a force field analysis should help planners anticipate such obstacles and develop strategies to overcome them. Such activities increase the probability of success.

The second set of difficulties concerns planning breakdowns, omissions, or deficits: one or more critical planning tasks have not been properly executed. The examples and case studies presented in Chapters 2 through 7 illustrate some of the most likely deficits in the planning process. We reiterate in Figure 8.1 some common difficulties at each stage.

Figure 8.1

Common Planning Deficits at Each Stage

Stage 1: Analyzing the Problem
- Insufficient information about the problem has been examined. We do not really know how big the problem is, where it is, or who is affected. We may not even have a clear definition of the problem.
- No theory guided the intervention. We do not know how or why the expected change should have occurred.
- Inadequate examination of previous interventions: we may have recreated the wheel, or recycled an old, broken wheel by failing to learn about previous attempts to change the problem.
- Important stakeholders were not identified or included in the planning process.
- Inadequate examination of the larger system or environment was conducted.

Figure 8.1, *continued*

Stage 2: Setting Goals and Objectives
- Goals and objectives were not clearly stated.
- Substantial disagreement about goals or objectives persisted among stakeholders.
- Incompatible goals or values in the larger system were not identified.
- Needs for interagency collaboration were not sufficiently addressed.

Stage 3: Designing the Program or Policy
- No specific intervention approach was identified.
- Target populations and selection were not adequately identified.
- Program components or policy provisions and procedures were unclear.
- Responsibilities of program staff or policy authorities were unclear.

Stage 4: Developing an Action Plan
- Required resources have not been properly identified.
- Required resources have not been acquired.
- Responsibilities for implementation have not been clearly assigned.
- Insufficient attention was devoted to maintaining support and anticipating resistance.

Stage 5: Developing a Plan for Monitoring Program/Policy Implementation
- No monitoring of program or policy implementation was attempted.
- Information systems for monitoring were inadequate.
- Monitoring instruments were unreliable.
- Responsibilities for data collection, storage, or analysis were unclear.
- Monitoring data was not used to make necessary adjustments to the program or policy.

Stage 6: Develop a Plan for Evaluating Outcomes
- Prerequisites for evaluation were not adequately met.
- Outcome measures were not reliable or valid.
- The research design was inadequate to determine outcomes.
- Confounding factors were not adequately addressed.
- Users of evaluation results were not adequately identified or consulted.

Stage 7: Initiating the Program or Policy Plan
- Inadequate review of the planning process was undertaken before implementation began.
- Substantial obstacles within the implementing agency or its environment subverted the aims of the program or policy.
- Planning breakdowns, errors, or omissions occurred.
- The change agent failed to learn and adapt during implementation.
- The change agent failed to properly execute plans.

Consider the following example. Implementation failure easily occurs when leaders overstate the goals of a program or policy (Stage 2) in order to garner support from stakeholders in the larger political environment (Stage 1). When innovations are oversold, stakeholders feel deceived and cheated. Todd Clear and his colleagues[4] observed with humor the range of promises attached to intensive probation services (IPS): "Advocates of IPS programs are not humble in the claims they made for these programs. Commonly, IPS is expected to reduce prison crowding, increase public protection, rehabilitate the offender, demonstrate the value of probation, and save money. Even a skeptic is bound to be impressed" (p. 32). These exaggerated objectives eventually spelled trouble for the evaluation (Stage 6). Petersilia and Turner[5] found in their evaluation of 14 IPS programs that the primary purposes of intensive supervision were rarely achieved:

- The programs did not alleviate prison crowding and may have increased it in some sites.
- They cost considerably more than is generally realized (Stage 5).
- They were no more effective than routine probation and parole in reducing recidivism.

The best that can be hoped for in the wake of such disappointing outcomes is a careful reassessment of the entire planning process followed by necessary adjustments (Stage 7)—especially a more realistic accounting of goals and objectives (Stage 2).

Planning for Success

The important point to keep in mind at the implementation stage is that the planning process has not yet ended. In fact, it never will. New information pertinent to the program or policy will emerge (some of it though evaluation research) that may suggest modification to the original design. This is what learning is about. The organization's capacity to learn will largely determine the extent to which the goals of the innovation are achieved. There are four tasks that need emphasis at this point in order to increase the chances of success.

1. *Communicate*: Continually communicate to constituents and potential opponents the need for the program or policy. Develop advocates for the program or policy among a wide range of public officials so that the vision of what you are up to is passed on to others who may be asked about the need for it. Publicize widely and frequently information on the program and its performance.

2. *Build internal capacities for leading and learning*: Those persons who are carrying out the activities articulated in the design are your most valuable assets. Their command of the vision, goals, and activities described in the design are critical to the innovation's success. Their ability to lead, support each other, think strategically, adapt to, and carry out their assigned tasks are essential to a program's success. Your organization needs to invest in their development.

3. *Study*: The need for information is essential for learning to occur. Data regarding implementation of the program or policy's design, data on performance, and data on changes in the environment need to be tracked and brought into discussions among key stakeholders.

4. *Increase the fit*: Purposefully permit the innovation to take shape as new information about the needs and characteristics of the environment emerge and as the capacities of the program or policy develop. The better it fits the needs and priorities of the political environment, the greater will be the level of acceptance.

Learning and Adapting

In Chapter 1, we mentioned the concept of *mutual adaptation*: the program (or policy) and the organizational environment in which it operates will both change during the implementation process. Programs change over time. Not only is there continual reshaping of a program design before it is put into action, programs continue to change following the point at which "the tire meets the road." It is this change in program characteristics that makes components of a program design poor predictors of program success. Then, too, program staff, program clients, and decisionmakers, rather than being passive participants in the implementation process, directly affect how the innovations are used, adapting the innovation to existing organizational structures and norms, and using them to serve their own purposes.

In addition, the same program design can produce drastically different results in different settings, thus supporting the conclusion that context is critical to outcome. You may recall from our discussion in Chapter 2 regarding systems analysis that the private sector has played a critical role in criminal justice for many years. Some local criminal justice systems, however, have had disastrous experiences with private-sector programs. In corrections, for example, the promised fiscal advantages of private corrections have not always materialized.[6]

It is not only innovations that undergo change during the implementation process, however; the organization within which the innovation is used also undergoes change. A new program for sex offenders is not installed in a vacuum; rather, this innovation must be accepted by a living system in which the balance is necessarily disrupted. Specifically with regard to a probation program in Texas, Markley[7] observed that when program management personnel changed, line staff became "demoralized." Their commitment to the program was dependent on the leadership provided by a few individuals. Other common disruptions include the transfer of personnel to a new program, the hiring of outsiders (new staff) to staff a new program, and the requirement that staff acquire new skills in order to continue doing their jobs.

Implementation of a program or policy in any organizational setting requires both adaptation by individuals and adaptation of the innovation in order for the implementation process to succeed.[8] This process of mutual adaptation implies that the same innovation can look very different across different settings.[9] The critical point to be made is that unless a program or policy is carefully tailored to the setting in which it is to be used, successful implementation is unlikely.

An excellent example of this kind of tailoring of the innovation can be seen in the approach that The Center for Alternative Sentencing and Employment Services (CASES) in New York City has taken to ensure that its clients fit their target population: jail-bound rather than probation-bound offenders. Data on sentencing in New York revealed that sentencing practices differed across the five boroughs. Judges in Queens, for example, require fewer misdemeanor offenses than do those in Manhattan before sentencing an offender to serve significant jail time. In order to prevent use of the CASES Community Service Sentencing Project (CSSP) from being used as a replacement for probation, criteria for accepting offenders into CSSP are adjusted to sentencing patterns at the borough level.[10]

Not only does tailoring itself promote effective adaptation, so do the structural characteristics of organizations. Decentralization of program control, for example, permits different sites to develop a program design at their own pace and allows the program to adapt to the idiosyncrasies of each site in ways that improve chances for successful implementation. It may be that a program is more effective under some conditions than under others, but it may also be the case that different modes of adaptation make it possible for an innovation to adapt to a variety of organizational environments.

It is critical during implementation to uncover any changes in the intended program or policy design and describe them. These changes are deviations from the original plan and must be understood before a sound evaluation can be conducted.

A Caution about Survival

Mutual adaptation also means that acceptance of and continued support for an innovation may serve the personal goals of decisionmakers. For example, if a program can screen cases and make admission decisions rapidly, life is made easier for referring agents such as probation officers and judges. A policy may be passed that gives prosecutors greater discretion (power). This has been the case in many mandatory sentencing schemes that allow charges to determine the sentence. David Rothman[11] refers to these latter motivations as *convenience* in contrast to the benevolent interests, what Rothman calls *conscience*, which may have served to motivate the creators of the innovation.

Unfortunately, even in the face of clear evidence that an innovation is failing, such interests of convenience may be powerful enough to sustain the innovation. Valuable resources can then be wasted that could be put to better use in the service of promising programs and policies. To counter this problem, evidence of what works and what doesn't should be shared as widely as possible. If evaluation data are not collected and results are not disseminated, or if they are kept confidential to protect the political interests of individuals, we run the risk of "convenience" (self-interest) winning out. Sharing outcome information among all stakeholders creates an environment in which system values can dominate policymaking.

The Tasks of Implementation

Implementing the program or policy plan (Stage 7) involves putting into motion the program design (Stage 3) and the action plan (Stage 4), monitoring implementation (Stage 5), and, if appropriate, evaluating outcomes (Stage 6). Once evaluation data are analyzed, feedback is provided to all stakeholders, and the program should be thoroughly reassessed to determine where revisions are necessary. At the end of the process, the change agent asks whether further adjustments are necessary to meet program objectives. What are the strengths and weaknesses of the program? Decisions may have to be made about whether the program should be continued and whether it should receive further funding. Reassessment and review of the program or policy should occur periodically from this point on.

Initiating the Program/Policy Design

In Chapter 4, we examined how a program or policy is constructed. Every program or policy must have a clearly defined design that includes: targets (e.g., eligibility, numbers to be served, access, screening, intake), program staff or individuals responsible for implementing the program or policy (e.g., selection, training, duties), and program components or policy provisions (e.g., specific goods, services, opportunities, or interventions to be delivered). Initiating the design, then, requires doing everything that was previously specified. Together with the action plan, the design lays out the major tasks for implementation.

Initiating the Action Plan

In Chapter 5, you learned how to develop an action plan that specified the entire sequence of tasks that need to be completed in order to successfully launch or implement the program or policy. These included technical and interpersonal tasks (e.g., identifying and acquiring the necessary resources, locating office space and/or meeting space, hiring and training staff, designing client intake and reporting forms, purchasing equipment and supplies, setting dates and assigning responsibility for the completion of specific tasks). The action plan is, in essence, a "blueprint" explaining how to translate a vision of the program or policy into reality.

Like the director of an orchestra, the change agent must coordinate the program or policy activities of all the different individuals and groups associated with the program or policy. Managers must hire and train their staff; they must build good relations with potential referral sources (e.g., police, schools, probation); they must train staff to use required intake forms and keep client records; they must build good relations with citizens and businesses in the neighborhood; and they must provide regular reports of progress to their funding providers. Remember three guidelines to ensure smooth coordination: (1) maintain consistency between staff job descriptions and actual tasks, (2) maintain clear and frequent communication among staff members, and between staff and supervisors; and (3) keep an eye on the time-line: make sure that activities required for successful progression from one step to the next are carried out on time (e.g., take care that staff are hired and trained by the dates specified in the action plan; make sure that all record-keeping forms are printed; ensure that procedures are clearly understood by staff).

Remember that some resistance is inevitable with the start-up of a new program or policy. Resistance may come from any of the participants involved: clients, targets, even the intervention's own staff (i.e., the action system). Resistance that appears should be dealt with fairly and seriously. Conflict is not something to be avoided at all costs. It may provide the opportunity to identify and resolve misunderstandings, and it may also point out difficulties in implementation that truly deserve attention.

Begin Monitoring Program/Policy Implementation

At Stage 6 (see Chapter 5), you laid out a plan for monitoring program or policy implementation. As program or policy operations begin, it is time to start monitoring. *Implementation* refers to the initiation, management, and administration of the action plan. Once the intervention actually begins, we want to minimize discrepancies between what was planned (i.e., the program or policy on paper) and what is actually done (i.e., the program or policy in action). *Monitoring* attempts to determine whether program/policy implementation is proceeding as planned. Monitoring is a process that attempts to identify any gaps between the program or policy on paper (design) and the program or policy in action (implementation).

For the target population, monitoring data should assess the following questions: What were the characteristics of the actual individuals targeted by the intervention? Were the targets selected truly in need or at risk? Is the intervention meeting its specified criteria in terms of target eligibility (e.g., age, sex, income, region) and numbers to be served? Were proper recruiting, screening, and intake procedures followed? How were referrals made? For program components, monitoring data should answer the following questions: who did what to whom in what order, how much, and how often? Were there variations in service delivery or activities? Did different staff deliver programming in a different manner? Was there more than one program site or location, and if so, were program activities administered consistently across different sites? Make sure that monitoring data also provide information about service tasks and responsible authorities: Were proper staff or authorities identified? Did they fit the specified roles and job descriptions? Did they understand their duties and perform them as expected?

Begin Evaluating and Providing Feedback to Users and Stakeholders

If any evaluation is to be useful, it should serve the information needs of the intervention and its stakeholders (see Chapter 2). Most notably, the program or policy's major stakeholder is its funding agency, but any intervention has multiple stakeholders such as the community, businesses, politicians, criminal justice agencies, volunteers, clients, and so on. The time spent previously (at Stage 1) identifying stakeholders should not be wasted. Evaluation (Stage 6) is a critical means of demonstrating accountability (and hopefully, effectiveness) to stakeholders. The change agent should now assign individual responsibility for packaging and communicating evaluation results to different users. If the results are to be useful—and used—one must create means of communication that can be understood and reacted to by the intended audiences.

Conclusion

Implementation is an ongoing process of adaptation, negotiation, and communication. In order to maximize the mutual fit between a program or policy and the environment within which it is initiated and allowed to develop, both the innovation and the environment must change.

At this point, we hope that students and practitioners have a good idea of the kind of analyses that should be done and questions that should be asked to figure out what works to reduce or prevent any specific problem. We have argued throughout this book that many criminal justice interventions fall short of their goals because of poor planning, poor implementation, and poor evaluation. What we truly need is not *more* programs and policies or *new* programs and policies, per se: we need *better* programs and policies. We need a better understanding of planned change to improve the effectiveness of criminal justice interventions. Such change is ubiquitous in governmental, community, private, and nonprofit agencies. This book has attempted to provide a systematic, seven-stage framework for analyzing and improving existing interventions, but also for planning new ones so as to maximize chances of success. Major steps of analysis were summarized in Figure 1.1.

Which of the following interventions are effective? How would you know, or how would you find out?

- Prisoner reentry initiatives and programs, including prison-based drug treatment and community aftercare, vocational and basic education, post-release employment assistance, and reintegration assistance.

- Drug Awareness Resistance Education (D.A.R.E.) for elementary, middle school, and high school students.

- Federal "Weed and Seed" Program (dual policy of first stamping out drug sales in specific communities, then "seeding" the communities with protective, economic, and social resources).

- Shelters, counseling, and victim assistance for abused women.

- Mandatory arrest policies for suspected spouse abusers.

- Juvenile waiver laws (serious juvenile offenses may be transferred to adult courts, or automatically tried as adult offenses).

- Comprehensive prisoner reentry and drug courts that provide assessment and treatment services in conjunction with traditional criminal sanctions

We reiterate a few major propositions to conclude this endeavor. First, we need a systematic plan for any change effort. Interventions both new and old need to be subjected to thorough scrutiny and analysis. Successful interventions are a product of hard work, careful planning, and a willingness to revise where necessary.

Second, good intentions are rarely sufficient to bring about successful change. Beware of the "activist bias,"[12] by which well-intentioned advocates of change assume that they already know what the problem is and what is needed. Such advocates may insist that we desist all this prolonged planning and simply "get on with it." The perils of unplanned or poorly planned change should by now be obvious: expensive, poorly articulated, poorly implemented, ineffective programs and policies that are unable to successfully compete for scarce funds.

Third, program or policy planning is an interactive and ongoing process. It is crucial to review and modify planning (where needed) at each stage of the analysis. This takes time, but it is time well spent.

Fourth, a rational planning approach provides a framework for developing logical and effective programs and policies. The default (all too commonly) is to use unarticulated and untested assumptions to guide planning. Finally, participation of and communication with all key actors or stakeholders (e.g., program staff, clients, individuals or agencies whose cooperation is needed, funding sources, citizens affected by the intervention, elected representatives, etc.) throughout the change process are keys to success. While careful planning and analysis cannot guarantee success, it will increase the probability of success.

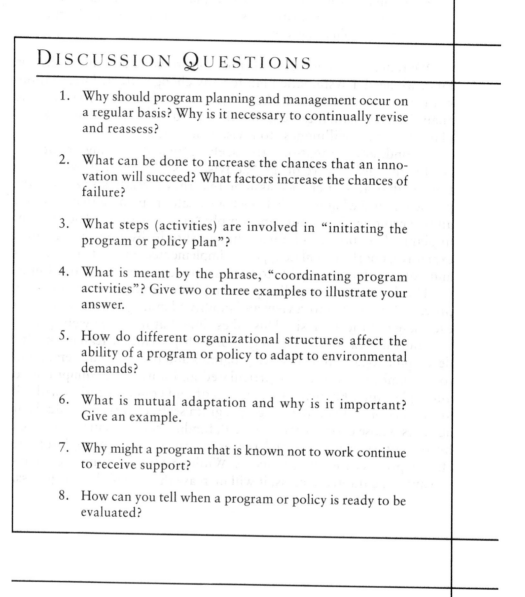

DISCUSSION QUESTIONS

1. Why should program planning and management occur on a regular basis? Why is it necessary to continually revise and reassess?

2. What can be done to increase the chances that an innovation will succeed? What factors increase the chances of failure?

3. What steps (activities) are involved in "initiating the program or policy plan"?

4. What is meant by the phrase, "coordinating program activities"? Give two or three examples to illustrate your answer.

5. How do different organizational structures affect the ability of a program or policy to adapt to environmental demands?

6. What is mutual adaptation and why is it important? Give an example.

7. Why might a program that is known not to work continue to receive support?

8. How can you tell when a program or policy is ready to be evaluated?

Case Study 8.1

Implementation Woes: Providing Residential Substance Abuse Treatment (RSAT) for Inmates in State Prisons

Instructions: *First read the background below, then read the article that follows. Answer the questions at the end of the case study.*

"The best laid plans 'o mice and men gang aft aglay . . .," Scottish poet Robbie Burns said it well. No matter how carefully "wee timorous beasties" or humans plan for the future, things never work out exactly as planned. Even when planned change is successful, it may not be permanent. Why not, you may ask? People who played critical roles ("stakeholders"), including leadership roles, come and go over time; initial enthusiasm abates; the political environment changes; the priority assigned to a specific public problem shifts; and the actual change that resulted may not have been sufficiently dramatic to maintain or recruit new support. Planned change is dynamic, like the problems it seeks to address. The need for substance abuse treatment among prison inmates is widely accepted. Developing effective methods to address those needs is quite another. The following case study summarizes some of the implementation problems that have been faced by a federally sponsored initiative.[1]

Background

The Residential Substance Abuse Treatment (RSAT) Program was created as part of the Violent Crime Control and Law Enforcement Act of 1994 to meet the needs of state correctional systems for resources to address a growing problem. Through the act, state authorities gained access to funds, technical assistance, and a network of innovators that could help them build their own local treatment programs. Every state took advantage of these funds, and by March of 2001, more than 2,000 RSAT programs were involved in providing services to adult inmates and parolees, as well as juvenile offenders.

With so many programs in place, the need to learn about the effectiveness of different treatment approaches was immense. Consequently, the federal government sponsored a national evaluation program. From a monitoring perspective, large numbers of inmates and parolees were receiving treatment, but to learn about what works takes time. Meanwhile, information regarding implementation was assembled and became part of the strategy for continued program development.

---

[1]   Harrison, L.D., and S.S. Martin (2003). *Residential Substance Abuse Treatment for State Prisoners: Implementation Lessons Learned.* NIJ Special Report (NCJ 195738, web-only document). Washington, DC: U.S. Department of Justice, Office of Justice Programs, National Institute of Justice. Available at: *http://www.ncjrs.org/pdffiles1/nij/195738.pdf* (retrieved March 17, 2004).

Case Study 8.1, *continued*

Implementation Lessons

Lana Harrison and Steven Martin[2] provided the following summary of the implementation difficulties encountered by RSAT programs.

Program Difficulties

The most severe problems reported by state officials involved locating or constructing appropriate facilities, recruiting trained treatment staff, and contracting with treatment providers under lengthy or complex bidding and proposal processes. More than one-half (53 percent) reported moderate or severe delays related to difficulties in locating facilities for the residential treatment program, and 37 percent reported delays resulting from the need to construct or physically alter existing structures. About one-fourth of states (28 percent) reported encountering difficulties as a result of state regulations, and one-fifth (21 percent) reported delays due to state bidding or competitive processes. Nearly two-thirds (62 percent) of the states reported difficulties in obtaining training for treatment staff.

Lack of aftercare. The National Evaluation's report expressed concern over the lack of aftercare, particularly because the RSAT Request for Proposal (RFP) for states emphasized that in-prison programs with aftercare services should be given preference. Aftercare was not funded, however, and RSAT funds could be used only for the residential treatment component. The National Evaluation found that work release (23%) or halfway houses (20%) were incorporated as aftercare programs in less than one-half of the RSAT programs. A few others had parole-supervised treatment as part of aftercare, but these numbers were not reported in the National Evaluation. The National Evaluation determined that 86 percent of RSAT in-prison treatment programs have either specified how graduates may continue treatment in the community or indicated their intention to do so. Continuity of care is an important element in treatment for offenders and is strongly linked to reductions in recidivism and drug use.

Merging of treatment components. The National Evaluation also expressed concern over the merging of treatment components. RSAT programs are "intended to develop the inmate's cognitive, behavioral, social, vocational, and other skills," which lends itself to a multifaceted approach. Yet the evaluators pointed out that therapeutic communities, and 12-step programs in particular, are based on different theories and practices. The 12-step programs are spiritually based, which is different from professional therapy. Nevertheless, 12-step programs have worked in conjunction with therapeutic communities for many years. The National Evaluation accurately pointed out that com-

---

[2] Harrison and Martin, p. 15.

> **Case Study 8.1,** *continued*
>
> bination treatments have not been fully evaluated and that many combinations may result in watered down components, leading to less effective treatment.
>
> **Other problems.** The National Evaluation showed that 55 percent of the RSAT programs lacked one or more operational treatment components, and 53 percent of program directors still considered their programs to be in the "shakedown" phase rather than stabilized at the RSAT midpoint. Programs had difficulty recruiting staff trained in the therapeutic-community and/or cognitive-behavioral methods as suggested in the RSAT RFP. Many states encountered difficulties employing ex-offenders and recovering addicts as counselors in prison therapeutic communities; often, individuals with criminal records were not allowed to enter the institutions to work or visit. Evidence regarding therapeutic community staff effectiveness, however, shows that staff should consist of a mixture of recovered therapeutic-community graduates and other counseling (social work, educational, or mental health) professionals.[3]
>
> ### Questions
>
> 1. Using the chart in Chapter 1 (Figure 1.1) as a guide, identify two major steps in the seven-stage model of planned change that could help explain what happened with the RSAT programs nationally. Use specific concepts from the text, and provide evidence from the article to support your answer.
>
> ---
>
> [3] Wexler, H.K. (1997) "Therapeutic Communities in American Prisons: Prison Treatment for Substance Abusers." In F. Cullen, L. Jones, and R. Woodward (eds.), *Therapeutic Communities for Offenders*, pp. 161–179. Chichester, NY: John Wiley and Sons.

Endnotes

[1]   Crichton, Michael (1990). *Jurassic Park*. New York: Ballantine.

[2]   Universal Films (1993). *Jurassic Park*. Directed by Steven Spielberg. Produced by Kathleen Kennedy and Gerald R. Molen. Written by Michael Crichton and David Koepp. Based on the novel by Michael Crichton. Photographed by Dean Cundey. Edited by Michael Kahn. Music by John Williams.

[3]   Doleschal, Eugene (1992). "The Dangers of Criminal Justice Reform." *Criminal Justice Abstracts*, (March) 133-152.

[4]   Clear, T., S. Flynn, and C. Shapiro (1987). "Intensive Supervision in Probation: A Comparison of Three Projects." In B. McCarthy (ed.), *Intermediate Punishments: Intensive Supervision, Home Confinement, and Electronic Surveillance*, pp. 31-51. Monsey, NY: Criminal Justice Press.

[5]   Petersilia, Joan, and Susan Turner (1990). "Comparing Intensive and Regular Supervision for High-Risk Probationers: Early Results from an Experiment in California." *Crime & Delinquency*, 36:87-111.

[6]   Shichor, David (1995). *Punishment for Profit: Private Prisons/Public Concerns*. Thousand Oaks, CA: Sage.

[7]   Markley, Greg (1989). "The Marriage of Mission, Management, Marketing and Measurement." *Research in Corrections*, 2.

[8]   Berman, P. (1981). "Thinking about Programmed and Adaptive Implementation: Matching Strategies to Situations." In H. Ingram and D. Mann (eds.), *Why Policies Succeed or Fail*. Beverly Hills, CA: Sage; McLaughlin, M. (1976). "Implementation as Mutual Adaptation: Change in Classroom Organization." In W. Williams and R.F. Elmore (eds.), *Social Program Evaluation*. Academic Press.

[9]   Ellickson, P., and J. Petersilia (1983). *Implementing New Ideas in Criminal Justice*. Santa Monica, CA: RAND.

[10] Neises, E. (1993). *Report: The Center for Alternative Sentencing and Employment Services*. New York: The Center for Alternative Sentencing and Employment Services.

[11] Rothman, David (1980). *Conscience and Convenience: The Asylum and its Alternatives in Progressive America*. Boston: Little, Brown.

[12] Sieber, Sam D. (1981). *Fatal Remedies*. New York: Plenum.

Appendix 1:
A Seven-Stage Checklist for
Program and Policy Planning

Stage 1: Analyzing the Problem

❏ **A. *Document the need for change***: Collect and analyze data to define what the problem is, where it is, how big it is, and who is affected by it. What evidence of the problem exists?

❏ **B. *Describe the history of the problem***: How long has the problem existed? How has it changed over time?

❏ **C. *Examine potential causes of the problem***: What causes the problem? What theories do we have? The intervention to be chosen must target one or more specific causes supported by research.

❏ **D. *Examine previous interventions*** that have tried to change this problem. Identify the most promising interventions and choose a preferred intervention approach.

❏ **E. *Identify relevant stakeholders***: Do different groups of people have different definitions of the problem? Who is affected by the problem?

❏ **F. *Conduct a systems analysis***: Conduct research on the justice system where the problem exists, and determine how the system may create, contribute to, or maintain the problem.

❏ **G. *Identify barriers to change and supports for change***: Who is likely to support a certain course of action? Who is likely to resist it?

Stage 2. Setting Goals and Objectives

❏ **A. *Write goal statements*** specifying the general outcome to be obtained. Consider the goals of criminal sanctions and normative values driving desired outcomes.

❏ **B. *Write specific outcome objectives for each goal***: These should include a time frame for measuring impact, a target population, a key result intended, and a specific criterion or measure of impact.

❑   C. *Seek participation* from different individuals and agencies in goal setting. Consider top-down versus bottom-up approaches.

❑   D. *Specify an impact model*: This is a description of how the intervention will act upon a specific cause so as to bring about a change in the problem.

❑   E. *Identify compatible and incompatible goals in the larger system*: Where do values of different stakeholders overlap or conflict?

❑   F. *Identify needs and opportunities for interagency collaboration.* Whose cooperation and participation is needed to achieve the goals of this program or policy?

Stage 3. Designing the Program or Policy

❑   A. *Choose an intervention approach*: Integrate the information collected at previous stages to decide what the substance of an intervention will be. Decide whether a program or policy approach is appropriate.

❑   B. **Program design** requires four major activities:

  ❑   (1) *Define the target population*: Who is to be served, or changed?

  ❑   (2) *Define client selection and intake procedures*: How are clients selected and recruited for the intervention?

  ❑   (3) *Define program components*: The precise nature, amount, and sequence of services provided must be specified. Who does what to whom, in what order, and how much?

  ❑   (4) Write *job descriptions* of staff, and define the *skills and training* required.

❑   C. **Policy design** requires four major activities:

  ❑   (1) *Define the target population of the policy.* Which persons or groups are included, and which are not?

  ❑   (2) *Identify the responsible authority.* Who is required to carry out the policy, and what will their responsibilities be?

  ❑   (3) *Define the provisions of the policy.* A policy should identify the goods, services, opportunities, or interventions that will be delivered, and the conditions that must be met in order for the provisions to be carried out.

  ❑   (4) *Delineate the procedures that must be followed.* Individuals responsible for implementing a specific set of rules must clearly understand the specific steps and actions to be taken to ensure that the policy is carried out consistently.

Stage 4. Developing an Action Plan

☐   A. *Identify resources needed and make cost projections*: How much funding is needed to implement a specific intervention? Identify the kinds of resources needed, estimate costs and make projections, and develop a resource plan.

☐   B. *Plan to acquire or reallocate resources*: How will funding be acquired? Identify resource providers, and be prepared for making adjustments to the resource plan.

☐   C. *Specify dates by which implementation tasks will be accomplished, and assign responsibilities to staff members for carrying out tasks.* A Gantt Chart is particularly useful for this purpose.

☐   D. *Develop mechanisms of self-regulation:* Create mechanisms to monitor staff performance and enhance communication, including procedures for orienting participants, coordinating activities, and managing resistance and conflict.

☐   E. *Specify a plan to build and maintain support*: Anticipate sources of resistance and develop responses.

Stage 5. Developing a Plan for Monitoring Program/Policy Implementation

☐   A. *Design a monitoring system* to assess to what degree the program or policy *design* (see Chapter 4) is being carried out as planned. Is the intended target population being reached? Are program/policy activities or provisions actually being carried out as planned? Are appropriate staff or responsible authorities selected and trained, and are they carrying out their assigned duties?

☐   B. *Design monitoring instruments to collect data* (e.g., observations, surveys, interviews). Collect data to find out what is actually being delivered to clients or targets. The purpose is to identify gaps between the program/policy on paper (design) and the program/policy in action.

☐   C. *Designate responsibility for data collection, storage, and analysis*: Ensure that there is no ambiguity about what information is to be collected, who is responsible for collecting it, or how it is to be collected, stored, and analyzed.

☐   D. *Develop information system capacities.* Information systems may consist of written forms and records that are filed, or fully computerized data entry and storage systems.

❏   **E.** *Develop mechanisms to provide feedback to staff, clients, and stakeholders.* Depending on the results of monitoring analyses, it may be necessary to make adjustments either to what is being done (the program or policy in action) or to the intended design (the program or policy on paper).

Stage 6. Develop a Plan for Evaluating Outcomes

❏   **A.** *Decide which type of evaluation is appropriate, and why.* Do major stakeholders (including those funding the evaluation) want to know whether the program or policy achieving its objectives (impact), how outcomes change over time (continuous outcomes), or whether it is worth the investment of resources devoted to its implementation (efficiency)?

❏   **B.** *Determine whether two prerequisites for evaluation have been met:* (1) Are objectives clearly defined and measurable? (2) Has the intervention been sufficiently well designed and well implemented?

❏   **C.** *Develop outcome measures based on objectives.* Good outcome measures should be valid and reliable.

❏   **D.** *Identify potential confounding factors* (factors other than the intervention that may have biased observed outcomes). Common confounding factors include biased selection, biased attrition, and history.

❏   **E.** *Determine which technique for minimizing confounding effects can be used—random assignment or nonequivalent comparison groups:* Each involves creating some kind of comparison or control group.

❏   **F.** *Specify the appropriate research design to be used.* Examples include: the simple pretest-posttest design; the pretest-posttest design with control group; the pretest-posttest design with multiple pretests; the longitudinal design with treatment and control groups; and the cohort design.

❏   **G.** *Identify users and uses of evaluation results:* Who is the intended audience, and how can results be effectively and efficiently communicated? How will the results be used?

❏   **H.** *Reassess the entire program or policy plan:* Review the entire planning process from start to finish, looking for any inconsistencies, contradictions, or inadequacies.

Stage 7. Initiating the Program or Policy Plan

❏   **A.** *Initiate the program or policy design and the action plan* developed at Stages 3 and 4. Make sure that specific individuals are responsible for coordinating all program or policy activities.

❏   B. *Begin monitoring program/policy implementation* according to plans developed at Stage 5.

❏   C. *Make adjustments* to program or policy design as monitoring detects gaps.

❏   D. *Determine whether the program or policy is ready to be evaluated.*

❏   E. *Implement the research design* developed at Stage 6. Collect and analyze evaluation data.

❏   F. *Provide feedback to stakeholders.*

❏   G. *Reassess the entire program/policy plan and make necessary modifications* to increase fit with the program or policy's environment.

About the Authors

Wayne N. Welsh is an Associate Professor of Criminal Justice at Temple University. He received his Ph.D. in Social Ecology from the University of California, Irvine, in 1990 and his M.A. in Applied Social Psychology from the University of Saskatchewan (Canada) in 1986. Undergraduate courses he has taught include Introduction to Criminal Justice; Violence, Crime, and Justice; Environmental Criminology; and Planned Change in Criminal Justice. Graduate courses include Violence, Crime, and Aggression; Criminal Justice Organizations: Structure, Process, and Change; and Rehabilitation, Reentry, and Recidivism. He is the author of *Counties in Court: Jail Overcrowding and Court-Ordered Reform* (Temple University Press, 1995) and *Criminal Violence: Patterns, Causes and Prevention*, with Marc Riedel (Roxbury, 2002). Recent articles have appeared in *Crime & Delinquency*, *Criminology*, *Justice Quarterly*, and *The Prison Journal*. Welsh served as Deputy Editor of *The Prison Journal* from 1993 to 2000. He has conducted research in two broad areas: (1) applications of organizational theory to criminal justice and examinations of organizational change, and (2) theories of violent behavior and intervention/prevention programs. His recent research has focused on prison-based drug treatment, school violence, and community-based delinquency prevention.

Welsh has been Principal Investigator on numerous federally and state-funded research grants, including "Building a Research Collaborative Between the Pennsylvania Department of Corrections and the Center for Public Policy at Temple University (1998-99)," "Evaluation of Prison-Based Drug Treatment in Pennsylvania (1999-2002)," and "Evaluation of Drug Treatment Programs at SCI-Chester" (2002-05). Based upon a collaborative research partnership between the Pennsylvania Department of Corrections and Temple University, these projects have examined critical interactions between inmate characteristics, prison-based treatment programs, and post-release outcomes such as relapse, recidivism, and employment. The development of an ongoing research relationship between DOC and Temple University has been a primary goal, increasing the capacity of both agencies to produce useful knowledge. Previous research projects included a school violence study titled "Building a Culture and Climate of Safety in Public Schools: School-Based Management and Violence Reduction in Philadelphia" (1993-1995). With a sample of more than 7,000 middle-school students and 400 teachers, this project examined multi-level predictors (individual, neighborhood, and school characteristics) of school violence in Philadelphia, and examined recommendations for violence prevention. Welsh was also principal investigator on a three-year study (1993-95) funded by the Pennsylvania Commission on Crime and Delinquency, "Reducing Over-Representation of Minorities in the Juvenile Justice System." This study evaluated nine community-based programs (five in Harrisburg, four in Philadelphia) designed to reduce the overrepresentation of minorities in the juvenile justice system.

Phil Harris is an Associate Professor in the Department of Criminal Justice at Temple University. He received his Ph.D. from the School of Criminal Justice of the University at Albany in 1979, where he worked most closely with Marguerite Q. Warren, creator of the Interpersonal Maturity Classification System. He has been a member of the Temple faculty since 1980, where he teaches courses on juvenile justice policy, criminal justice organizations and management, and urban minorities and crime. Prior to coming to Temple, Harris spent four years as a juvenile correctional administrator in Canada. There he directed the assessment department of a large private agency, developed training for staff, provided training to staff from Canadian and American juvenile justice systems, and designed the agency's management information system. He has directed research on police and correctional decisionmaking, evaluations of juvenile delinquency programs, and the development of management information systems. From 1989 to 1995, Harris also directed the Juvenile Corrections Leadership Forum, the platform for launching the Council of Juvenile Correctional Administrators (CJCA). He continues to support CJCA as a consultant. Beginning in 1992, he and Peter Jones designed and have now implemented an information system, ProDES, that provides a continuous flow of outcome information on all programs that receive youths from Philadelphia's Family Court.

In 1999, ProDES was chosen as a finalist from among 1,609 submissions in the Innovations in American Government competition, sponsored by Harvard University and the Ford Foundation. Harris's current research focuses on the matching of juvenile offenders to programs. In addition to the first edition of this volume, he has contributed more than 80 book chapters, journal articles, and research reports on juvenile justice, classification of juveniles, program implementation, and information systems. He has also provided consultation and technical assistance to police departments, courts, juvenile delinquency programs, probation departments, criminal justice advocacy groups, and professional organizations. In 2001, the American Evaluation Association selected Harris as winner of the Alva and Gunnar Myrdal Government Service Award.

Index

Access, in target selection, 130
Accountability, of agencies, 8-9
Action plan. *See also* Developing an
    action plan, in the seven-stage
    model
    defined, 152
    initiating, 258
Action research, 57, 217
Action system, in identifying stake-
    holders, 47
Activist bias, 34
    in planned change, 27
Advocacy efforts, 8
African-Americans. *See also* Minorities
    mandatory sentencing and, 115-121
    "three-strikes" laws and, *viii-ix*
After-school program, program of
    planned change, 5
Aggregate matching, 226
Analysis, preliminary, 34
Analyzing the problem, in the seven-
    stage model, 1
    activities during, 13-15
    checklist for, 267
    Club Drugs case study, 61-67
    conduct a systems analysis, 33
        assessment activities, 50
        change agents and, 48
        elements of, 50
        examples, 49
        guidelines for, 49-54
        information sources for, 51
        model for, 49-54
        steps, 50, 52-54
        system, defined, 48
    describe the history of the problem,
        33
        critical incidents list, 40-42
        events as perception of, 40
        lawsuits as perception of, 40

legislation as perception of, 40
        questions to ask, 39
    document the need for change, 33
        apply boundaries, 35-36
        data collection techniques, 37
        differentiate need from prob-
            lem, 34-35
        incidence vs. prevalence, 36
        narrow definition of problem,
            36
        need, defined, 34
        problem, defined, 35
        questions to ask, 34
        school violence example, 35
        social indicators, 36-38
    Domestic Violence, case study, 59-
        60
    examine potential causes of the
        problem, 33, 43. *See also* Prob-
        lems
        domestic violence example, 44-
            45
    examine previous interventions, 33,
        46
    family-oriented theories, 45
    identify barriers to change and sup-
        ports for change, 33
        "action research" and, 57
        examples, 55
        force field analysis, 55-57
        forms of resistance, 54-55
        Kurt Lewin and, 55-57
        resistance to change and, 55-57
    identify relevant stakeholders, 33,
        46-48
    Incorporating Restorative Commu-
        nity Justice into American Sen-
        tencing and Corrections case
        study, 68-86
    individual-oriented theories, 44

organizational theories, 45
planning deficits during, 252
prostitution example, 16
questions to ask, 13
social structural perspectives, 45
system analysis and, 14-15
systematic approach, 14
"three-strikes" legislation example,
    viii
Andrews, Don, 129
Attica prison riot (1971), 40

Balbus, Isaac, 107
Barnum, Richard, 129
Berk, Richard A., 225
Bias
    activist, 34
    in data, 38
Biased attrition, 223
Biased selection, 223
Blacks. *See* African-Americans
Boot camps, *vii*, 94
    components of, 130
    program design of, 19
    program of planned change, 5-6
    program/policy and, 6
Bottom-up format, in approach to goal
    setting, 100
Bouffard, Jeffery A., 22
Boundaries, in analyzing the problem,
    35-36
Brady Act, *vii*, 1
    Monitoring Presale Firearm Checks
        Under the Brady Act case study
        (developing a plan for monitor-
        ing program/policy implementa-
        tion), 200-209
    resistance to changes by, 55
    Why Action Planning is Needed case
        study (developing an action
        plan), 170-175
Bratton, William, 39
Budgeting, 153-155. *See also*
    Resources
Bush, George H.W., 6

Causality, establishing, 221-222
Center for Alternative Sentencing and
    Employment Services (CASES),
    256
    as example of mutual adaptation, 27
Center for Effective Public Policy, 49-
    50

Challenge of Crime in Free Society
    (1968 President's Commission
    report), 12
Change. *See also* Analyzing the problem,
    in the seven-stage model; Force
    field analysis; Planned change
    barriers to and supports for, 54-57
    bottom-up format, 100
    documenting need for, 33, 34-39
    resistance to, 10, 11-12, 54-55, 162
    top-town format, 100
Change agents, 1
    defined, 11
    goals and values and, 93
    identification of sources of resist-
        ance by, 11
    as participants in goal setting, 99-
        100
    planned change and, 4
    resource plan adjustment by, 157-
        158
    successful, 11
    in systems analysis, 48
Change agent system, in identifying
    stakeholders, 47
Change process, roles of participants
    in, 47-48
Checkmate Program of Philadelphia
    case study (designing a program or
    policy), 138-145
Clear, Todd, 254
Client system, in identifying stakehold-
    ers, 47
Club Drugs case study (analyzing the
    problem), 61-67
Cohort design, 229
Cohorts, defined, 229
Collaboration, 91. *See also* Interagency
    collaboration
Collaborative strategies, 1
    defined, 11
    for handling resistance, 11-12
    planned change and, 1
Columbine High School shooting, 35
Community Corrections Acts (CCAs),
    134
Community forum, in documenting
    need for change, 37
Community justice
    compatible and incompatible goals
        and, 103-104

Incorporating Restorative Community Justice into American Sentencing and Corrections case study, 68-86
Community policing, in weed and seed programs, 178
Community survey, in documenting need for change, 37
Comprehensive drug courts, 1, 2
Computer crime, 10
Computerized fingerprint identification systems, 10
Computerized information systems, 218
Conflict resolution, 162
Conflict strategies
  costs associated with, 11
  defined, 11
  for handling resistance, 11-12
  planned change and, 1
Confounding factors (confounds), 215, 222
  biased attrition, 223
  biased selection, 223
  history, 224
  potential, in Minneapolis Domestic Violence Experiment, 225
  techniques for minimizing
    nonequivalent comparison groups, 226
    random assignment, 224
Constrained-flexible guidelines, in policies, 5
Construct validity, 221
Correctional Program Assessment Inventory (CPAI), 193-199
Corrections, Incorporating Restorative Community Justice into American Sentencing and Corrections case study, 68-86
Cost-benefit analysis, 218-219
Cost-effectiveness analyses, 218-219
Costs
  of conflict strategies, 11
  intervention approach choices and, 126-127
  projections of, in action plan, 153-155
"Creaming," 223
Crime control model, of criminal case processing, 95
Criminal justice, as a "system," 48

Criminal justice interventions, *vii. See also* Planned change
  essence of, 2
  examples, 1, 2
  falling short of goals, 2-3
  maximizing success of, 3
  poorly planned, 4
Criminal justice planning, 251
Criminal justice system, as a "nonsystem," 48, 106
Criminal justice system assessment, 50
Criminal sanctions. *See* Sanctions, criminal
Critical incidents list, 40-42

Data. *See* Developing a plan for monitoring program/policy implementation, in the seven-stage model
Data collection techniques, 37. *See also* Developing a plan for monitoring program/policy implementation, in the seven-stage model
Data guide method (observational data technique), 184-185
Delinquency prevention program, action plan development of, 20-21
Department of Homeland Security, 108
Designing the program or policy, in the seven-stage model, 1
  activities during, 17-19
  boot camp example, 19
  checklist for, 268
  choosing an intervention approach, 125
  costs of options, 126-127
  critical elements of, 136
  description, 17-19
  major activities for policy design, 125, 131-132
    define the target population, 133
    Getting Tough with Juvenile Offenders case study, 146-148
    identify the responsible authority, 133-134
    specify policy provisions and procedures, 134-135
  major activities for program design, 125, 127
    assess risk and needs, 129
    Checkmate Program case study, 138-145

define program components,
130-131
define target population, 128-
129
define target selection and
intake procedures, 129-130
information needed, 128
write job descriptions of staff,
and define skills and training
required, 131
planning deficits during, 253
systematic approach, 14
"three-strikes" legislation example,
ix
Deterrence
general, *viii*, 95
as a goal of criminal sanctions, 94
specific, *viii*, 95
Developing an action plan, in the
seven-stage model, 1
action plan, defined, 152
activities during, 20
The Brady Act: Why Action Planning is Needed case study, 170-
175
checklist for, 269
delinquency prevention program
example, 20-21
develop mechanisms of self-regulation, 151
coordinating activities, 160-161
managing resistance and conflict, 162
orienting participants, 160
estimate costs of resources, 153-155
Halfway Houses in Ohio: Costs and
Benefits case study, 165-169
identify resources and make cost
projections, 151, 153-155
planning deficits during, 253
plan to acquire or reallocate
resources, 151, 155
adjust resource plan, 157-158
funding sources, 156-157
Gantt Chart example, 158-159
resource plan, defined, 153
specify a plan to build and maintain
support, 151, 163
specify dates for task accomplish-
ment, 151, 160
systematic approach, 14
"three-strikes" legislation example,
ix-x

Developing a plan for evaluating outcomes, in the seven-stage model, 1
activities during, 24
checklist for, 270
develop outcome measures, 215,
221-222
evaluability assessment, 220-221
Evaluating Outcomes of Community-Based Delinquency Prevention case study, 237-241
Evaluation of Prison-Based Therapeutic Community Drug Treatment Programs in Pennsylvania
case study, 242-245
identify potential confounding factors, 215, 222-224
identify users and uses of evaluation
results, 215, 230
Kansas City Gun Experiment example, 24-25
nonequivalent comparison groups,
215
planning deficits during, 253
prerequisites for evaluation, 215,
220
ProDES—An Information System
for Developing and Evaluating
Services to Delinquent Youths
case study, 218, 233-236
purpose of, 215
random assignments, 215
reasons not to evaluate, 216
reassess the entire program plan,
215, 230-231
specify research design, 215, 226
cohort design, 229
diagrams of, legend for, 227
longitudinal design with treatment and control groups,
228-229
pretest-posttest design with
control group, 227-228
pretest-posttest design with
multiple pretests, 228
simple pre-post design, 227
systematic approach, 15
techniques for minimizing confounding effects
Minneapolis Domestic Violence
Experiment, 225
nonequivalent comparison
groups, 226
random assignments, 224

"three-strikes" legislation example, *x-xi*

types of evaluation
  efficiency, 216, 218-219
  impact, 215, 216, 217
  meta-analysis, 215, 219-220
  performance (outcome-based information systems), 216, 217-218

Developing a plan for monitoring program/policy implementation, in the seven-stage model, 1
  activities during, 22
  checklist for, 269-270
  description, 21-23
  designate responsibility to collect, store, and analyze data, 177, 188-189
  design instruments to collect data, 177, 182
    observational data, 184-186
    participant data (targets), 187-188
    service provider data (staff), 187
    service record data (documents), 186-187
  develop information system capacities, 177, 189-190
  develop mechanisms to provide feedback to stakeholders, 177, 190
  implementation, defined, 180
  intentions and actions, gap between, 178-180
  monitoring
    analysis (chart), 183
    defined, 177, 180
  Monitoring Presale Firearm Checks Under the Brady Act case study, 200-209
  Operation Weed and Seed example, 178-180
  outline the major questions for monitoring
    program components or policy provisions, 181, 183
    staff to implement the policy, 182
    target population, 181
  planning deficits during, 253
  prison-based therapeutic community (TC) drug treatment programs example, 22-23

"process evaluation," 21

Program Monitoring: The Correctional Program Assessment Inventory (CPAI) case study, 193-199

systematic approach, 15

"three-strikes" legislation example, *x*

Why Drug Courts Need Good Information Systems case study, 210-212

Dickey, Walter, *vii, viii*

Discretion, rules and, 5

Disproportionate minority confinement (DMC), 40-42

DNA testing, 10

Documents, as information source for criminal justice systems analysis, 51

Doleschal, Eugene, 251

Domestic violence
  advocacy efforts and, 8
  analyzing the problem, in the seven-stage model case study, 59-60
  causes and correlations of (analyzing the problem), 44-45

Dosage, 130

Drug Abuse Warning Network (DAWN), 64

Drug Awareness Resistance Education (DARE), as criminal justice intervention, 2, 7, 187

Drug courts, *vii*, 1

Drug testing equipment, 10

Drunk driving laws, goals and objectives for, 17

Due process model, of criminal case processing, 95

Ecstasy Anti-Proliferation Act of 2000, 64

Effect size, 219

Efficiency evaluation, 216, 218-219

Electronic monitoring equipment, 10

Emergency Release Acts, 135

Environment of policies and programs, changeable, 255. *See also* Mutual adaptation

Equity
  as a normative value, 96
  "three-strikes" laws and, *viii-ix*

Etiology, of a problem, 43

Evaluability assessment, 220-221

Evaluating Outcomes of Community-Based Delinquency Prevention case study (developing a plan for evaluating outcomes), 237-241

Evaluation. *See* Developing a plan for evaluating outcomes, in the seven-stage model

Evaluation of Prison-Based Therapeutic Community Drug Treatment Programs in Pennsylvania case study (developing a plan for evaluating outcomes), 242-245

Failure, planning for. *See* Initiating the program/policy plan, in the seven-stage model

Family-oriented theories, in problem analysis, 45

Federal Gun Control Act (GCA), 170-175

Feedback, to stakeholders, 177

Fingerprint identification systems, 10

Firearm Inquiry Statistics (FIST) program, 200-209

Firearms
  Brady Act, *vii*
  Kansas City Gun Experiment (developing a plan for evaluating outcomes), 24-25
  Monitoring Presale Firearm Checks Under the Brady Act case study (developing a plan for monitoring program/policy implementation), 200-209

Force field analysis
  defined, 55
  intervention approach and, 126
  steps in, 56

Functional budgeting, 154

Funding sources, 156-157

Gantt chart, 158-159

Gendreau, Paul, 219

General deterrence, *viii*, 94

Getting Tough with Juvenile Offenders case study (designing a program or policy), 146-148

Giuliani, Rudolph, 39

Goal conflict, within criminal justice system, desirability of, 106

Goals and objectives. *See* Setting goals and objectives, in the seven-stage model

Goals, defined, 16, 92

Goals of Mandatory Sentencing case study (setting goals and objectives), 115-121

Goal statements, 91, 92-93

Government services. *See* Accountability

Grisso, Thomas, 129

Gun control, 1

Guns. *See* Firearms

Hagan, John, 107

Halfway Houses in Ohio: Costs and Benefits case study (developing an action plan), 165-169

Hare, Robert, 129

Harris, Philip W., 233-236

Hispanics, mandatory sentencing and, 115-121

History (confound), 224

Hoge, Robert, 129

Homicides, by juveniles, 35

Humane treatment, as a normative value, 96

Impact evaluation, 215, 216, 217

Impact models, 91
  defined, 101
  for Department of Homeland Security, 108
  example of, 102
  key elements in, 101
  outcomes and, 221-222
  reentry program example, 102
  steps of, 101

Implementation, defined, 180. *See also* Initiating the program/policy plan, in the seven-stage model; Developing a plan for monitoring program/policy implementation, in the seven-stage model

Implementation Woes: Providing Residential Substance Abuse Treatment (RSAT) for Inmates in State Prisons case study (initiating the program/policy plan), 263-265

Incapacitation, as a goal of criminal sanctions, 94

Incidence, defined, 36

Individual matching, 226

Individual-oriented theories, in problem analysis, 44

Individual records, in target selection, 130

Information gathering, sources for, 36-38

Information system capacity, 177
guidelines for developing, 189-190

Information systems
computerized, 217
defined, 189

Initiating the program/policy plan, in the seven-stage model, 1
activities during, 26
Center for Alternative Sentencing and Employment Services (CASES) example, 27
checklist for, 270-271
criminal justice planning example, 251
exporting jobs and the global economy example, 250
Implementation Woes: Providing Residential Substance Abuse Treatment (RSAT) for Inmates in State Prisons case study, 263-265
learning and adapting, 249, 255-254
mutual adaptation, 26-27
planning deficits during, 253
planning for failure, 249
breakdowns, omissions, or deficits, 252, 254
obstacles, 252, 254
planning deficits at each stage, 252-253
planning for success, 249, 254-255
program and policy survival, 249, 257
systematic approach, 15
tasks of implementation, 249
evaluating and providing feedback to users and stakeholders, 259-260
initiating the action plan, 258
initiating the program/policy design, 257-258
monitoring program/policy implementation, 259

Initiator system, in identifying stakeholders, 47

Intake procedures, in target selection, 129-130

Interagency collaboration, needs and opportunities for, 104-108

Intervention approach, choosing, 125, 126-127

Intervention hypothesis (impact model), 101

Interventions. *See also* Criminal justice interventions
of criminal justice, 2
failure of, 92
notable and recent, *vii*

Jail overcrowding, as "systems" problem, 49

Johnson, Lyndon, "War on Poverty," 5

Jonesboro, Arkansas, school shooting, 35

Jones, Peter R., 233-236

Juvenile Justice and Delinquency Prevention (JJDP) Act, 40
funding for, 126

Juveniles
getting tough with, 146-148
homicides by, 35

Juvenile violence prevention, 5

Juvenile waiver laws, 1
as criminal justice intervention, 2

Kansas City Gun Experiment (developing a plan for evaluating outcomes), 24-25

Key informant approach, in documenting need for change, 37

Knowledge, expansion of, 9-10

Law Enforcement Assistance Administration (LEAA), 12-13

Lewin, Kurt, 55, 217

Lipsey, Mark, 219

Longitudinal design with treatment and control groups, 228-229

Loose coupling, 106-108

Mandatory arrest, for suspected spouse abusers, 2

Mandatory sentencing, goals of, 115-121

Massachusetts Boot Camp Program, as example of designing a program or policy, 19

Massachusetts Youth Screening Instrument, Second Version (MAYSI-2), 129

Matched control groups, 218

Mediation of interests and system adaptation (goal conflict), 106

Meta-analysis, 215, 219-220

Minneapolis Domestic Violence Experiment, 98, 225
  observational data techniques and, 184
Minorities
  disproportionate minority confinement (DMC), in juvenile justice, 40-42
  mandatory sentencing and, 115-121
Model, defined, 12
MonDay Community Correctional Institution, 195-199
Monitoring. *See also* Developing a plan for monitoring program/policy implementation, in the seven-stage model
  analysis (chart), 183
  defined, 177, 180
Monitoring implementation. *See* Developing a plan for monitoring program/policy implementation, in the seven-stage model
Monitoring Presale Firearm Checks Under the Brady Act case study (developing a plan for monitoring program/policy implementation), 200-209
Moore, Mark, 12-13
Multiple cohort design, 217
Mutual adaptation, 26-27, 255-257

Narrative method (observational data technique), 184
National Crime Victimization Survey (NCVS), 35
  purpose of, 36-37
National Criminal Justice Reference Service (NCJRS), 46
National Household Survey on Drug Abuse, 221
National Instant Criminal Background Check System (NICS), 55
National Institute of Corrections, 37
National Institute of Justice, 216
Need, defined, 34
Needs, defined, 129
Negotiation, principled, 162
"NIMBY" ("not in my back yard"), as resistance to change, 55
Nonequivalent comparison groups, 215, 226
Normative values. *See* Setting goals and objectives, in the seven-stage model

Objectives
  components of, 97-98
  defined, 16, 92, 97
  distinction between process and outcome, 99
Observational data, collecting
  data guide method, 184-185
  narrative method, 184
  structured rating scheme, 185-186
Office of Juvenile Justice and Delinquency Prevention, 111-114
Omnibus Crime Control and Safe Streets Act of 1968, 12-13
Operation Weed and Seed, 178-180
Organizational theories, in problem analysis, 45
Outcome-based information systems, 217-218
Outcome measures, 215, 221-222
Outcome objectives, 91
  defined, 99
  for goals, 97-99
Outcomes
  goals and objectives for, 16-17
  of goals and values, *viii-ix*
Outcomes, evaluating. *See* Developing a plan for evaluating outcomes, in the seven-stage model
Output, defined, 131

Parsimony, as a normative value, 96
Participant data, 187-188
Pennsylvania Commission on Crime and Delinquency (PCCD), 138-145
Performance evaluation, 216, 217-218
Petersilia, Joan, 127, 254
Planned change. *See also* Seven-stage model for planned change
  "activist bias" and, 27
  approaches to, 1, 5-7
  change agent, defined, 11
  characteristics of, 4
  collaborative strategies and, 1, 11
  components of, *vii*
  conflict strategies and, 1, 11
  defined, 3
  need for, 1
    accountability and, 7, 8-9
    declining resources and, 7, 8
    expansion of knowledge and technology and, 7, 9-10
  perils of, 10-12
  problem-solving model as basis for, 12-13

trends causing need for, 7-10
unplanned change vs., 1, 3-4
Planning, poor, "three-strikes" legislation example of, vii-xii
Plea bargaining, "three-strikes" laws and, *x*
Police brutality, conflict strategies and, 11-12
Policy
   birth of, examples, 3
   components of, 181
   defined, 5
   design of, activities for, 18-19
   programs' relation to, 7
Policy and program development and analysis, systematic approach to, 14-15
Policy approach to planned change, 1, 5
Policy implementation, staff for, 182
President's Commission on Law Enforcement and Administration of Justice, 12-13
Pretest-posttest design with control group, 227-228
Pretest-posttest design with multiple pretests, 228
Pretest-posttest, simple, 27
Prevalence, defined, 36
Principled negotiations, 162
Prison-based therapeutic community (TC) drug treatment programs, 22-23
Prisoner reentry initiatives, *vii*, 1
   as criminal justice intervention, 2
   impact model example, 102
Privatization, 103-104
Problem analysis, faulty, *vii-xii*, 13. *See also* Analyzing the problem, in the seven-stage model
Problems. *See also* Analyzing the problem, in the seven-stage model
   boundaries to, 35-36
   defined, 35
   etiology of, 43
   examining information about, 34
   levels of, causes of, 43
   need differentiated from, 34-35
   perceptions of and reactions to, 34
   social indicators leading to definition of, 37-38
Problem-solving model. *See* Seven-stage model for planned change

Process evaluation, 21. *See also* Developing a plan for monitoring program/policy implementation, in the seven-stage model
Process objectives, 99
ProDES—An Information System for Developing and Evaluating Services to Delinquent Youths case study (developing a plan for evaluating outcomes, in the seven-stage model), 218, 233-236
Program-based budgeting, 153-154
Program Monitoring: The Correctional Program Assessment Inventory (CPAI) case study (developing a plan for monitoring program/policy implementation), 193-199
Program or policy, designing. *See* Designing the program or policy, in the seven-stage model
Program or policy implementation. *See* Developing a plan for monitoring program/policy implementation, in the seven-stage model
Programs
   birth of, examples, 3
   boot camp design, 19
   components of, 181
   defined, 5
   design of, activities for, 17-18
   distinguished from projects, 6-7
   effectiveness of, debate over, 7
   planned change and, 5-6
Projects
   defined, 6
   distinguished from programs, 6
   planned change and, 6
Proportionality, as a normative value, 95
Prosecutors, "three-strikes" laws and, *x*
Prostitution, analyzing the problem, in the seven-stage model, 16
Psychopathy Checklist—Youth Version (PCL-YV), 129

Race. *See* African-Americans; Hispanics; Minorities
Random assignment, 215, 224
RAND report (1994), "three-strikes" legislation and, *xi*
Reentry program. *See* Prisoner reentry initiatives

Reflective diversity (goal conflict), 106
Rehabilitation, as a goal of criminal
    sanctions, 93
Reiss, Albert J., 38
Reliability, of a measurement, 222
Research design, 215. *See also* Devel-
    oping a plan for evaluating out-
    comes, in the seven-stage model
Resistance to change, 10
    forms of, 54-55
    managing, 162
    strategies for handling, 11-12
Resource plan. *See also* Resources
    adjusting, 157-158
    defined, 153
    goals of, 153
Resources
    acquiring or reallocating, 151, 155
    declining, trend causing need for
        planned change, 8
    funding sources, 156-157
    identifying, for action plan, 153-
        155
Restoration, as a goal of criminal sanc-
    tions, 94
Restorative justice
    compatible and incompatible goals
        and, 103
    Incorporating Restorative Commu-
        nity Justice into American Sen-
        tencing and Corrections case
        study (analyzing the problem),
        68-86
Retention, in target selection, 130
Retribution, as a goal of criminal sanc-
    tions, 93
Ridge, Tom, 108, 146
Risk/needs assessment, 129
Rosenberg Self-Esteem Scale, 221, 226
Roth, Jeffrey A., 38
Rothman, David, 257

Sanctions, criminal
    deterrence, 94
    incapacitation, 94
    purposes of, 93
    rehabilitation, 93
    restoration, 94
    retribution, 93
Scared Straight, 94
School Crime Supplement (SCS), 35
School violence (analyzing the prob-
    lem), 35

Screening, in target selection, 130
"Second-strike" felonies, *ix*
"Seeding," 178-180
Self-regulation, of program or policy,
    151
    coordinating activities, 160-161
    managing resistance and conflict,
        162
    orienting participants, 160
Sentencing
    disparities in, as "systems" problem,
        49
    Incorporating Restorative Commu-
        nity Justice into American Sen-
        tencing and Corrections case
        study (analyzing the problem),
        68-86
September 11, 2001, 108
Service delivery, 130
Service provider data, 187
Service record data, 186-187
Setting goals and objectives, in the
    seven-stage model, 1
    activities during, 16-17
    checklist for, 267-268
    description, 16-17
    drunk driving laws example, 17
    goals, defined, 92
    goals of criminal sanctions
        deterrence, 94
        incapacitation, 94
        rehabilitation, 93
        restoration, 94
        retribution, 93
    Goals of Mandatory Sentencing case
        study, 115-121
    identify compatible and incompati-
        ble goals in larger system, 91
        examples of, 102-104
        guidelines to, 104
    identify goals and values, 92-93
    identify needs and opportunities for
        collaboration, 91, 104-108
    normative values
        crime control model, 95
        due process model, 95
        equity, 96
        four value orientations, 95-96
        humane treatment, 96
        parsimony, 96
        proportionality, 95
        "right" goals and values, 96-97
    objectives, defined, 92

planning deficits during, 253

purpose of sanctioning, 93

seek participation in goal setting, 91, 99-100

specify an impact model, 91, 101-102

systematic approach, 14

"three-strikes" legislation example, *viii-ix*

top-down versus bottom-up approaches, 100

Top-Down versus Bottom-Up Goal Setting: Responding to Negative Information about Conditions of Juvenile Confinement case study, 111-114

write goal statements, 91, 92-93

write specific outcome objectives, 91

   distinction between process and outcome objectives, 99

   measurable and specific, 97

   objective components, 97-98

   objectives, defined, 97

Seven-stage checklist for program and policy planning

analyzing the problem, in the seven-stage model, 267

designing the program or policy, in the seven-stage model, 268

developing an action plan, in the seven-stage model, 268

developing a plan for evaluating outcomes, in the seven-stage model, 270

developing a plan for monitoring implementations, 269-270

initiating the program or policy plan, 270-271

setting goals and objectives, in the seven-stage model, 267-268

Seven-stage model for planned change. *See also* Analyzing the problem, in the seven-stage model; Designing the program or policy, in the seven-stage model; Developing an action plan, in the seven-stage model; Developing a plan for evaluating outcomes, in the seven-stage model; Developing a plan for monitoring program/policy implementation, in the seven-stage model; Initiating the program/policy plan, in the seven-stage model; Setting goals and objectives, in the seven-stage model

key points, 27-28

poor planning example (three-strikes legislation), *vii-xii*

summarized, 1

Shelters, for abused women, 2

Sherman, Lawrence W., 225

Shock incarceration programs, 94

Simple-complex rules/guidelines, 5

Social change, 56

Social constructions, 34

Social indicators

biases in, 38

in documenting need for change, 36-39, 37

examples of, 36-37

as information source for criminal justice systems analysis, 51

problems with, 37

Social structural perspectives, in problem analysis, 45

Sourcebook of Criminal Justice Statistics, 38

Specific deterrence, *viii*, 94

Spouse abusers, mandatory arrest as criminal justice intervention, 2

Stakeholders

defined, 46

feedback for, 177, 259-260

goals and values and, 93

identifying, 33

identifying, for problem analysis, 46-48

as information source for criminal justice systems analysis, 51

as participants in goal setting, 99-100

Structured rating scheme (observational data technique), 185-186

Success, planning for, 254-255

Supreme Court. *See* U.S. Supreme Court

System adaptation (goal conflict), 106

System, defined, 48

Systems analysis, 33

assessment activities, 50

change agents and, 48

conducting, 48-54

criminal justice as a "system," 48-49

elements of, 50
examples, 49
guidelines for, 49-54
intervention approach and, 126
model for, 49-50
restorative justice case study, 50,
    68-86
sources for information, 51
steps, 50, 52-54
system, defined, 48

Target populations
defining, for a policy, 133
defining, for a program, 128-129
for intervention, 4
in monitoring, 181
in policy design, 18
in program design, 17-18
for "three-strikes" laws, *ix*
Target selection, 129-130
Target system, in identifying stakehold-
    ers, 47
Taxman, Faye, 22
Technology, expansion of, 9-10
Terrorism, federal government
    response to, 108
Theory, defined, 43
Therapeutic community (TC) drug
    treatment programs, 22-23
"Three strikes and you're out" legisla-
    tion, 1
    as criminal justice intervention, 2
    deterrent effects of, *viii*
    effects of, on crime, *xi*
    intent of, *viii*
    plea-bargaining and, *x*
    poor planning of, *viii-xii*
    problems with, *vii*
    prosecutors and, *x*
    seven-stages of planning and, *viii-xii*
*Thurman et al. v. City of Torrington,
    Conn.*, 40
Tonry, Michael, 119
Top-down approach to goal setting,
    100

Top-Down versus Bottom-Up Goal Set-
    ting: Responding to Negative
    Information about Conditions of
    Juvenile Confinement case study
    (setting goals and objectives), 111-
    114
Turner, Susan, 254

Uniform Crime Reports (UCR)
    biases in, 38
    contents of, 36
Unplanned change, 1, 4. *See also*
    Planned change
USA Patriot Act (2001), 3, 10-11
U.S. Bureau of the Census, 37
U.S. Department of Justice, 6, 38, 46
User fees, 156
U.S. Supreme Court, discretion, excep-
    tions to, 5

Validity, of a measurement, 221
Violent Crime Control and Law
    Enforcement Act of 1994, 6
Vision, for crime control, 12-13

"War on Drugs," 6
"War on Poverty," 5
Weed and seed programs, *vii*, 6
    as criminal justice intervention, 2
    Operation Weed and Seed (1991),
        178-180
"Weeding," 178-180
"What works" in criminal justice, 2
    lack of consensus concerning, 7
Why Drug Courts Need Good Informa-
    tion Systems case study (develop-
    ing a plan for monitoring
    program/policy implementation),
    210-212
Women's shelters, as criminal justice
    intervention, 2
Wright, Kevin, 105, 106

Youth Level of Service/Case Manage-
    ment Inventory (YLS/MI), 129